CARDUS ON CRICKET

CARDUS

on

CRICKET

A selection from the cricket writings of
Sir Neville Cardus, chosen and introduced
by SIR RUPERT HART-DAVIS

SOUVENIR PRESS

First published 1949

This edition Copyright © 1977 Souvenir Press Ltd
43 Great Russell Street, London WC1B 3PA

Reprinted October 1977
Reprinted June 1979
Reprinted February 1983

ISBN 0 285 62284 6

Printed in Great Britain by
Ebenezer Baylis & Son Ltd
The Trinity Press, Worcester, and London

CONTENTS

ACKNOWLEDGMENTS

THE compiler and the publishers are grateful to the editor of *The Guardian*, to Messrs. Longmans Green & Co., and to the Richards Press for permission to include material of which they control the rights.

Capt Rose's XI v G.P. Dewhurst's XI
At See-Ily Hill. May 11-12 1910

G.P. Dewhurst's XI

1st Innings		2nd Innings	
W.B. Burns, b Cardus	0	b Cardus	72
A.F. Spooner, c Sugden b Cardus	18	b Jones	18
H.D. Stanning, b. Cardus	12	b Jones	0
F.H. Hollins, c Jones b Dykes	3	c & b Jones	3
Smoker, b Dykes	7	b Cardus	10
T.A. Higson, c Fleming b Dykes	0	b Cardus	1
W. Birchenough c Mallinson b Cardus	24	b Cardus	3
W.L. Winser, b Cardus	0	b Cardus	2
R.H. Stanning, b Dykes	51	b Cardus	0
G.P. Dewhurst, b Dykes	18	lbw b Cardus	12
W.H. Sell not out	8	not out	6
Extras	10	Extras	3
Total	151		130

Bowling

Dykes	15.1	— 3	— 61	— 5		5	- 0	- 28	- 0
Cardus	16	— 4	— 52	- 5		15.1	- 2	- 59	7
Jones	5	- 1	— 10	- 0		12	— 4	31	3
Wilson	6	- 0	— 18	- 0					
G. de St Croix						2	- 0	— 9	- 0

Capt. Rose's XI

T. Mallinson, c Winser b Smoker	21
W.L. Jones, b Birchenough	0
C.C. Fleming, b Birchenough	39
G. de St Croix, c & b Higson	18
A. Crowther, b Smoker	170
A.P. Wilson c&b R.H. Stanning	61
J.D. Sugden, not out	37
Extras	17
Total (for 6 wkts)	363

Smoker took	2 for	108
Birchenough "	2 "	93
Higson "	1 "	49
H. Stanning "	1 "	30
Sell "	0 "	41
Burns "	0 "	25

Capt Rose's XI WON by Innings & 82 runs

This Book is Dedicated by its Compiler
To the Happy Memory of

BARBE EDE

A compulsive cartoonist, Sir Neville Cardus was always drawing lightning caricatures of any subject he was discussing. The above illustration is of players in a cricket match of nearly 70 years ago in which, as a spinner, he took 12 wickets in the match.

INTRODUCTION TO THE 1949 EDITION

NEVILLE CARDUS was born in 1890 at Rusholme, a poor suburb of Manchester. His maternal grandfather was a pensioned ex-policeman with lumps on his head, caused by Charlie Peace's crowbar. The family took in washing, but soon the three Cardus girls discovered that lovers were more fun than laundry-work, and much more rewarding. Neville's father, whom he never knew, played the violin in an orchestra.

Although the boy loved his mother, and adored his Aunt Beatrice (the gayest and most extravagant of the sisters, whose brief career included a successful action for breach of promise against the Turkish Consul in Manchester), he was, as he still is, at heart a solitary, an introvert by temperament and circumstance alike. He was a delicate boy with poor eyesight, though this was not discovered until he was nineteen. After four years at a Board School, he began to gather knowledge in a wider field, and before he was fourteen he had earned money as a pavement artist, by pushing a builder's handcart, by boiling type in a printing works, and as a chocolate-seller in a Manchester theatre.

At the age of ten he somehow discovered Dickens, and thereafter, like Silas Wegg, all print was open to him. (Dickensians will recognize an occasional echo of the Master in Cardus's style to this day.) Every moment he could snatch from his various employers was spent in the Public Library or Reading Room. And then, when he was twelve or so, he first visited Old Trafford cricket ground, and saw A. C. MacLaren at the wicket. The grace and style of this great batsman fired his imagination and gave him a glimpse of aesthetic beauty in general, and the genius of cricket in particular, which was to remain with him always.

There had been no cricket at the Board School, but there were plots of waste ground, and failing all else the streets, to play on. The boy was interested in the game and was becoming something of a bowler, but it was his first sight of MacLaren, 'the noblest Roman', that, without his knowing it, determined the course of his life.

His next move was to a Marine Insurance office, where he worked for seven years. His salary began at eight shillings a week and worked

11

up, by the time he was twenty-one, to a pound. On this he somehow managed to live in the back room of a lodging-house and continue his education. He attended free lectures on all kinds of subjects at the University; he went to the theatre, Miss Horniman's and others; he planned a cultural 'Schema' of study for himself, embracing literature, philosophy, economics, comparative religion and goodness knows what; finally, he determined to be a writer.

But what should he write about? This perennial problem of youth was resolved on an April evening in 1907 when, at the Princes Theatre, Manchester, he listened to a performance of Edward German's opera, *Tom Jones*. Even as MacLaren had opened his eyes, so did German (of all unlikely composers) open his ears. Suddenly, almost instantaneously, he comprehended music, and knew that this was his allotted theme. Thereafter, as he stood in the street opposite the *Manchester Guardian* office, and he often did so stand, waiting to catch glimpses of the great men who worked there—C. P. Scott, Allan Monkhouse, C. E. Montague and the rest —it was the music critic, Samuel Langford, whose job he wildly and hopelessly coveted. Music was now added to the 'Schema', and his first published writing was an article on 'Bantock and Style in Music', for which *Musical Opinion* paid him seven shillings and sixpence in 1910.

By 1912 the time had clearly come for him to leave Marine Insurance. By a lucky chance he answered an advertisement for an assistant cricket coach at Shrewsbury School. The engagement was for the summer term only, but he reckoned that he could save enough from his salary of two pounds ten a week to keep him through the winter. He had never, in all his twenty-one years, travelled more than a few miles from Manchester, and it was a rapturous youth who set off for Shrewsbury on May Day, taking with him his worldly goods (mostly books) in a battered tin box, his off-break, and his immortal longings.

*

He spent five happy summers at Shrewsbury, and something of the peace and delight he found there shines out from his 'Shastbury' sketches. The old cricket pros under whom he worked, Attewell of Notts and Wainwright of Yorkshire, also reappear in his writings. One evening the head master, Dr. C. A. Alington, discovered the studious-looking young cricket pro reading a Gilbert Murray translation of Euripides under a tree, and when in August 1914

Cardus was refused for the Army, he found himself installed as Alington's secretary.

The head master's cultivated learning, irony, wit, kindliness and sense of drama made a deep impression on Cardus, as they did on thousands of other young men. Thirty years later he said that Alington had been 'an influence that inspired and corrected at one and the same time; not by precept but by example', and his liking seems to have been reciprocated, for when Alington was appointed head master of Eton in 1916, he asked Cardus to go along with him.

The plan miscarried, since Cardus was liable to undergo a further Army Medical Board and, as he found to his discomfiture, no one was anxious to engage a young man who might be removed at any moment. He returned sadly to Manchester, where lack of money compelled him to accept a job as canvasser for a Burial Society. From the depths of his despair he wrote to the Editor of the *Manchester Guardian*, the great C. P. Scott, asking for a humble job in the counting-house. Few editors would even have answered such a letter, but Scott immediately summoned Cardus to his home, employed him as a secretary and eventually, in March 1917, appointed him to the staff of the *Guardian*. A year in the reporters' room was followed by promotion to the editorship of the Miscellany column and the back-page article, and then to the unexpected post of dramatic critic, assistant to C. E. Montague.

In June 1919, Cardus was recovering from an illness, and W. P. Crozier, the News Editor, suggested that he should spend a few days in the open air at Old Trafford and amuse himself by writing about the cricket. In so casual a fashion was the greatest of all cricket-writers set on his way. By May 1920 he was 'Cricketer', the paper's full-time correspondent with a roving commission over all the cricket fields of England. And so he continued until the Second World War caused stumps to be drawn for six years.

Meanwhile, whenever there was an opportunity, he was allowed to write musical criticism as second string to Samuel Langford, and when that remarkable man died in 1927, Cardus took over. He had thus reached the happy position of being paid for doing the two things he liked best, watching cricket and listening to music. Several attempts were made by London papers to lure him from Manchester, but he preferred the freedom and the tradition of the *Guardian*.

In 1940 he sailed for Australia, where he spent the next seven years, writing and broadcasting about music, and composing his autobiography. He was happy in Sydney, but there was nothing there to take the place of the Long Room at Lord's, and when the Australian cricket team of 1948 played its first match in London, Neville Cardus was there to see.

*

The cricket writings fall neatly into three periods, each exemplified by two books: the first by *A Cricketer's Book* (1922) and *Days in the Sun* (1924); the second by *The Summer Game* (1929) and *Cricket* (1930); the third by *Good Days* (1934) and *Australian Summer* (1937).

We have seen that Cardus came to write on cricket by chance, and it was natural that in later days the early writings of his first period should seem to him flowery and overwritten. When we read the essays from *Days in the Sun* we should remember that they are not the work of a cricket reporter turned literary, but the first flights of a new prose-writer whose subject happened to be cricket. Most of the literature of the game has been contributed by players, ex-players or regular commentators. Occasionally a Nyren or a Pycroft has cropped up, but usually we read old cricket books for the deeds they chronicle rather than for their authors' style. Many professional men of letters, in particular Andrew Lang, E. V. Lucas and Edmund Blunden, have touched on cricket in the course of their writings, but Cardus was the first literary man to devote the whole of his stored mind and eager pen to the great English game.

Approaching the second period and *The Summer Game*, we find that our author has learnt restraint. His eye is more often on the ball, and less often on his images and metaphors. He has not yet mastered the bowling, but his eye will soon be in.

The books of his third period show the full flowering of his gifts. I am prepared to uphold *Good Days*, with its uninspiring title, as one of the two best books ever written about cricket,[1] and I use the word 'written' advisedly. Here Cardus is absolutely sure of what he wants to say, and of how he means to say it. He has mastered irony and controlled his romanticism, though occasionally the old Adam, albeit regenerate, pops out, as in the lovely essay on Woolley (page 110 of this book), with its undertones of poetry and George Meredith. (Incidentally, when Cardus read the essay to Woolley himself, the great batsman took the sentence: 'So with Woolley's

[1] The other is Edmund Blunden's *Cricket Country*.

14

cricket; the lease of it is in the hands of the special providence which looks after the things that will not look after themselves' as a reflection on his back-play!)

*

I have tried to make the selection as representative as possible of the whole body of Cardus's work. This has meant allowing only one innings each to 'Shastbury', to village cricket, and to most of the great players whom he has so often described. I have omitted the essay called 'A Sentimental Journey' (which Cardus has declared his own favourite and in which he conducts Galsworthy's Jolyon Forsyte to Lord's), preferring 'The Greatest Test Match' as an example of imaginative reconstruction. The arrangement is chronological, except that I have placed first the extracts from *Cricket*, so that this volume may fittingly open with the one called 'Prelude'. The pieces from the *Manchester Guardian* in 1938 are here for the first time presented in book form.

The author has given his approval, in part somewhat reluctantly, to my choice. Left to himself he would probably have refused entry to anything written before *Good Days*, though as he approaches his sixtieth year I detect a more tolerant, indeed almost a tender, look in his eye when he contemplates his own youthful exuberance.

*

In person he is slight, lean and spectacled: in character, ascetic, unbusinesslike and diffident. The two strains in his nature mingle in an embracing wit, invoking now the earthy humour of a north country pro, now the lightning repartee of his friend Sir Thomas Beecham. He is an enchanting companion, but I suspect that at heart he is seldom sorry to be left alone. For all his expressed desire to dissociate himself from cricket, almost any fine summer's day will find him at Lord's, high in the Press Box, wandering from the Tavern to the Long Room and back, or sitting alone in one of the stands. Even those minor games for which the match-card used to promise 'Band if Possible' draw him in. He smokes a pipe and carries a book under his arm. Often he seems not to be watching the players at all, but experience has shown that little escapes him. If one eye is on the Eternal Verities, the other is firmly fixed on Denis Compton.

It is impossible in a few pages to give more than a brief and superficial account of the man, his life and his work. I had hoped to supplement this introduction with some chapters from the *Autobiography*, but that has proved impossible. Nevertheless I believe that in the essays here assembled will be found sufficient of the quiddity of Cardus, man and writer, to justify the book's title.

January 1949   RUPERT HART-DAVIS

POSTSCRIPT

When this book was first published in 1949 as *The Essential Neville Cardus* it contained four of his essays on music, and in my introduction a paragraph on his work as a music critic. Now that these have been removed, and the book deals with cricket only, I should be vexed by my old friend's gentle ghost if I failed to make it plain that music was just as important to him as cricket, and that he was greatly esteemed as a music critic. That is a subject on which I am not qualified to judge, but of one thing I am quite certain; that in the literature of cricket he has no equal.

November 1976   RUPERT HART-DAVIS

CRICKET

PRELUDE

EVERY summer I travel north, south, east and west to watch
cricket. I have seen the game played far down in Kent, at
Dover, near the cliffs trodden by King Lear. There, one late
August afternoon, I said goodbye to a cricket season on a field which
lay silent in the evening sunshine; the match, the last of the year,
was over and the players gone. I stayed for a while in the failing light
and saw birds run over the grass as the mists began to spread. That
day we had watched Woolley in all his glory, batting his way through
a hundred felicitous runs. While he batted, the crowd sat with white
tents and banners all round—a blessed scene, wisps of clouds in the
sky, green grass for our feet to tread upon, 'laughter of friends under
an English heaven'. It was all over and gone now, as I stood on the
little field alone in the glow of the declining day. 'The passing of
summer,' I thought. 'There can be no summer in this land without
cricket.'

Whenever I am in love with cricket's beauty and sentiment I
always think of the game as I saw it go to an end that day in Kent, as
though to the strain of summer's cadence. Cricket, as I know and
love it, is part of that holiday time which is the Englishman's heritage
—a playtime in a homely countryside. It is a game that seems to me
to take on the very colours of the passing months. In the spring,
cricketers are fresh, and eager; ambition within them breaks into
bud; new bats and flannels are as chaste as the April winds. The
showers of May drive the players from the field, but soon they
are back again, and every blade of grass around them is a jewel in the
light. I like this intermittent way of cricket's beginning in spring
weather. A season does not burst on us, as football does, full grown
and arrogant; it comes to us every year with a modesty that matches
the slender tracery of leaf and twig, which belongs to the setting of
every true cricket field in the season's first days.

When June arrives, cricket grows to splendour like a rich part of
the garden of an English summertime. In June the game is at the
crown of the year; from Little Puddleton to London the fields of
village and town are white with players in hot action. Batsmen move
along their processional way to centuries at Lord's, while in a

17

hundred hidden hamlets far and wide some crude but not inglorious Hobbs flings his bat at the ball, and either misses it or feels his body tingle as willow thwacks leather. Bowlers set their teeth and thunder over the earth, seeing nothing in the world but a middle stump. And when a wicket falls, fieldsmen in the deep give themselves to the grassy earth, stretch their limbs, and look up into the blue sky. Now is the time of cricketer's plenty—June and July. Let him cherish every moment as it passes; never will he be so young again.

With the advent of August, cricket loses the freshness and radiance of its heyday. Colour and energy begin to leave the game, even as colour and energy begin to leave summer itself. Cricketers grow weary; ambition wanes as the sun wanes. The season goes to its end with a modest and lovely fall. It does not finish rhetorically, as football does, vaunting a cup-tie final before a million eyes. One after another the cricketers say goodbye in the darkening evenings of late summer; they fold their tents and depart, and nobody sees them. The noisy crowds have left the game for the new darling with the big ball. Down at Eastbourne (it may chance to be) the season comes to an end on a quiet day, on which the crack of the bat sends out a sweet melancholy. As the cricketer leaves the field, not to set foot again on his game's carpet for months and months to come, he has his moments of private sentiment. He glances back to take a last look at the field as the hours decrease and autumn grows in everything. He is glad that cricket belongs to summer, comes in with the spring, and gets ready to go when the trees are brown. Other games can be played in different parts of the world. Cricket is a game which must always be less than its true self if it is taken out of England and out of the weather of our English summer.

So much for the season and the setting, the time and the place. The game itself is a capricious blend of elements, static and dynamic, sensational and somnolent. You can never take your eyes away from a cricket match for fear of missing a crisis. For hours it will proceed to a rhythm as lazy as the rhythm of an airless day. Then we stretch ourselves on deck-chairs and smoke our pipes and talk of a number of things—the old 'uns insisting that in *their* time batsmen used to hit the ball. A sudden bad stroke, a good ball, a marvellous catch, and the crowd is awake; a bolt has been hurled into our midst from a clear sky. When cricket burns a dull slow fire it needs only a single swift wind of circumstance to set everything into a blaze that consumes nerves and senses. In no other game do events of import hang so bodefully on a single act. In no other game does one little mistake lead to mischief so irreparable. You get another chance at football if you foozle a kick; but Hobbs in all his majesty must pass out of the scene for hours if for a second he should fall into the error that hedges all mortal activity. Many a great match has been lost by a missed catch; terrible are the emotions of long-on when the ball is driven high towards him and when he waits for it—alone in the world—and the crowd roars and somebody cries out, ' 'E'll miss it— 'e'll miss it!' Years ago, in a match for the rubber in Australia, Clem Hill and Victor Trumper were making a mighty stand, turning the wheel of the game against England. Here were two of the greatest batsmen of all time thoroughly set, scourging the English attack with unsparing weapons. Hour after hour they cut and drove right and left. Wilfred Rhodes, who seems always to have been playing cricket, tossed up over after over, angling for the catch in the deep. And at the very moment when the fortunes of the battle were on the turn, moving definitely Australia's way—at this moment of fate, Clem Hill let his bat swing at a ball for all he was worth in valour and strength. Up into the sky the ball went, and it began to drop where A. E. Knight was standing. All eyes rested on Knight; the vast Sydney multitude were dead still as the ball fell like a stone. Knight held his catch, but as he did so, he was seen to go down on one knee, and bow his head. Some of the English players, thinking Knight was ill, moved towards him. But as they approached, Knight raised himself, made an explanatory gesture, swallowed emotion in a gulp, and said to his anxious colleagues, 'It's all right, it's all right; I was only thanking my Maker.' Cricket can mean much to a man: responsibility can weigh down the strongest.

The laws of cricket tell of the English love of compromise between a particular freedom and a general orderliness, or legality. Macdonald's best break-back is rendered null and void if he should let his right foot stray merely an inch over the crease as he wheels his arm. Law and order are represented at cricket by the umpires in their magisterial coats (in England it is to be hoped these coats will never be worn as short as umpires wear them in Australia, much to the loss of that dignity which should always invest dispensers of justice). And in England umpires are seldom mobbed or treated with the contumely which is the lot of the football referee. If everything else in this nation of ours were lost but cricket—her Constitution and the laws of England of Lord Halsbury—it would be possible to reconstruct from the theory and the practice of cricket all the eternal

Englishness which has gone to the establishment of that Constitution and the laws aforesaid.

Where the English language is unspoken there can be no real cricket, which is to say that the Americans have never excelled at the game. In every English village a cricket field is as much part of the landscape as the old church. Everybody born in England has some notion of what is a cricket match, even folks who have never had a cricket bat in their hands in their lives (few must be their number since it is as natural to give a cricket bat as a present to a little boy as it is to give him a bucket and spade when he goes to the seaside). I should challenge the Englishness of any man who could walk down a country lane, come unexpectedly on a cricket match, and not lean over the fence and watch for a while. Has any true Englishman ever resisted the temptation, while travelling on the railway, to look through the carriage window whenever the train has been passing a cricket field? The train rushes round a curve just as the bowler is about to bowl; in a flash we are swept out of sight of the game, and never can we know what happened to that ball! Cricket is not called the 'Sport of Kings'; it is the possession of all of us, high and low, rich and poor. It was born in a small place and it has conquered all the habitations of our race. Wherever cricket is taken, England and the flavours of an English summer go with it. The game's presiding genius is W. G. Grace, dead and therefore immortal. He gave his heart and soul to cricket, stamped the English stamp on it, and caused it to loom with his own genial bulk in the eyes of his country-men for all time. Today, when it is regarded right and proper for the nation to pay honour to all heroes of the open air, Grace would have been knighted. But the very idea of 'Sir W. G. Grace' is comical. You see, he was an institution. As well might we think of Sir Albert Memorial, Sir National Debt, Sir Harvest Moon—or Sir Cricket!

FOWLER'S MATCH

GIVEN a setting of smooth grass, the true and cultivated scene of the game, then boys' cricket is cricket at its best. If there is the image of a match laid up for all time in heaven it will be not one of a Test match, or even one of a match between Sussex and Kent; it will be a match between Eton and Harrow at

Lord's that the eternal mirrors reflect. And the image will be of Fowler's match, played in 1910. If a writer of boys' stories had narrated the tale of this game, with Fowler in the traditional role of Captain of the School—well—our author would have been told that he had overdone at last the 'manly and fearless hero' business. 'In real life', his critics would have maintained, 'things don't turn out quite so glamorously.'

On the first day of Fowler's match, Harrow scored 232. Then Eton lost five wickets for 40 runs, before bad light stopped play. The scene of Lord's that evening stays always in the mind. Two batsmen at bay—one of them Fowler—against conquering bowlers. Over the ground came the cries of 'Play up, Harrow!' On the edge of the field a sequence of top hats was to be observed standing upside down; Etonian brows required cooling.

The next morning Eton collapsed; they were all out for 65. Only Fowler, with 21, reached double figures for Eton, who had to follow on 165 behind. Again did Eton collapse, five wickets going for 65. Etonians of great age were unable to watch the issue now. During the lunch interval I saw, in one of the boxes near the Nursery end, a well-preserved earl attending to his colours with a hammer in his hand. I imagined he was battling with emotion. To this day I have wondered in what manner the hammer and nails came into the possession of one whose life so obviously was removed from the paths of labour. Did he bring the implements to Lord's himself?— in the depths of his coat-tails. Or did he, with great foresight, remind Perkins the night before, as he was going to bed: 'There's the chicken and tongue, Perkins; there's the trifle and champagne— and, oh, Perkins, don't forget the hammer and nails. The same hammer we had last year will do; no doubt you will be able to find it somewhere.' Strange that memory of Fowler's match should cling to the sight of an aristocrat performing with a hammer! Out in the middle, at Lord's that day, youth measured itself with the giants of history. Eton, only five wickets in reserve, were wanting 100 runs to save defeat in a single innings. Fowler flung his bat about him, each quick circling of it a flash of defiance in the sunlight. He hit eight boundaries and scored 64. He and Wigan added 42 for the sixth wicket in fifty minutes; with Boswell, Fowler held the seventh wicket for three-quarters of an hour and made 57. Yet, when all these deeds were done, Eton were beaten to their knees, beaten to the world. When the last man came in, the innings defeat had barely been avoided; with only one wicket to fall Eton led by four runs! It is at this point of truth's story of the skill and courage displayed at Lord's on July 9th, 1910, that our romantic writer of boys' tales would take fright and jib. Eton's last wicket—held by Lister-Kaye and Manners—cut and drove 50 runs in twenty minutes. A crowd of 10,000 were there to see it, the most aged and most silvery-haired of them a boy again for the while, piping of voice, blessèd of vision. Harrow were left with 55 to win. Fowler bowled off-breaks, hit the stumps five times, and took eight wickets for 23. Harrow were all out for 45; Eton won by 9 runs—a cricket match in which none of us would now be believing for a moment if there were not figures extant to prove that it actually took place. Some of the boys who played in the Eton and Harrow match of 1910 gave their lives shortly afterwards in the Great War. But at Lord's on that Saturday afternoon they fought on a battleground where wages for ever the chivalrous combat of character against the challenge of circumstances. Their souls entered the Valhalla of cricketers—which is the Lord's pavilion, noble and murmurous with history.

THE CHAMPION

SOME seventy years ago, on any summer morning, an orchard in Gloucestershire stood fresh and silent in the light of dawn. The birds had it to themselves for a while, and the dew sweetened every leaf and spray of blossom. The English countryside spread all around; imagination today feels that it was a simple and quiet land, the soil of it going into the nature of the men who lived on it.

As the sun grew warmer, this little orchard began to echo with noises, shouts of healthy boys at play, the crack of a cricket bat, the barking of a dog. The labourer on his way to the fields, walking along the track by the orchard's side, heard these sounds and probably said to himself: 'There be the Graces playing at bat and ball again.' But he could not have guessed that in the green beauty of the orchard—a familiar enough part of the landscape—the greatest of cricketers was being cradled. W. G. Grace learned to play in a scene which we can imagine was not unlike the unsophisticated Hambledon meadow. Before his long career was half over he organized the technique of the game into a science; he orchestrated the folk music of cricket, so to say. Yet with all his orthodoxy, his shrewd logic of execution, he never sundered from the west country; to the end there was sap in his cricket. The plain, lusty humours of his first practices in a Gloucestershire orchard were to be savoured throughout the man's gigantic rise to a national renown. He dominated cricket in every corner of England, whether the occasion were a village green at Thornbury or a Test match at Lord's. He rendered rusticity cosmopolitan whenever he returned to it. And always did he cause to blow over the fashionable pleasances of St. John's Wood the hearty west wind that is not afraid to upset all manners that are less than human. He was a giant in build, with a big beard. I have never seen a portrait of Grace—not even amongst those taken of him when he was a boy—that did not show him bearded like the pard. By dint of his skill and the gusto of his love for each day's play, he made cricket come home to the nation at large. He was not the least eminent of the Victorians. And he shared their view that authority was a matter to be exploited drastically. The sweep of his energy was so tremendous that he caused cricket to expand beyond the scope of a game; his bulk and stride carried cricket into the country's representative highways; it became part of the Victorian epoch. In my home, when I was a boy, there were no cricketers, and little talk of any form of sport, but most summer mornings at breakfast the name of W. G. Grace was pronounced with that of Mr. Gladstone. When Grace was 'not out' at lunch at Lord's the London clubs quickly emptied and the tinkle of hansom cabs along the St. John's Wood Road had no end. People not directly interested in cricket found the presence of Grace occasionally looming into their social consciousness. The Royal Family inquired about the health of Grace from time to time. Small boys, playing primitively in fields or on the pavements of growing cities, struck defiant attitudes with their bats and said they were 'W.G.'. It has been told that outside a cricket field it was often possible to read the following sign: 'Admission threepence; if Dr. W. G. Grace plays, admission sixpence.' For he did not give his genius only to select and fashionable scenes and company. In those days the line between county and country cricket was slenderly drawn. Grace journeyed right and left, playing with the greatest and the humblest—now at Lord's against the Australians, now at Thornbury against the lads of the village. When he turned for a while from the glamour of the towns and revisited the little fields of Gloucestershire, the whole countryside would go forth to see him, on foot or on horse, Hodge and Squire. A blissful picture for the modern mind to dwell upon.

Once in a rustic game Grace had scored twenty or so runs. He played in these modest engagements with all the keenness he put into a Test match. Having scored twenty, on this occasion he was brilliantly stumped by the local wicket-keeper. Grace had played forward and lifted his right toe only for a fraction of a second. 'H'zat?' shrieked our yokel wicket-keeper, in a panic of triumph, seeing himself rendered immortal by his cleverness against 'The Champion'—'H'zat?' 'Not hout!' replied the umpire without loss of time. 'Not hout—and look'ee here, young feller, the crowd 'as come for to see Dr. Grace, and none of your monkey tricks.'

Grace was fifteen years old when, in 1863, he made 32 against the All-England XI and the bowling of Jackson, Tarrant and Tinley. He established himself as a master batsman in a period of fast, slinging bowling. And in those days the pitches were often dangerously rough. Grace killed the 'brute strength' school of attack; he always revelled in a fast ball. One afternoon at Lord's the crowd rose as one man and cheered him for stopping four consecutive shooters. This ball, the deadliest of all, because no batsman can possibly anticipate it, was common enough in Grace's heyday. If and when the modern batsman receives a shooter he looks aggrieved to the soul; usually the groundsman is called up after the match and cross-examined by his committee. In cricket, when there is the possibility of a shooter coming along, the skill even of a Grace is hedged round by mortality all the time; it is as though a Kreisler were playing the violin beautifully on a platform which might at any moment collapse. 'How do you stop a shooter?' somebody once asked Grace. Though the Old Man (as he came to be called) was no theorist, he replied with a true Victorian relish of First Principle: 'Why, you put your bat to the ball.' A blade of willow was Grace's chief weapon, in offence or in defence. He kept his left leg so close to the bat when he played forward, that as an old professional once told me, 'not a bit of daylight could be seen between them'. He played back in defence with his right foot near to the line of the ball. But he seldom deliberately moved both of his legs over the wicket while stopping a good ball, and he did not make a habit of glancing the good-length delivery on the leg stump to fine leg. He taught the gospel of the straight bat, the left shoulder forward to all well-pitched bowling. 'The first time I ever saw Grace play,' Mr. A. C. M. Croome has written (and he is the soundest of living authorities on the technique of W. G.), 'was in August 1876. He celebrated the occasion by taking 318 not out off the Yorkshire bowlers. Earlier in the week he had made 177 against Nottinghamshire at Clifton, and on the preceding Friday and Saturday 344 at Canterbury for M.C.C. against Kent. It is on record that he made over twelve hundred runs in first-class cricket during that month of August; and he found time before September came to run up to Grimsby and score 400 not out for the United South against twenty-two of the district. That would be a normal month for him if he would begin again today, knowing what even bowlers and wicket-keepers know now of back strokes, played with the second line of defence, and enjoying the advantages so plentifully bestowed on his successors—truer wickets, longer overs, shorter boundaries.'

It is argued by any sceptic of the present time that W. G. Grace never was called on to play the googly and the swerve. In the 'eighties, Walter Wright and Shacklock could make a ball swerve, but not sufficiently to trouble the Champion. He never had the chance to show, while at his best, what he could do against a googly. There is no evidence in his career to suggest he would not have used the ball as he used every other. The man who could stop four consecutive shooters was, I fancy, capable of anything on a cricket field.

The history of the technical development of cricket has not yet been written and probably never will be, because not until recently has day-by-day criticism taken the trouble to examine the machinery from within. Cricket reports in Grace's time were concerned only with the facts as discerned from the score desk. Little has been recorded of the Master's fine shades of method and style. Perhaps it's as well; I tremble to think what W. G. would have had to say of any modern writer who wrote of his play in terms of either the poet or the pedant. 'You just put your bat to the ball,' we can imagine him telling us. 'And who the hangment was Zeus?' The remarkable fact about the great players of Grace's day was that they won their immortality without the aid of that school of literary criticism which at the present time is ready to 'write up' the next honest flock of geese as so many handsome and immortal swans. Today the word 'great' is attached to each and every innings of a hundred runs scored industriously on a flawless wicket in four hours. The newspapers must be able to get out a flamboyant headline, and it wouldn't do to print: 'Another dull innings by Bloggs.' Not long ago I had occasion to hunt amongst the files of a newspaper of the summer of 1895. I found a report of a match between Gloucestershire and Middlesex. It was set in very small type. Grace scored more than

150 in this engagement. The headline in the paper, to the account of this match, stated soberly and minutely (small type), 'Another good innings by Dr. Grace'. If today we think of the cricket of Grace's long reign in terms of character, personality—then surely there must have been really big men in action; for they contrived to fix themselves in the country's imagination and memory by deeds that had no fancy writing to give them a fair start on the road to notoriety.

Scanty though our materials are for a technical study of Grace's batsmanship, we can be positive about two attributes of his play which, though perhaps he inherited them from other years, he made his own. I allude to his ability to place his strokes almost to a yard; and to his ability to see and treat every ball strictly on its merits. 'I puts the ball where I likes,' was the comment of J. C. Shaw, a master of length bowling; 'and the Old Man, he puts it where *he* likes.' If you look at the painting of W. G. Grace in the pavilion at Lord's, you will see that his stance at the wicket was organized alike for defence and offence. You will see how cleverly the artist has suggested that as Grace stands ready for another ball, he has an open mind as to what manner of ball it is going to be. Grace at any hour of the day was likely to receive a vicious shooter; very well, then, after he stopped it he did not assume that the succeeding delivery was bound to be unplayable also. The average modern batsman is sent into his shell for a long time by one really deadly ball. A. P. Wickham, the old Somerset stumper, relates how Grace in an innings of over 200 did not allow half a dozen balls to pass the wicket unplayed. Grace's mastery over fast bowling is a fact enshrined in the heroic poetry of cricket. He smashed the alarming round-arm slingers of the 'sixties. And thirty-five years later, in the year of his Jubilee, he cut and drove the lightning bowling of C. J. Kortright and scored 126 out of his side's total of 203. Towards the end of his life, after his days in the cricket field had come to an end, he sat with a company of friends in his house one winter night. The conversation touched on fast bowling. Grace maintained that Tarrant of the 'sixties was one of the fastest bowlers he had ever known. 'But', remonstrated somebody who was jealous of more modern reputation, 'what about Ernest Jones?' The Old Man stroked his beard in contemplation. 'Jones?' queried he. 'Jones—ah, I remember him. The Australian fellow. Yes, I bear him in mind; the first ball he bowled at me pitched halfway down and went through my whiskers for four byes. Yes, I remember Ernest Jones—and I daresay he *was* fast—ay, I'd call him a fast bowler.' He gave

Ernest Jones the benefit of the doubt. Grace hit the fast bowlers in front of the wicket; he learned the thrilling trick from his brother, E. M. Grace, a cricketer who for gusto and humour turned every game in which he played into a chapter from Dickens. E. M. was the first to go out at fast bowling. Having a wonderful eye, he could hit forward the swiftest balls, and as he constantly drove them over the bowler's head the fieldsmen had to be placed in the long field. 'When I began to play in first-class cricket I followed the same tactics.' This was W. G. Grace's own tribute to his brother, whose natural genius for cricket would have laughed at the sophistication of C. B. Fry's Aristotelean book on 'Batsmanship'.

From all that we can find out about those cricketers who played with and knew Grace, he was very dogmatic in his faith in himself. 'Get at the bowler before he gets at you,' was one of his favourite sayings. Round about 1884 the Australians came to England with a new bowler, of whom it was advertised that he mingled with the arts of spin the black magic of devils. Grace came to Lord's one morning and went into the Australians' dressing-room. 'So you've got a new bowler?' he asked. 'Ay, Doctor,' was the reply; 'he's a marvel. You'll have to watch out this time.' 'What does he do?' said Grace, 'spin 'em, or what?' 'Oh,' came the propagandist reply, 'he mixes 'em, he mixes 'em.' 'Oh, he does, does he?' retorted Grace. 'Very well, I'll have a look at him this afternoon.' That afternoon Grace took guard for the M.C.C., and the new 'mystery' bowler attacked. During his first few overs, Grace's bat was like a stout door bolted against evil; he watched every ball as though Satan were behind it. Then, suddenly, he hit three fours and a three in one over from the unknown weaver of spells. And as Grace went up and down the wicket, he turned to his colleague and cried out in his high voice: 'Run up, Dick, run up; we'll mix 'em for him, we'll mix 'em for him!'

Grace's career in first-class cricket began with seven completed innings in 1865, his age then being seventeen. Without the break of a single summer it continued until 1908. In all, he scored 54,896 runs, at an average of 39.55. He also bowled to the tune of 2664 wickets, at an average of 17.99. It is often written and said of Grace that he invented modern batsmanship. The phrase has grown habitual amongst the Master's admirers. But it is to be doubted whether they are all fully aware how close to the truth the compliment comes. When Grace began to play, round-arm bowling had been the fashion for only some thirty summers. The amount of cricket played each

season in those times could today be got into six weeks. Grace
inherited a batting technique formed out of an obsolete attack. He
at once elaborated it and rendered it equal to every change that
happened to bowling in rapid sequence, after the bowler's arm was
permitted by law to be raised higher than the shoulder. How can we
doubt what Grace, with genius's adaptability, would have achieved in
batsmanship on modern turf? It has been written that he was not
too clever against slow bowling. Well, in 1871, he made 2739 runs
at the incredible average (in those days) of 78.90. The next best
batsman that year was Daft, whose average was 37 for 565 runs.
Only one other batsman in 1871 scored 1000 runs; that was Jupp,
and he batted nine times oftener than Grace. Tom Emmett was
playing cricket then; in this season of Grace's plenty, Emmett was
by no means an inconsiderable bowler. It would have been interesting to have his candid opinion, in good Yorkshire, of the notion that
Grace was not as good as he ought to have been against slow
bowling. Emmett used to wake up at night in a hot perspiration after
dreaming that W. G. had driven one of his balls hard back at him.

If Grace adhered to the principle of the more or less rigid right
foot in his batting, we must take it for granted, from the greatness
he carved out of the game, that the principle suited all the needs and
the circumstance of cricket as he met them. The technique of no
artist can be considered in the abstract; we must examine it in relation to the problems a man has to tackle, and in relation to the work
he needs to do. It is uncritical to argue that the technique of a
Palestrina is not as 'advanced' as that of a Wagner. In his middle
years, when he had grown rather unwieldy of body. Grace found he
could not thrust his left foot across to the off-side ball as quickly as in
earlier years. He therefore learned to pull the ball to the on side—
and by the acquisition of this stroke he began a new lease of
prosperity.

The attack of Grace on fast bowling had important consequences
to the game at large. But before I look into these consequences, let
me pay, in the words of an old Yorkshire cricketer, a tribute to the
Master's vehemence. This veteran was one of the slinging bowlers
whom Grace put severely in his place—at Lord's on a fiery wicket.
'I shall remember it to my dying day,' said the ancient from Yorkshire. 'I were only a young lad, and I was bowlin' then like the wind.
Nobody could stop me, and they asked me to play for t' Players
agaenst t' Gentlemen. I went to Lord's, and I can see misen goin' to
t' ground yet, all on a sunny mornin'. When I come to t'gates at

t'main entrance, a hansom cab drove up and the Doctor he got out. He were dressed in navy blue clothes, I think, and he looked big as Goliath. Before t'match began he comes into our dressin'-room and says to our captain: "So you've got a new fast bowler, eh?" And t'skipper says, in a loud voice, so as to encourage me, for I was only a young 'un: "Ay, Doctor, he can send 'em down." "All right," replies the Old Man, "I'll have a look at him." And, by gum, 'e did! When t'Gentlemen batted, I bowled at him for all as I was worth. And t'faster I bowled the more he cracked me. Hey, but he did and all!' (The old man's eyes glistened; he seemed unaware that he was telling of Grace's glory at his own expense.) 'All over the field he cracked me; he cut me into ribbons. He broke mi heart, and when I got back to my hotel I couldn't eat mi dinner. I went up to mi room, took off mi boots, and let mi feet cool on t'oilcloth. Then I got into bed and cried like a babby.' I do not know that a more eloquent or more generous acknowledgment than this has ever been made of the Master's ability.

The batsmen learned, from Grace's example, how to hit fast bowling in front of the wicket. Moreover, the pitches were by gradual stages more solicitously prepared, though not for many years yet were all the rough places to be made smooth. In the early 'seventies, bowlers began to contemplate the vanity of mere energy. As the hand got higher, the off-break was practised and deployed with some strategy. The school of Alfred Shaw began to teach almost axiomatically the virtue of accuracy in length and direction. When the summer of 1877 came, slow bowling was as widely practised as fast bowling. Grace was not in himself the cause of all cricket's deepening culture during the years of his progress to a national institution. Indeed, without an extension and subtilization of the technique of bowling from within itself Grace could not have transformed batsmanship from (to use Ranjitsinhji's phrase) 'the single-stringed instrument into the many-chorded lyre'. Even had Grace never lived at all cricket would have grown out of its Hambledon cradle and have marched over the English-speaking world. Had Bach never been born we should have had music rich and abundant enough. Daft and J. C. Shaw, V. E. Walker and Emmett, Carpenter and Lillywhite, each of these natural cricketers was giving cricket a push of his own on the road to where waited Hobbs and Rhodes, Hammond and Tate.

As soon as the arm of the bowler rose above the shoulder, a new world opened before cricketers—batsmen, bowlers and fieldsmen.

Grace was not the one and only fount that made the brooks of his heyday to flow. But lacking Grace, the period would have seemed to us today much as the eighteenth century would have seemed had it not known Dr. Johnson. In the absence of Johnson, there would still have been Boswell, Burke, Reynolds and the others! Grace's English humours, drawn out of West Country sunshine and wind and rain, passed into cricket itself. It will be a sad day when the juice of the man has run dry. He is not a fit subject for a technical study; he is not to be considered in the language of an abstract technical discussion. We must also see the man (as we must see Falstaff) against a background of historical circumstances. As he grew to power, cricket grew to power in proportion. The game was his kingdom, and we must see him like a monarch bestriding it. The counties met in tourney as though to break lances in his honour, for did not his authority lend to the counties identity? Was it not his goings up and down the land that first discovered cricket for the multitude in the counties? His parliament was Lord's, and he had great ministers, Lord Harris one of them. But he was the G.O.M. of Cricket; the crowd named him so.

More concretely still must we try to see this most palpable of Englishmen. Picture him on guard against Spofforth, the forked lightning threatening the great oak—another eternal attitude! Picture him as he runs over the earth to bowl, shaking it: 'An enormous man, rushing to the wicket, both elbows out, a black beard blowing on both sides of him, a huge yellow cap on the top of a dark, swarthy face.' He was the most dominating man ever seen on a cricket field. He was shaggy, gigantic. When a wicket fell he overtopped everybody that gathered in a group to look at the fallen stump. Always will cricket hold on to the memory of him as Lord's saw him on countless July days. A blue sky, torrents of sunshine, a match between the Gentlemen and the Players, and somebody just out. Grace standing amongst famous men, Lucas, Steel and Stoddart, his high voice chuckling. 'Well bowled, well bowled!' Or, best of all, let us keep him in mind playing the game on a field in Gloucestershire at the end of a murmurous first-class season, his enthusiasm and energy fresh yet, as though the month were May. It was in such a match that he put one of the most shrewd and comical leading questions ever devised by man of wit. He was playing for Thornbury, and after the match had been in action for a quarter of an hour, and after Grace had batted himself in comfortably, he hit a ball far to the deep field. As the ball was dropping well beyond a low wall, which was the boundary, long-on leaned against it and held the catch. There was tremendous hubbub at the wicket. 'Not out, not out,' towered the Old Man's high voice, 'that ball was over the boundary when it was caught. Put it down a four, scorer; not out, not out!' Altercation proceeded for a quarter of an hour, at the end of which period the matter was submitted to the jurisdiction of the umpire. 'Come here, George,' said W. G. to the rustic in the white coat. 'Come here, George. Now how many times have I told you—?!' To labour W. G.'s question further would spoil it. He learned cricket in the fresh air of Gloucestershire; he ripened cricket in his long lifetime. I see all of his days with the west country for a background. Morning after morning the summer's sun rose for him, and he went out into the fields to play cricket. Each springtime found him eager and not old. Surely something of the man's rich juice went for good and all into cricket to ensure that the game shall always, as the years come and go, have a springtime.

MACDONALD

THE present age knows Spofforth only as a legend. But they have seen Macdonald, who, not less than the 'Demon' bowler, sums up in his own skill and psychology the Australian cricketer today and for ever. He has Spofforth's pace, though not his many masks and contrivances. When Macdonald bowls slow he is not really on the kill. Macdonald also lacks Spofforth's unappeasable appetite; there are moments when he will not spend his energy on the small fry of batsmen. But how true to the traditional 'cornstalk' Macdonald holds himself. The sunshine of his land has gone into his body, making warm music of motion play throughout his suppleness. That sunshine, though, has not entered his mind. He is indeed the true Australian by reason of a want of juice in his temperament; the sun of Australia dries up the humours that breed urbanity in a man (there has never been an Australian humorist who was not satirical). Macdonald bowls fast and destructively, not out of the gusto of a Walter Brearley. When Brearley was upsetting wickets he reminded us of the hearty gale that turns head over heels the old woman and her apple stall. Macdonald's speed is seen by the imagination as a cold spear, flashing to destroy. Look at him as he runs to bowl: immediately his power is to be felt by all. We never have need to argue the fact of greatness; it knocks you over at first sight. Macdonald is under no obligation to be in form to convince us of his genius; personality transcends the utilitarian values. Judge the artisan by results, not the genius. Macdonald is possessed by an incalculable spirit; he does not always seem himself to understand the comings and goings of the forces within him. One day sees him masterful; it is then that his right arm is a wheel of war and pestilence. On another day his demon sleeps; now he is an ineffectual Lucifer of fast bowlers, 'dispossessed, chucked down.' Little use for Macdonald's captain to try to goad him out of his moments of majestic indifference. He rises in such periods beyond the Australian type; he is not reponsive to the call for a rally, an 'effort'. As well might a demand be made on Mount Etna when Mount Etna is sleeping.

At his best Macdonald will be remembered as one of the great fast bowlers of all time. When in 1921 he attacked for Australia with Gregory, we saw a sight as thrilling in its contrasted beauty as any ever witnessed on a cricket field—Gregory thundering over the earth, shaking it, and leaping up at the wicket by a great act of strength; Macdonald at the other end running along a curve silently, his arm sinuous, his wrist poising the ball before letting it go—the cobra's poise. Gregory bowled until he was dead tired; like Tom Richardson, he was one of nature's toilers under the sun, though he lacked Richardson's action, and wasted much of his gusto on the air. Macdonald's attack is always under the influence of a man mixed in his elements. Against a bad batting side Macdonald is as likely as not to bowl with a contemptuous slackening of his fires. I have seen him toss up slow off-breaks to frail batsmen, toss them up sardonically by the hour. Then I have seen him sweep these weaklings out of sight by sudden strokes of speed, as though he had impatiently said: 'Out of my way, scum!' In his prime, he was at his greatest against a great batsman. I have known him confront Hobbs at the Oval like one who for a long time has awaited this moment. He has taken the ball as though by right—before his captain has given it to him. He has seemed to cry out: 'This man is mine!'

Australia had her fast bowlers before Macdonald was given to her. But, like Gregory, they belonged to what George Lohmann called 'the brute force' school. Remember Cotter and Ernest Jones. ('Yes, I'd say he *was* a fast bowler all right!') Macdonald's pace, like that of all the game's really genuine fast bowlers, was the product of a rhythmical body action, and flexible wrists and fingers. His greatness resided wholly in his fast bowling—graceful and lissome fast bowling. The man has never been seen to make an awkward or angular movement; even when he tossed the ball up the pitch to the bowler at the other end, the curve of the flight through the air seemed somehow more beautiful than when other men threw. When he was on the kill, in the 1921 Test matches, his superb mingling of the rhythm of life with the dissonances of temper and conquest, rendered him the Australian cricketer seen *sub specie æternitatis.* There never was a cricketer of loftier disdain. At Trent Bridge I saw him at the end of a sweltering day. Notts had scored nearly 400 and it was six o'clock. Macdonald's captain—he was playing for Lancashire now—asked him for one final onslaught before close of play. Macdonald had bowled for hours, but he bowled again. He sent down an over of brutal bumpers. An honest yeoman named Flint hit three of these bumpers for four; the last ball of the over he hooked to the square-leg ropes for six. Macdonald, even before Flint's mighty stroke was finished, turned on his heel indifferently and slouched to his position in the field at mid-off. He did not even look where Flint's hit had gone. And somehow it was Flint that seemed the futile man. An onlooker in the crowd said: 'There's the Australian for you, all over.' Macdonald spat on the grass—the 'Digger' from head to foot.

DAYS IN THE SUN

THE GREATEST TEST MATCH

ON a bright day in the spring of 1921 I went to Lord's, hoping to see the first practice of the Australians. But the place was deserted, save for the man at the gates. He told me Armstrong's men were being entertained that afternoon somewhere in the City, and that they wouldn't be in the nets till after tea. Still, he added, with a touch of human nature not too common at Lord's, if I liked I could enter the ground and sit and enjoy myself in the sun till they came.

I sat on a bench with my feet spread out so that they touched the soft grass. A great calm was over the field. The trees beyond the Nursery were delicate with fresh green, and the fine old pavilion seemed to nod in the sunshine. It was an occasion for a reverie, and I fell to affectionate thoughts upon the great days of cricket, of the history that had been made on the field which stretched before me. I thought of Grace, of Spofforth, of Hornby, of A. G. Steel . . . Maybe I dozed for a while. Then I was conscious of a voice. 'Would you mind moving up a little? This seat is rather congested.' I looked around and saw sitting by my side a man in a tight black coat which buttoned high on his chest. He had sidewhiskers and wore a low turned-down collar and a high bowler hat. A handkerchief was showing from a breast pocket in his jacket. Not quite awake yet, I moved up. 'Thank you,' he said. 'I'm sorry I disturbed you. A nap carries one comfortably through a long wait at these matches. What a crowd there is!' I looked round. I was in the middle of a big crowd indeed. In front of me sat a parson. He was reading *The Times*. I glanced over his shoulder and saw the headline: 'Egyptian Campaign: Sir G. Wolseley's Dispatch.' The man at my side said, 'Were you here yesterday, sir?' and before I could reply he added, 'It was a considerable day's cricket, and the *Post* has an excellent account. Perhaps you've seen it?' He handed me a copy of the *Morning Post*, and, thanking him, I took it. The paper was dated August 29th, 1882. In a column headed 'England v. Australia' I read that, on the day before, Australia had been dismissed for 63 by Barlow and Peate, and that England, captained by A. N. Hornby, had made in reply 101. Then I understood my situation. And what is more I now understood it without the slightest astonishment. Even the aspect of the ground, which told me it was Kennington Oval and not Lord's, did not embarrass me. It was enough that I was one of the crowd that was to witness the second day's cricket in the ninth Test match—the most famous Test match of all.

I gave the *Post* back to my companion in silence. 'A considerable day's cricket indeed, sir,' said the parson. 'But England ought to have made more runs. Our batting was distinctly mediocre—almost as bad as the Australians'.' A loud cheer disturbed his argument. Down the pavilion steps walked the England Eleven in single file, led by Hornby. With him was 'W. G.', and he passed along the field with an ambling motion, and the wind got into his great black beard. He spoke to Hornby in a high-pitched voice and laughed. Then he threw the ball to a tall, graceful player just behind him and cried, 'Catch her, Bunny.' Following Grace and Hornby were Lucas, C. T. Studd, J. M. Read, the Hon. A. Lyttelton, Ulyett, Barlow, W. Barnes, A. G. Steel and Peate. The crowd quietened, awaiting the advent of Australia's first two batsmen, and I again heard the parson's voice ' . . . The English total was distressingly poor. Rarely have I seen poorer batting from an All England Eleven. The fact is, sir, that for some little time now English cricket has been deteriorating. Our batsmen don't hit the ball as hard as they used to do, and even our bowling . . . ' Another cheer drowned his discourse. 'Bannerman and Massie,' said my companion. 'I should imagine Bannerman's the youngest man in the match.' The parson was prompt with his correction. 'I believe S. P. Jones, who was twenty-one on the 1st of the month, is the junior member of the two teams. Studd is, I fancy, eleven months older than Jones. Bannerman is twenty-three at least, and Giffen is six days younger than Bannerman.' My companion was silenced, but I ventured a question. 'How old is Spofforth?' Pat came the answer, 'Twenty-seven on the ninth of next month.'

The crowd, including even the parson, went as quiet as a mouse as Barlow began the English bowling to Bannerman. Lyttelton, behind the wicket, crouched low. It was exactly a quarter past twelve. The next half-hour was a tumultuous prelude to the day. Bannerman was all vigilance, while Massie played one of the great innings of Test cricket. He hurled his bat at every ball the slightest loose, and his hits crashed ponderously to the boundary. He was the living image of defiance as he faced the Englishmen, glaring round the field his challenge. At one huge drive from Barlow's bowling my companion murmured, 'I've never seen a bigger hit than that at the Oval.' But the parson overheard him. 'When the Australians were here in '78,' he said, 'W. H. Game, playing for Surrey, hit a ball from Spofforth to square-leg right out of the ground.' Still, he admitted that this Massie fellow hit them quite hard enough. In half an hour England's advantage of 38 was gone. Hornby called up bowler after bowler, Studd for Barlow, Barnes for Studd. Steel tried his hand at 56—the sixth bowler in less than three-quarters of an hour. When Australia's score was 47 Massie lifted a ball to long-on. 'Lucas is there,' said the parson; 'he'll get it all r——. Good Lord!' For Lucas dropped the ball and blushed red as the crowd groaned out of its soul.

'Sixty-six for none,' murmured the man at my side; 'they're 28 on with all their wickets intact. If Massie prevails—ah, bravo, sir; well bowled, well bowled!' A ball from Steel had tempted Massie, and just as he jumped out it broke back and wrecked the wicket. Massie walked to the pavilion, roared home by an admiring but much relieved crowd. His innings was worth 55 to Australia, made out of 66 in less than an hour.

Bonner came next, and the English out-fields dropped deep and had apprehensive thoughts. Would not Massie's example make this bearded giant a very Jehu? But Hornby has an inspiration. He asks Ulyett to bowl instead of Steel. And Ulyett moves to the wicket like a man ploughing against a breaker, puts the last ounce of his Yorkshire strength into a thunderbolt of a ball that sends Bonner's middle stump flying. The crowd is only just getting back the breath lost in approval of this feat when Bannerman is caught by Studd at extra mid-off. Bannerman has batted seventy minutes for 13. 'Quick work for him!' says the parson. And with the broad bat of Bannerman out of the way the English bowlers begin to see daylight. Peate's slow left-hand deliveries spin beautifully, as though controlled by a string. The Australians now, save Murdoch, are just guessing. The fourth wicket falls at 75, the fifth at 79. Australia are all out 122. 'Only 85 to win,' says the parson. 'It's our game after all, though Lucas did his best to lose it.'

It was a true autumn afternoon going to its fall in grey light when 'W. G.' and Hornby went to the wicket to face Spofforth and Garratt. The crowd filled the ground, but so silent was it as Grace took his guard that one could hear the tink-tink of a hansom cab coming closer and closer along the Vauxhall Road. Spofforth's first over was fast—he let the ball go with a quick leap, dropping his arm at the moment of release. Blackham 'stood back' when Grace was batting, but crept up for Hornby. 'Beautiful wicket-keeping', murmured my companion. 'Pinder was not less gifted,' said the parson. And he added, 'I have not seen Spofforth bowl as fast as this for some time. He has latterly cultivated medium-pace variations.' Both Hornby and Grace began confidently, and at once the tension lifted. Hornby made a lovely cut from Spofforth and a dainty leg stroke for a couple.

Spofforth uprooted Hornby's off stump with England's score 15, and with his next ball clean bowled Barlow. The crowd gave out a suspicion of a shiver, but the advent of bluff George Ulyett was reassuring, especially as Grace welcomed him with a fine leg hit from Garratt for three and a beautiful on drive to the boundary from Spofforth. 'Thirty up,' said my companion; 'only 55 to get.' England was still 30 for two when Spofforth crossed over to the pavilion end. Now I was behind his arm; I could see his superb break-back. And he bowled mainly medium pace this time. With each off-break I could see his right hand, at the end of the swing over, finish near the left side, 'cutting' under the ball. Sometimes his arm went straight over and continued straight down in the follow-through—and then the batsman had to tackle fierce top spin. There was the sense of the inimical in his aspect now. He seemed taller than he was a half-hour ago, the right arm of him more sinuous. There was no excitement in him; he was, the parson said, cold-blooded. Still Ulyett faced him bravely while Grace, at the other end, time after time moved from his crease with a solid left leg and pushed the ball away usefully. 'Fifty up,' said my companion, 'for two wickets. It's all over—we want only 34 now.' And at 51 Spofforth bowled a very fast one to Ulyett, who barely snicked it. It served though; Blackman snapped the catch, and his 'H'zat!' was hoarse and aggressive. Lucas came in, and with two runs more 'W. G.' was caught at mid-off. 'What a stroke!' said the parson. 'I'm afraid he's not the Grace he was.' Four for 53, and Lyttelton and Lucas in. Lyttleton hits out big-heartedly, but the field is like a net tightly drawn. It is suddenly understood by every man of us that the game is in the balance. 'The wicket must be bad,' says somebody.

Lucas stonewalls, with a bat as straight as a die. Spofforth bowls a maiden; Boyle bowls a maiden; Spofforth bowls another maiden. The air is growing thick. 'Get runs or get out, for the Lord's sake,' says somebody. The field creeps closer and closer to the wicket. Spofforth and Boyle are like uncanny automatons, bowling, bowling,

bowling . . . Six successive maidens. 'This,' says the parson, 'this is intolerable.' One's heart is aching for an honest boundary hit . . . And the human bowling machines send down six more successive maidens. Think of it; twelve successive maidens, and the game in that state, the crowd in that purgatory. 'When Grace was a boy of eighteen I saw him make 50 on this very ground and he played every ball he got.' It was the parson again, but he sounded a little strained, a little unhappy. At the end of the twelfth successive maiden, a hit was purposely misfielded that Spofforth might have a 'go' at Lyttelton. The batsmen fell into the snare. Four more maidens, and spinning is Lyttelton's wicket. 'Anyhow, that's over and done with!' thankfully breathes the crowd. Better all be dead than dying! England five for 66—19 needed. Steel comes next and Lucas hits a boundary. Roars the crowd 'Bravo!' then catches breath. Steel caught and bowled Spofforth none—Maurice Read clean bowled second ball. England seven for 70. 'Incredible!' say 20,000 people in dismal unison. Barnes, the next man, hits a two. Thirteen to win. Heaven bless us, Blackman has blundered! He allows three byes. Run Barnes, run Lucas! Spofforth is inscrutable as the crowd makes its noises. His next ball is too fast for eyes at the boundary's edge to see. Lucas comes down on it, though—hard, determined. And the ball rolls ever so gently on to the wicket and disturbs the bail. Poor Lucas bows his head and departs, and blasphemy is riot throughout the crowd and is communicated by stages to the outer darkness of Kennington Road. The stars are set against England—our cricketers are for the first time on English soil face to face with a victorious Australian XI. With ten to struggle for, Blackman catches Barnes off his glove, and the last man is here—poor Peate, who is the best slow bowler in England and not a bit more of a cricketer than that, and what good are his mysteries of spin now? Studd is there yet, though; only ten runs and it is our game. Perhaps *he*—Peate has hit a two. It was audacious, but maybe the ball was a safe one to tackle. A bad ball's a bad ball at any time. Peate has nerve (so we are telling ourselves, desperately): he's the right man: he'll play the steady game to good stuff and leave the job to Studd . . . The stark truth is that Peate hit out wildly yet again at a slow from Boyle, missed it, and was bowled. There was a hollow laugh somewhere as the wicket went back, but whether it came from this world or the next I couldn't say. Studd did not get a ball. 'Why, man, did you try to hit: why couldn't you just stop them?' they asked Peate. 'Well,' he replied, 'I couldn't trust Maister Studd!'

38

As Peate's wicket was broken, ten thousand people rushed the rails and hid the green field. Spofforth was carried shoulder-high to the pavilion, and there the mob praised a famous man. I, too, wanted to get up and shout, but somehow I was rooted to my seat. I was probably the only man in that multitude on the pavilion not standing up, and as I sat there I had a strange sense of making a lonely hole in a solid black mass. The parson was standing on the seat beside me. His boots were not more than two feet from my eyes and I could see the fine ribbed work on the upper edge of the soles. The cheering came downwards to me, sounding remote. I lost grip on events. It seemed that I sat there till the ground was almost deserted, till over the field came a faint mist, and with it the vague melancholy of twilight in a great city. Time to go home, I thought . . . a great match . . . great days . . . great men . . . all gone . . . far away . . . departed glory . . . A hand of someone touched my shoulder and I heard him say: 'The Orsetralians are on the way, and they'll be in the nets at four o-clock. Nice in the sun, isn't it?'

TOM RICHARDSON

ON June 26th, 1902, Old Trafford was a place of Ethiopic heat, and the crowd that sat there in an airless world saw J. T. Tyldesley flog the Surrey bowlers all over the field. Richardson attacked from the Stretford end, and at every over's finish he wiped the sweat from his brow and felt his heart beating hammer strokes. Richardson had all his fieldsmen on the off-side, save one, who 'looked out' at mid-on. And once (and once only) he bowled a long hop to Tyldesley, who swung on his heels and hooked the ball high and far into the on-field. The Surrey fieldsman at mid-wicket saw something pass him, and with his eye helplessly followed the direction of the hit. 'One boundary more or less don't count on a day like this,' it was possible to imagine the sweltering fellow telling himself. 'Besides, Johnny's plainly going to get 'em anyhow.' The ball slackened pace on the boundary's edge. Would it just roll home? The crowd tried to cheer it to the edge of the field. Then one was aware of heavy thuds on the earth. Some Surrey man, after all, had been fool enough to think a desperate spurt and a boundary saved might be worth while, blistering sun despite. Who on earth was the stout but misguided sportsman? Heaven be praised, it was Richardson himself. He had bowled the ball; he had been bowling balls, and his fastest, for nearly two hours. His labours in the sun had made ill those who sat watching him. And here he was, pounding along the out-field, after a hit from his own bowling. The writer sat on the 'popular' side, under the score-board, as the ball got home a foot in advance of Richardson. The impetus of his run swept him over the edge of the grass, and to stop himself he put out his arms and grasped the iron rail. He laughed—the handsomest laugh in the world—and said 'Thank you' to somebody who threw the ball back to him. His face was wet, his breath scant. He was the picture of honest toil. With the ball in his hands again he trotted back to the wicket and once more went through the travail of bowling at J. T. Tyldesley on a pitiless summer's day.

This was Tom Richardson all over—the cricketer whose heart was so big that even his large body hardly contained its heroic energy. And this hot June morning the crowd mused about a day that had dragged out an intolerable length six years earlier—in 1896—on which England had struggled bitterly with Australia at Old Trafford, and Tom Richardson had touched as sublime a heroism as ever cricketer knew. This Manchester Test match of July 1896 seems now to have been fought on so vast a scale that it might well be thought none but giants could have sustained the burden of it. Yet when Richardson's part in it is retold he was a very colossus that made pygmies of the others—made even Ranji a pygmy, despite that he played the innings of his life.

Australia batted first and scored 412. England—with Grace, Ranji, Stoddart, Abel, Jackson, J. T. Brown, MacLaren, Lilley and Briggs to look to for runs—were all out for 231, and the Australian captain sent us in again. And once more the English cracks were reduced to littleness—all save Ranji, who, in Giffen's term, 'conjured' an innings of 154 not out, out of the total of 305. Australia needed 125 for victory—a mere song on the wicket. Old Trafford gave itself up to the doldrums as soon as Iredale and Trott had comfortably made a score or so without loss. Then it was that Richardson's face was seen to be grim—his customary happy smile gone. In Australia's first innings he had bowled 68 overs for seven wickets and 168 runs. Yet he was here again, bowling like a man just born to immortal energy. And four Australian wickets were down for 45 in an hour. If only England had given the Australians a few more runs, the crowd wished out of its heart—if only Richardson could keep up his pace for another hour. But, of course, no man could expect him to bowl in this superhuman vein for long . . . Thus did the crowd sigh and regret. But Richardson's spirit *did* go on burning a dazzling flame. The afternoon moved slowly to the sunset—every hour an eternity. And Richardson *did* bowl and bowl and bowl, and his fury diminished not a jot. Other English bowlers faltered, but not Richardson. The fifth Australian wicket fell at 79, the sixth at 95, the seventh at 100. The Australians now wanted 25, with only three wickets in keeping. McKibbin and Jones—two rabbits—amongst them. 'Is it possible? whispered the crowd. 'Can it be? Can we win . . . after all? . . . Why, look at Richardson and see: England must win. This man is going to suffer no frustration. He has bowled for two hours and a half, without a pause. He has bowled till Nature has pricked him with protesting pains in every nerve, in every muscle of his great frame. He has bowled till Nature can no longer make him aware that she is abused outrageously, for now he is a man in a trance, the body of him numbed and moving automatically to the only suggestion his consciousness can respond to—'England must win, must win, must win' . . . With nine runs still to be got by Australia, Kelly gave a chance to Lilley at the wicket and Lilley let the ball drop to the earth. The heart of Richardson might have burst at this, but it did not. To the end he strove and suffered.

Australia won by three wickets, and the players ran from the field —all of them save Richardson. He stood at the bowling crease, dazed. *Could* the match have been lost? His spirit protested. Could it be that the gods had looked on and permitted so much painful striving to go by unrewarded? His body still shook from the violent motion. He stood there like some fine animal baffled at the uselessness of great strength and effort in this world . . . A companion led him to the pavilion, and there he fell wearily to a seat. That afternoon Richardson had laboured for three mortal hours without rest. In the match he bowled 110 overs and three balls, for 13 wickets and 244 runs. He never bowled again in a Test match at Manchester.

This man Richardson was the greatest cricketer that ever took to fast bowling. Lockwood had nicer technical shades than Richardson —a guile which was alien to the honest heart of Richardson. But Lockwood had not a great spirit. He was a bowler at the mercy of a mood; an artist with an artist's capriciousness. Richardson bowled from a natural impulse to bowl, and whether he bowled well or ill that impulse was always strong. His action moved one like music because it was so rhythmical. He ran to the wicket a long distance, and at the bowling crease his terminating leap made you catch breath. His break-back most cricketers of his day counted among the seven wonders of the game. He could pitch a ball outside the wicket on the hardest turf and hit the leg stump. The break was, of course, an action break; at the moment of 'release' his finger swept across the ball and the body was flung towards the left. And his length was as true as Attewell's own. But who is going to talk of Richardson's art in terms of the 'filthily technical', as Mr. Kipling would call it? His bowling was wonderful because into it went the very life-force of the man—the triumphant energy that made him in his heyday seem one of Nature's announcements of the joy of life. It was sad to see Richardson grow old, to see the fires in him burn low. Cricketers like Richardson ought never to know of old age. Every springtime ought to find them newborn, like the green world they live in.

CRICKET FIELDS AND CRICKETERS

THERE is surely some interaction between a cricket team and the ground it mainly lives on—does not the play of the side assume tone and colour from the scene? Yorkshire cricket has the aspect of Bramall Lane and Leeds—dour, and telling of stern competitive life with smoke and real industry about. Can you imagine the shrewd Lancashire game quite at home under a June sky at the Saffrons? Does not there come through the cricket of Sussex the brown and sunny flavour of Eastbourne and Hove when the time of day is noon and the earth seems humming with heat? The plain homeliness of the Midlands is expressed by Leicester-shire cricket: it has no airs and graces, no excessive refinements. See an innings by Cole, of Leicestershire, and you ought not to be long guessing from the smack of rotund nature about it that he has passed the main portion of his days in the sun on a field with rustic benches running intimately round. No, it is not mere fancy to say: 'Show me a cricket team in action and I'll tell you where is its native heath.'

Take Lord's, for example. The country spirit, the circumscribed life denoted by country, is not for Lord's. For your good cricketer the ends of the earth have come to a resting-point at Lord's, and wherever he may be at the fall of a summer's day his face should turn religiously towards Lord's. Lord's is the Cosmopolis of cricket. And which county do you find playing the bulk of its games at Lord's? Why, naturally enough, the team that, less than them all, gives us the definite county flavour. Middlesex has ever been as cosmopolitan as Lord's itself—a side gathered from the earth's corners, West Indians, Australians, even Yorkshiremen! A man from Huddersfield sat in the crowd at Lord's a season or two ago, and as he watched Middlesex beating his own county he was stirred to a protective derision—a derision which he cultivated as balm for the wound that defeat at cricket must always bring to Yorkshiremen. 'Middlesex?' he asked of the throng around him. 'Wheer's Middlesex? Is it in Lundon?' His barb was well directed; London obliterates the county boundaries, and neither at Lord's nor at the Oval do you feel the clannishness that stings you in the atmosphere of Old Trafford or Bramall Lane. To be eloquent of authentic county demands a certain narrowness, a contentment with those things of the earth, and that part of the earth, which Providence has placed immediately at one's doorstep. County means nature—and at Lord's cultivation borne on the winds of the world has rather expelled nature. Watch Hearne move fastidiously towards a century; watch Bruce or Crutchley batting, and you are looking on cricket played in the drawing-room of civilized men and women. And at those times when Bosanquet bowled at Lord's there came into the game the touch of exquisite decadence that marks a true Cosmopolis. Frankly, I have never yet been able to fix Hendren into my notion of Lord's; he is quite indecently provincial in his relish of a thumping boundary.

There is, of course, in the life of a civilized cricketer little that is sweeter than a summer morning at Lord's, a morning when the sky is a blue awning blown out with soft wind, and the trees at the Nursery End make a delicate motion. 'The Nursery End at Lord's!' The phrase sets memory astir, for have we not read in days of old in those evening papers our boyish eyes scanned that 'Richardson went on at the Nursery End', that 'Ranjitsinhji glanced Noble to the rails at the Nursery End'? Because Max Beerbohm has never written an essay called 'Going to Lord's on a July Morning' we have proof he has never in his life walked down the St. John's Wood Road with a day of cricket in sunny weather before him. But perhaps it is not given to the man who lives only round the corner from Lord's and can visit it every day to feel its appeal as keenly as the man from the north, who not more than three or four times a year walks down the

St. John's Wood Road. Let the morning be quiet and mellow and there seems in the air about the St. John's Wood Road, at least to one not too familiar with the place, a sense of the dead old days, causing a melancholy which no doubt one ought to be ashamed of. The mind is made by this something in the St. John's Wood air to play with .ancies of Victorian greatness hanging about the spot; of a gleaming hansom cab at the entrance and a black-bearded man, looking mountainous in everyday clothes, getting out while folk standing round murmur ' "W. G." !'; of simple-faced men in wide, uncreased trousers proceeding along the pavement—the names of them, likely enough, Lockwood, Lohmann, Richardson—all keen to 'get at the old 'un'. No lover of cricket as he wanders about Lord's can very well keep the thought of Grace from his mind, for though Grace was a Gloucestershire man surely he larded the green earth at Lord's till the very spirit of him may be said to have gone into the grass. You see, just as Lord's is too large in spirit to stand for any one county or for any one space of time in cricket's history, so did the amplitude of Grace transcend Gloucestershire and his little day. At Lord's with a June morning spending its warmth, one feels a kind of resentment that there should ever have been a bourne put by nature on W. G.'s capacity to endure and play the game till he was utterly tired of it. Is not Lord's here for him now just as ever it was, and a summer day here also, one so fresh that it casts clean out of the understanding the thought of years that pass away? Why should it ever happen to a cricketer that a June morning comes on which the sun begins in the old comfortable way to climb the sky, and Lord's stands in the light, full of summertime animation, and he no longer there to know of it?

II

Leave Lord's one day and tomorrow discover Bramall Lane and you enter another world. Frankly, the cricket field at Sheffield is a blasted heath, but, as Shakespeare knew, it is on blasted heaths that matters of grim moment come to pass. A Lancashire and Yorkshire match is not to be thought of at Lord's; here at Sheffield the scene tells a plain tale of the stiff energy of north country life, and it provides the right setting for a battle between ancient hosts where the informing spirit is of a dour and combative blood feud. Squat chimneys outside the ground loom black, and even on a Bank Holiday the air contains a hint of furnaces and steel smelters. And

44

to the man who likes his cricket moving dramatically on the right stage the Bramall Lane crowd is a work of art. It is a multitude which seemingly throws out a white heat and causes the game to boil over prodigiously. Who at Sheffield on Whit Monday in 1922 will ever forget the great crowd that watched Yorkshire struggling for a first innings advantage over Lancashire the day long? It was a crowd unashamedly partisan. No room had the red-hot ranks for the equanimity that can look on an issue and say: 'May the best side win.' This vast gathering lived the violent afternoon through to one thought, to one thought alone: 'Down with Lancashire. Trample the Red Rose in the dust.' Here we had a partisan temper which sought to persuade events in Yorkshire's way. There was surely not a man on Bramall Lane's desolate plain that afternoon who would not have held up his hands to the sky till pain scourged him had he believed that such a martyrdom would keep the hurly-burly favourable to his county. Not magnanimous, you might well say; still, there is an aspect to partisanship as brittle as this which is not entirely to be despised. If the Sheffield crowd cannot attend to the amenities at the sight of an advance by the ancient foe, if it is driven in the hour of Yorkshire's adversity to a fury and apprehension that have no use for a magnanimous admiration of the skill of the conquerors, we may wish ourselves far away from such a crowd, and thank our stars cricket does not breed many like it, but we certainly cannot deny that here is 'character', here is rich red blood and abundant spirit.

I have heard folk from the south say of cricket at Sheffield that it simply is *not* cricket. Their preference has been for the game as it is played with trees and country graciousness around. But why put a limit to cricket's appeal; why deny her infinite variety? Lancashire and Yorkshire at Bramall Lane is not less cricket than any match in an old meadow at Little Slocombe on the laziest day in June. Cricket, indeed, has many facets; it can satisfy most of the human animal's interests and emotions, and, as we have seen, it is sensitive to most of our moods and our habitations. It can stir one, at Sheffield, into a very man of war; it can soothe one, at Tonbridge, to the sweetest peace. In turn, it can sound a clarion note that sets the combative spirits in the blood running agog like hey-go-mad, as Tristram Shandy would say; and in turn it can capture the summer's own music.

III

Kent cricket, as you may see from a mile's distance, was born of Canterbury and Tonbridge—an innings by Woolley is a pastoral. And those who have Miss Mitford's eyes for the summer game will find cricket at Worcester lovable. The pretty field there, true, is overshadowed by the town and its industry, but all the bricks and mortar of the place are huddled at one side cosily, and there is the cathedral to look at. The Worcester cricket ground is in the midst of meadow-land; the scent of grass is here all day and a wide space of sky above. Here a cricket-lover may seek out a corner of the field, lie down at full length and watch the game from a distance. (There is some enchantment about watching the movements of men in white through the sun's haze from a long way off.) And well does Worcestershire cricket suit countryside ease and humour. It is even a virtue in a place so full of green loveliness as this that Worcestershire often cannot play severely expert first-class cricket. The rough conflict of the championship manner would seem surely to mock Worcester's drowsy landscape. This is a cricket field apt for the country club game, and it is the happy country club cricket Worcestershire plays.

Looked at from strict first-class standards, Worcestershire's bowling these last few years has been rather a joke. Better far to look at it from the tolerant country club view. Let us talk of the Worcestershire bowlers not with the names they are known by in the list of first-class averages, but by names like Smith, Jones, Brown and Robinson—all names of jolly good fellows for a country club match. Smith we all know; he possesses strong views on the leg-break, but somehow it never comes off 'in the middle'. Jones has a complete mastery over the principles of the googly—in the smoke-room when he is playing matches over again in reminiscent mood. Brown once got a wicket against the M.C.C., and of course there is always a chance that he will some day do it again. And Robinson boasts an ability to swerve with a new ball; he goes on at the outset of the innings, and will be ready again when the 200 is up! How they must enjoy their summers down at Worcester!

IV

The world of Kent and Worcestershire cricket and the world of Yorkshire cricket might appear far apart, yet Lancashire manages to make the best of both. At Old Trafford the game has a hearty sportsmanship, yet this is an efficiently ordered ground, which never lets you forget that Manchester knows a thing or two about getting and spending. Old Trafford, like Lancashire cricket, is both utilitarian and human. Makepeace, who plays the game as a machine might play it, is at home at Old Trafford, but so was Johnny Briggs, a cricketer who was always smiling. Old Trafford possesses a nice name, and more of the open air gets into it than into Kennington Oval, for there still are fields outside Old Trafford, so that its beautiful stretch of turf does not cause you to ask, as the turf at the Oval does: 'How on earth did it get here?'

The Old Trafford crowd is fond of Lancashire cricket, but not so jealous of it that there will not be generous applause for a triumphant invading host. When Lancashire collapses the Old Trafford crowd will simply curse the county players heartily for a while and ease its heart that way. But at Leeds one afternoon, when Yorkshire collapsed against Notts, though the crowd took a rather lasting sorrow with it to tea, no word of complaint or distrust was uttered against Yorkshire cricket. There, in a word, is the difference between a Lancashire crowd's regard for its county XI and the Yorkshire crowd's. The one is based on the notion that after all cricket is only a game and hence need not ever be an occasion for a gnashing of teeth; the other sees in cricket—that is, in Yorkshire cricket—one of the finer passions of life, a possession of the clan not to be rudely handled. The Yorkshireman's intolerance of an enemy's prowess is simply the measure of the Yorkshireman's pride in his county's genius for cricket.

The Australians find the best light in the country at Old Trafford —no nonsense about waving trees there! And at Old Trafford the Australians have made history. The writer, for one, will always remember Armstrong sitting on the grass at Old Trafford, refusing to go on with the game until the crowd, which was in a bad temper, for a wonder, stopped barracking him. He will also never forget the innings Darling played at Old Trafford in the 1902 Test match—a small innings numerically, but how lion-hearted! It was a day of lowering clouds and Australia was in an awkward situation. Darling came in and played a death or glory innings, the fitful sun glinting on his bat. Not in great Test matches, though, has Old Trafford found its true heart, but when Hornby and Barlow were at the wicket and we all looked devotedly on as 'the run-stealers flickered to and fro'. Perhaps Old Trafford is less Lancashire than Manchester; there is not much in its prosperous shape—the pavilion is the

image in stone and mortar of your successful Manchester man—
that tells of the county's scrambling little mill towns where cobbled
streets go up and down hill. None the less it is more like Lancashire
county than Kennington Oval is like Surrey county. For if Lord's is
cosmopolitan, the Oval is distinctly metropolitan. One of the ironies
of the game, surely, is that Surrey, with its hills and downs, has in
cricket come to be associated with Kennington and a setting of
bleak tenements and confident announcements (on hoardings) about
somebody's pale ale and dry gin. Little of breezy country air passes
over the Oval. And so, because the Oval incessantly comes to mind
when one thinks of Surrey cricket, one is driven to thinking of the
Surrey team as made up wholly of the stuff of Cockaigne. Bobby
Abel was the personification of Surrey cricket seen through the air
of the Oval; the pert lift of the cap on his head, the slick dexterity of
his play, with bat at an impudent angle—all these gave cricket a
Cockney accent. Poor Tom Richardson, with his sun-tanned face
and black hair, was, I can hardly think, rarely in his heart's home
with the odours of modern Vauxhall about him. Why cannot Surrey
find for occasions a pleasant field somewhere, say, near Cranleigh?

V

Nottinghamshire cricket has never been unfaithful to Trent
Bridge. That perfect pitch at Trent Bridge went a long way towards
the making of the Nottinghamshire cricket tradition. For on a
cushion of Trent Bridge marl, batsmanship was tempted to proceed
comfortably along the lines of least resistance. The poor bowler was
at a discount at Trent Bridge in fine weather; no long and keen
challenge was sent from him to the batsman. 'Keep your wickets up,
lads, and runs will come', seems usually to have been the easy
philosophy of Nottinghamshire cricketers—dwellers for a season's
better part on Trent Bridge, a Lotus-land for batsmen, a place
where it was always afternoon and 360 for 2 wickets. That guileless
turf at Nottingham accounted for Shrewsbury, whose every innings
was the stately blank verse of batsmanship; accounted for Attewell,
pitching the ball on a sixpenny piece's circumference till soothing
monotony came over the onlooker; accounted for Scotton, the
stonewaller: 'Block, block, block at the foot of thy wicket, O
Scotton!' In its heyday Nottinghamshire cricket was fit for heaven
and eternity. You could admire it like unflawed marble, but, being
human, you could not live with it for long. How powerfully the

Trent Bridge pitch contributed to the cold Nottinghamshire cricket tradition of the past may best be understood if we look at the doings of the Nottinghamshire XI in 1907—a wet summer. In that season Notts won the championship by cricket as brilliant as Kent cricket. The rain took from the Trent Bridge wicket its customary ease-fulness; no longer could a batsman dawdle on it all day while his score mounted almost without a thought from him, his innings growing in the warmth like a plant. No; he had now to get runs by art and quick wit against a spinning ball, and the Nottinghamshire XI responded beautifully to the stimulus of the new environment. Today, one believes, the wicket at Trent Bridge is no longer as delicately nurtured on marl as it was in the old times: Nature in the grass is given a better chance of asserting herself. If this is the truth, we can hardly put it down to accident that nowadays Nottingham-shire cricket has perhaps a more lively habit of mind, a freer gait than ever it had: that A. W. Carr, wearing the mantle of A. O. Jones, is leading his batsmen from its ancient flat lands to slopes romantic-ally uneven.

VI

You can't get away from it—cricket does turn sensitively to sun and the setting, moves to the passing of summer in England. True, they play cricket in Australia and South Africa; the game, in fact, has gone round the wide world. But not in the lands of dry light and parched brown earth is cricket the game we know and love here. Cricket as a combat and as a display of skill would be fascinating in the Sahara, no doubt; in England only does the soul of it unfold. You have never even wooed cricket, let alone won it, if you have looked on the game merely as a clever matter of bat and ball which, given a fine day and expert players, might be appreciated at any time of the year like football, which is as good to watch in December as in April or May. One, indeed, has heard folk ask for winter cricket, to be played in some glass-domed Olympia brilliant with electric light. The cricketer of soul knows better than this. He knows that whoever would appreciate cricket rightly must have a sense, as he sits in the sun (there can be no real cricket without sunshine), that he is simply attending to one part, and just one part, of the pageant of summer as it slowly goes along, and yet a part as true to summer as villages in the Cotswolds, stretches of gleaming meadow-land, and pools in the hills. Cricket in high summer is played with the mind of the born lover of it conscious the whole time that all this happy English life is around him—that cricket is but a corner in the teeming garden of the year. Pycroft in *The Cricket Field* writes of 'those sunny hours . . . "when the valleys laugh and sing",' and plainly the memories of them as he wrote his book were as memories of some sweet distillation of cricket itself. You see, at cricket there is a chance to bask in a comprehension of the summertime setting and spirit; the game more often than not is a leisurely game. And so the watcher may be mindful, as the men in white come on to the field at the fresh of the morning, that the sun is beginning a lazy journey up the sky; that, while the game pauses in the hour for rest and lunch, the earth is smoking in the heat of noon; that at the fall of day, with its shadows and peaceful night—why, then the watcher of the game may also see the peach bloom come in evening skies. All things that matter are these to cricketers of heart and to our delectable game. Only on dull days and in dull places is cricket dull.

BY THREE RUNS
(The Greatest Test Match at Old Trafford)

THE most thrilling finish of all the Test matches over fought at Old Trafford happened on the Saturday afternoon of July 26th, 1902. It was the decisive game of the rubber, and Australia won it by three runs, snatching the spoils from the lion's mouth. The match at the end seemed to get right out of the control of the men that were making it; it seemed to take on a being of its own, a volition of its own, and the mightiest cricketers in the land looked as though they were in the grip of a power of which they could feel the presence but whose ends they could not understand. As events rushed them to crisis even MacLaren, Ranjitsinhji, Trumper, Noble and Darling—most regal of cricketers—could only utter: 'Here we do but as we may; no further dare.' The game, in Kipling's term, was more than the player of the game.

The match was designed, surely, by the gods for their sport. Even the victors were abominably scourged. On the second day, when the issue was anybody's, Darling played an innings which, as things turned out, must be said to have won Australia's laurels as much as anything else. Australia in their second innings had lost 3 wickets—those of Trumper, Duff and Hill—for 10 runs and now possessed an

BY THREE RUNS

advantage worth no more than 47. Under a sky of rags, the fitful and sinister sunlight coming through, Darling let all his superb might go at the English attack. His hitting had not the joyfulness of mastership in it; its note was desperation. He plainly felt the coils of circumstance about him; he plainly was aware of the demon of conflict that had the game in grip. And the defiant action of his bat was like a fist shaken at the unfriendly heavens. It was in this innings of Darling's that the gods played their first cruel trick. For with Darling's score only 17 he was impelled to sky a ball to the deep field —a high but easy catch. And who was the wight that the ironic powers had decreed should shoulder the responsibility of taking that crucial catch? His name was Tate—Tate of Sussex, a kindly fellow who never did harm to a soul. The humour of the gods really began when this cricketer was asked to play for England instead of George Hirst. Tate was a capital bowler, but as soon as he was seen in the company of the great the question went out: 'What is he doing in this galley?' Tate had not the stern fibre of character that can survive in an air of high tragedy; his bent was for pastoral comedy down at Horsham. Tate missed the catch, and never looked like holding it. As he stood under the ball, which hung for a while in the air—an eternity to Tate—and then dropped like a stone, his face turned white. Darling survived to make 37 out of a total of 86. Had Tate held the catch Australia could hardly have got a score of more than 50, for Lockwood and Rhodes, that Friday afternoon, bowled magnificently. Yet when Tate laid himself down to rest in the evening, can he not be imagined as saying to himself: 'Well, it's nearly all over now, and as far as Tate of Sussex is concerned, the worst must have happened. I never *asked* to play for England—they thrust greatness on me—and I'll be well out of it this time tomorrow, back to Brighton, and who'll remember my missed catch after a week? What's a muff in the field in a cricketer's career?—everybody makes them.' If Tate did console his spirit in this way the poor man did not know he was born. The gods had not finished with him; the next day he was to be put on the rack and have coals of fire heaped on his head.

On the Saturday England were left with 124 to get for victory. A tiny score—with the cream of batsmanship at hand. But there had been five hours of rain in the night, and Trumble and Saunders were bowling for Australia. Still, England seemed nicely placed at lunch; the total 36 for none and MacLaren and Palairet undefeated. The crowd took its sustenance light-heartedly; everybody lived at

51

ease in a fool's paradise as rosily lighted as Tate's. Here, again, was the humorous touch of the gods: men that are taken suddenly out of contentment are the more likely to writhe in Gehenna. After lunch the sun got to work on the wicket, and straightway Palairet was bowled by an intolerable break from Saunders. Tyldesley came in, and, with MacLaren, the game was forced. The play of these two batsmen gave the crowd the first hint that all was not yet settled in England's favour, for it was the play of cricketers driven to desperate remedies. The runs, they seemed to say, can only be got if we hurry; there's the sun as well as Trumble and Saunders to frustrate. Tyldesley jumped to the bowling; he hit 16 runs in quick time before he was caught in the slips. England 68 for 2—56 wanted now, And, said the crowd, not yet sniffing the evil in the wind, *only* 56, with Ranji, Abel, Jackson, Braund and Lilley to come, to say nothing of Rhodes and Lockwood. Why, the game is England's! Four runs after Tyldesley's downfall MacLaren was caught by Duff in the long field. An indiscreet stroke, yet whose was the right to blame the man for making it? It had come off time after time during his priceless innings of 35, and England could not afford to throw a single possible run away. MacLaren had played like a gambler at a table—not looking as though he were making runs, but rather as one who had ample boundaries at his bat's end to bank on every throw of the dice.

Abel and Ranji were in when at last the multitude unmistakingly saw the evil day face to face. For what sort of a Ranji was this? Palsy was on him. You could have sworn that he shook at the knees. It looked like Ranji; his shirt rippled in the wind even as it did on that day at Old Trafford six years earlier than this, the day on which he conjured 154 runs out of the Australians. Yes, it looked like Ranji—the same slight body, the same inscrutable, bland face. Alas! the spirit had gone—here was a deserted shrine. Thousands of eyes turned away from Ranji and looked to Abel for succour. Ah, this is better—the pertness of little Abel lightened the soul. He made gallant runs—a boundary over Hill's head. 'Cheeky' work this—batsmanship with *gaminerie*. 'Bravo–Bobby!' shouted the Old Trafford crowd. At 92 Ranji was out, leg-before-wicket to Trumble. Well, the sophist crowd told itself, that was bound to happen; he never looked good for any at all. But 5 runs more and Trumble bowled Abel. England 97 for 5—27 needed. 'It's quite all right,' said a parson on the half-crown stand; 'there's really no cause for anxiety. To doubt the ability of Jackson, Braund, Lilley, Lockwood and

Rhodes to get a paltry 27 runs would be scandalous. Besides, I do believe that fellow Tate is a batsman—he has an average of 16 for Sussex.' The century went up with cheers to herald it—the crowd made as much of joyful noise as it could, presumably in the hope that cheering would put a better face on the scoring-board. Jackson, who made a century in the first innings, scored seven in his best 'Parliamentary' manner—neat, politic runs. Then he was caught by Gregory, and now the cat was indeed out of the bag; sophistry passed away from the heaped-up ranks. 'Who'd 'a' thowt it?' said a man on the sixpenny side. Who, indeed? At that very moment of agony at Old Trafford, people far away in the city read in the latest editions, 'England 92 for 3,' and agreed that it wasn't worth the journey to Old Trafford, that it had been a good match, that the Australians were fine sportsmen, and jolly good losers.

Sixteen runs—four good boundaries or four bad ones—would bring the game into England's keeping when Lilley reached the wicket.

He was frankly and unashamedly in some slight panic. He hit out impetuously, as who should say: 'For the Lord's sake let it be settled and done with quickly.' Braund was overthrown at 109, and Lockwood made not a run. Lilley lashed his bat about like a man distraught. Rhodes is his companion now, and stands on guard ever so cool. Eight runs will do it, and 'There goes four to them!' affirms the red-hot crowd as Lilley accomplishes a grand drive into the deep. 'Well hit, sir!' shouts our parson. 'Nothing like taking your courage in both hands against these Australian fellows. Well hit, sir!' Clem Hill is seen running along the boundary's edge as though the fiend were after him. Trying to save the four, is he?—even from as certain a boundary hit as this! Extraordinary men, Australians; never give anything away. Hill, in fact, saved the boundary in the most decisive manner in the world by holding the ball one-handed before it pitched. The impetus of his run carried him twenty yards beyond the place where he made the catch—a catch which put incredulity into the face of every man and woman at Old Trafford that day. 'A sinful catch,' said the parson. Tate, the last man in, watched Rhodes ward off three balls from Trumble, and then rain stopped play. Yes, rain stopped play for forty minutes—and England eight runs short of triumph with the last men in. But though it was heavy rain there was always a bright sky not far away— another piece of subtle torture by the gods, for nobody could think that the weather was going to put an end to the afternoon. It would clear up all right in time; the agony had to be gone through. The crowd sat around the empty field, waiting, but hardly daring to hope. The tension was severe. Yet surely there were calm minds here and there. Why, under a covered stand sat two old gentlemen who were obviously *quite* indifferent to the issue. One was actually reading to the other the leading article from one of the morning papers. Moreover, he was reading it in a controlled and deliberately articulated voice. 'Sir M. Hicks-Beach argued yesterday,' he read, 'that even if Ireland was overtaxed in 1894, its grievance was less today, because taxation had not increased quite so rapidly in Ireland as in the United Kingdom.' And the other old gentleman, so far was he from troubling his head needlessly over a mere cricket match, promptly took up the points in the argument, and he too spoke in a perfectly controlled and deliberately articulated voice. 'Two wrongs,' he commented, 'do not make a right.' Excited about England and Australia? Not a bit of it, sir! We trust we are old and sensible enough to put a correct valuation on a game of cricket.

In the pavilion Tate was dying a thousand deaths. All depended on him—Rhodes was safe enough. In his head, maybe, notions went round and round like a wheel. 'You've only to keep your bat straight,' he might well have said to himself time after time. 'Don't even move it from the block-hole. I've heard tell if you keep your bat quite still it's a thousand to one against any ball hitting the wicket' . . . At six minutes to five the Australians went into action again. Saunders bowled at Tate—a fast one. Tate saw something hit the ground and he made a reflex action at it. Click! Tate looked wildly around him. What had happened? A noise came to him over the wet grass, sounding like a distant sea. The crowd was cheering; he had snicked a boundary. Another snick like that and the game is England's and Tate safe for posterity! The ball was returned from the ring, and Darling slightly but impressively rearranged his field, the while Saunders bent down to a sawdust heap. Bloodless, calculating Australians they were. Tate got himself down on his bat once more, and the wheel in his poor head went round faster and faster. ' . . . Bat straight . . . don't move . . . can't hit wicket . . . block-hole . . . don't move . . . Bat straight . . . can't hit wicket . . . ' And the gods fooled him to the top of his bent—to the last. Saunder's fourth ball was not only good enough for Tate's frail bat; it was good enough for the best bat in England. It was fast through the air and— it was a shooter. It broke Tate's wicket, and, no doubt, broke Tate's heart and the heart of the crowd.

54

In twenty minutes Old Trafford was deserted save for one or two groundsmen who tended to the battlefield. The figures on the scoreboard had revolved, obliterating all records of the match from the face of it, which now looked vacantly over the grass. The gods had finished their sport—finished even with Tate. Yet not quite. A week later, on the Saturday afternoon following this, Tate met the Australians again in his beloved Sussex, and he was graciously permitted to play an innings of 22 not out against them—and a capital innings at that.

CRICKET AT BRAMALL LANE

(Notes from a Diary)

[Being an account, written 'on the spot', of the play in the Lancashire and Yorkshire match at Sheffield on Whit Monday, 1922—the wildest day of cricket in the writer's experience. Yorkshire were batting nearly all the time, eager for points on the first innings, Lancashire's score having been 307.]

LIFE no less than art achieves now and again an expressive picture. In the scene at Bramall Lane we had a typical representation of Lancashire and Yorkshire cricket; the stern spirit of it was given significant form by the crowd's mountainous bulk, the hard antagonism of the play, the ugliness of the setting of chimneys and huddled tenements, all of them telling of the competitive life that is led in this part of England. Almost the only note in the cricket that went on to a ceaseless roar from the multitude was the note of conflict, harsh indeed. Almost, one says, but not wholly. Scourging though the fight, one cricketer there was to remind us of the grace which is the game's very soul. Sutcliffe's bat made sweet curves, and, like the true artist, he was aware of the beauty he was fashioning. The contrast of his batting with the dominant unloveliness of the morning's action moved one romantically; it made one think of the jewel in the toad's head.

The Lancashire bowlers got their first taste of blood after half an hour's work, Holmes attempting to cut Cook's fast ball and sending it into slip's hands. And from then for some gruelling ninety minutes onwards no other satisfaction came to Lancashire. In a stand for Yorkshire's second wicket Oldroyd and Sutcliffe added 92 runs, playing with a confidence that put the crowd into a state of blessedness. Yet it cannot be said that the batsmen, any more than

the bowlers, were ever masters: the issue was dramatically even—
one got the sense from the play now of a violent tug-of-war, the rope
taut, with no man giving ground at this end or that.

A solitary boundary hit came in the first hour. Cook's bowling had
matchless length: in sixty-five minutes he bowled 13 overs, 5
maidens, for 20 runs and 1 wicket. The Sheffield roar went into the
sky as Yorkshire reached the first hundred, after some hundred
minutes' toil. Lunchtime was nigh, and vast appetites eager for it,
when a disaster fell on Yorkshire which turned to vanity the crowd's
thought of meat and drink. Oldroyd pushed a ball to the off-side, and
to every Yorkshireman's dismay Sutcliffe dashed down the pitch.
Stung to madness he was by the very imp of mischief that pricked
Makepeace to ruin on Saturday. Oldroyd did not budge an inch,
and Sutcliffe saw his wicket broken far away behind him—in sad
perspective indeed must his wicket have looked to him, for he was
in Oldroyd's crease when the stumps were broken. A Lancashire
man witnessed Sutcliffe's unhappy downfall with mixed feelings—
it provoked gladness because a dangerous Yorkshire stand had been
ended, but sorrow also at the sight of so much grace trapped in a
snare.

Sutcliffe batted for two hours and a half. He is one of the most
artistic professional batsmen in the country. Forward play is his
main game, and he manages it with an elegant thrust of the left leg,
the most easeful swing of the bat, with the wrists putting polish on
the stroke at the penultimate second. There is indeed a pretty little
flick of his bat at every stroke's end: it is the artist's way of expres-
sing delight in work well done—one sees it and thinks of Dickens's
flourish of a signature, Whistler's vain but charming butterfly.
Sutcliffe perhaps is wanting the power necessary to handle an attack
drastically and so win a match. But amongst defensive batsmen he
stands apart; he gives Utility coloured feathers to preen. The score
at lunch was Yorkshire 138 for 2. In the two hours and a quarter's
play of the morning the Lancashire bowlers sent 57 overs down,
including 17 maidens, for 110 runs. In this time only nine boundaries
were hit.

From the first ball after lunch Roy Kilner was leg-before-wicket
to Richard Tyldesley. Rhodes and Oldroyd added 44, then Rhodes
was caught, fourth out at 182. Seven runs later Oldroyd fell to a
cunning ball by Richard Tyldesley, and, with Yorkshire's total
unchanged, Robinson was leg-before-wicket. Thus in quick time the
game suffered yet again one of those convulsions which strike fire

out of a lover of cricket. We had all imagined the play in the morning strenuous enough, but soon it was apparent we had been living in a place becalmed. For the match waxed fit for the fighting gods. The two sides set teeth grimly in a struggle for a first innings lead—for points that might well have a critical value. As Norman Kilner and Wilson bent low on their bats the pot started a-boiling. One seemed to feel the heat of the antagonistic fires that were setting it in motion. The batsmen were plucky and attacked the bowling. Runs came from cracking bats, and the roars of the crowd were like the wind in the woods on a wild day. It was war to the knife now; art and method were not heeded by batsman or bowler. Nothing but naked conflict mattered in this hour: grit and brute strength were pitted openly against grit and brute strength. Surely cricket has never been played more fiercely than these rivals played it at this period; surely it has never had its airs and graces so ruffled!

For three-quarters of an hour the pace of the game was too giddy for eyes to follow. One got only an impressionistic picture of it— bowlers scowling and heaving themselves at the wicket; bats handled drastically; fieldsmen agitated and awry; snicks through conster- nated slips, taking your breath away; heavy thuds to the boundary. And all the time a packed mass of 26,000 Yorkshire folk turning the sunny afternoon into Bedlam. Madder and madder went the speed of the match. The batsmen were getting on top by sheer desperation and quick eyes. And suddenly the Lancashire fielding went to pieces. With Yorkshire's score 237 happened one of the craziest kettles of fish ever witnessed in the cricket field. Kilner and Wilson got into a muddle over a run and discovered themselves in the same crease. Blomley, the Lancashire stumper, had the ball in his hand and needed but to throw it to the other end to run Kilner out by half the length of the pitch. But as Kilner dashed down the wicket confusion fell upon Blomley, who, instead of sending the ball through the air after Kilner, rolled it along the grass, like some old gentleman on a bowling green. Kilner stumbled, but none the less he got home in time.

The howls of the crowd as Kilner fled to his crease, the ball following him, were the howls of the furies. Never, indeed, has one known a crowd so explosive as this, never has one known on a cricket ground such noise as this crowd made at every ball bowled. The passions of the mob passed like hot fluid through the ranks; it was a Shakespearean crowd in the sudden changefulness of its emotions. Cheers greeted a good hit; mockery fell on the fieldsman that bungled. In the Wilson-Kilner stand Parkin's bowling was punished severely and the crowd taunted him. And when at last Parkin gave way to Cook and the batting went into comparative quiet again, the crowd shouted: 'Put Parkin on! Put Parkin on!'

The seventh Yorkshire wicket fell at 244, Kilner falling to a magnificent catch by Hallows. At tea Yorkshire's score was 263 for seven. Forty-five were needed by Yorkshire for a first innings victory when the game went on. Macaulay and Wilson played capitally, tackling the bowling with true Yorkshire pugnacity. The total reached 283 before Macaulay was caught on the leg-side. Dolphin, next man in, hit a lusty on-side boundary; Wilson, still playing a resolute game, cut a ball from Richard Tyldesley through the slips for four. At 296 Dolphin fell in Richard Tyldesley's leg-before-wicket trap. One Yorkshire wicket to fall and a dozen wanted. Waddington came in now as calm as a master batsman. 'Put Parkin on!' again moaned the crowd. Kenyon arranged and rearranged his field, and trusted to his length bowlers.

Cook went at it with all his heart; Richard Tyldesley controlled his leg-break with amazing steadiness. Still, the batsmen persisted; seven overs they withstood, and at the finish of them Yorkshire were 306, one run behind. Tyldesley now got himself ready to bowl at Waddington; the Lancashire field crept close to the wicket. And the crowd got itself ready to roar out Yorkshire's victory to the world. The ball which Tyldesley at length bowled was slow, well pitched in the air, and so spun as to break away as it hit the turf. And how did the man Waddington play it—Waddington, who had so far been all composure, all confidence? He jumped recklessly out of his crease, missed the break and was stumped. The match so far was Lancashire's. At the vision of this lunacy of Waddington's the crowd did not believe its myriad eyes. It had been ready to move Sheffield with a shout of triumph; its pent-up breath passed out of its ranks like air from a pricked bladder. A silence fell over the field more significant even than the loudest of the afternoon's thousand ear-splitting noises; it was the silence of men and women sick at heart through hope outraged.

Much of the anxiety Lancashire passed through during the afternoon was of the team's own making. Good fielding would have put an end to Yorkshire's innings long before the race became neck and neck. After the fall of Yorkshire's sixth wicket the fielding fell into slovenliness. An easy chance of stumping given by Oldroyd when he was 34 went begging. Wilson was missed in the slips with his score

21. The frenzy of the crowd seemed to upset the Lancashire men badly. Before lunch the bowling had all-round excellence; in the crisis during the afternoon Richard Tyldesley alone, and perhaps Cook, kept a cool head. Parkin was a big disappointment, and it seems as though this Sheffield crowd will be the death of him. Three years ago he bowled against Yorkshire at Bramall Lane and had no wickets for 99. This afternoon 74 runs were hit from his bowling, and again his wickets were none. Thus his record at Bramall Lane is none for 173. Yet before lunch today he bowled really well, and at least one catch was missed from him. James Tyldesley on the whole possessed little length or direction. Cook was mainly his own steady self. But had Richard Tyldesley not been present Yorkshire might easily have left Lancashire a hundred behind. He bowled all day with the coolest art, using his leg-break with the nicest judgment and keeping a length astonishingly accurate for a bowler with his spin.

The stormy day—the stormiest the writer has ever known at cricket—proceeded to a calm end, with Hallows and Makepeace putting confident bats to the Yorkshire bowling. As the crowd beat up the dust on the homeward journey at close of play one felt a touch of disillusionment somewhere. And if I have written of the crowd in this account almost as much as I have written of the cricket itself, my excuse must be that the crowd acted a considerable part in the day's play. It was, indeed, the villain of the piece.

A NOTE ON CHAPMAN

WHEN Chapman played for the Gentlemen in 1920, though he then made but a score or so, he was written down as an England batsman of tomorrow or the day after. For a while Chapman, true, did not uphold this promise; judged by the test of averages he was a failure in 1921. One or two cricketers had the sense to see that Chapman's mistakes in this period were the mistakes of a batsman in whom spirit was stronger than craft. The impulse of genius often comes before mastery over technique has been established: Chapman suffered many a fall, just as a fresh-born bird does—but with the same excuse. He knew he was destined to soar sooner or later; he felt it in his young blood.

In 1921 Chapman could boast but a tiny band of friends with

faith in him, and the writer was soundly taken to task by one of the oldest and most experienced umpires in cricket for suggesting that Chapman had greatness in him, despite his failures.

> Your makers of quite new men, producing them
> Had best chalk broadly on each vesture's hem
> The wearer's quality.

Chapman in 1921 was spendthrift while yet lacking the dower experience brings; but the next summer saw him come into his own. At Lord's in the University match he made a century against an indifferent Oxford attack, and a few days later he made another against the Players, carving a way to glory out of the finest professional bowling in the land. In this innings his play was hailed even by old judges of the game—those jealous guardians of the fame of ancient days—as the best left-handed batsmanship displayed on an English cricket field by an amateur since the days of F. G. J. Ford.

In Australia, critics were able to appreciate the fine points of Chapman's art, for in Australia left-handed batsmen have set up illuminating standards. Hill, Bardsley, Ransford and Darling have all exhibited superb left-handed batsmanship in recent years. Yet even these cricketers hardly spilled a brilliance of Chapman's lustre. Hill and Bardsley, indeed, must be classed with the utilitarians. They fought by the book of arithmetic; even their most masterful cricket seemed to have in it the canny Australian nature. Darling touched heroic poetry at times, but he knew little of the joyous cavalier mood of Chapman; Darling at his most challenging was a Titan, struggling with odds and scattering them by a strenuous act of energy. Ransford's play gave us a sense of the artist's satisfaction that the end of beauty as well as the ends of utility were being served, but it was not so rapturously youthful as Chapman's.

Here we are at the crowning glory of Chapman's cricket—it is the cricket of youth. He looks the young cricketer all over—tall, sturdy, pink-cheeked, and fair of hair. He goes to the crease like one in search of adventure. The good ball that baffles him and just misses his wicket does not dismay him; he invariably has a smile for the bowler, and larger impudence for the next ball.

He has rarely given us a game more in keeping with his nature than his little innings of 48, made in the North *v.* South match at Manchester the other summer. He was always up to mischief, like some scamp of a schoolboy. Barratt from Notts, knowing no doubt of Chapman's love of playing wantonly at off-balls, bowled fast outside his off stump to a field containing no fewer then five slips. The charm of this innings of Chapman was that he would not be dismayed by the sight of those five crouching slips. He met Barratt's challenge in the happiest and most adventuresome heart; once, twice, thrice he jumped at Barratt's bait, flashed his bat at the flying ball—and gleefully eluded the slips.

None of us could grumble because this innings was not flawless in execution. Cold perfection is no ideal for a rosy young man like Chapman to pursue; for him, who has youth nipping sharp in the blood, an innings must needs be a big adventure, with every stroke an escapade. This is not to suggest that Chapman cannot achieve beautiful and skilful batsmanship. Of course he can. The point is that his finest strokes are just as spontaneous, just as impulsive, as his bad ones. He does not achieve a perfect hit by taking more thought than he takes when he blunders into a mishit; good, bad, or indifferent, his cricket is a quick, unpremeditated expression of the youth in him, and he comes by his beautiful strokes, just as he comes by his indiscreet strokes, simply because beauty and indiscretion are the proper accompaniments of youth. Some day Chapman will grow up into one of the most finished batsmen in England; but for my part I would have him remain a boy for ever.

THE SUMMER GAME

OUR VILLAGE

ON Saturdays at high noon in a certain village of the Cotswolds, a little cricket field stands silent in the sun. Over the grass walks an old horse, pulling a roller and led by an old man. There is to be a match this afternoon, and though everywhere is quiet, the preparations are going forward. Organization is in the air. The click of a latch on the ground's wooden gate is suddenly heard. Mrs. Renshaw and her daughter walk along the path carrying a tea-urn. They keep carefully to the path, for, not being themselves cricketers, they would not dream of putting foot on the grass. Yet Mrs. Renshaw, her daughter, and the tea-urn, are week by week, summer after summer, indispensable parts in the whole of Ludbury's cricket team. That fact is never overlooked by the XI itself and those who lead the XI to victory and defeat. At every annual meeting of the Ludbury cricket team, held in the schoolroom on a dark February evening, the Rev. W. G. Soames, after he has performed the distribution of medals for good batting, bowling and fielding, will conclude his remarks by an allusion to Mrs. and Miss Renshaw. And invariably he will add, with a display of the jocular, 'Where, indeed, would the Ludbury cricket team be without the ladies?' One year this question was most suddenly and startlingly answered from the back of the hall by George, the club's ancient umpire, who cried out in a loud voice, 'Why, zur, we'd be having to make our own cups of tea, we'd be!' Having accomplished this interruption, George appeared all at once to see something funny in his words; he burst into a great guffaw, and set the whole meeting guffawing too, which was not good for the Rev. Soames's speech.

George is the 'official' umpire of Ludbury C.C. That is how he himself puts it. I do not think George is a good umpire; to say the truth he is not impartial. At the finish of every season the Ludbury XI is photographed in flannels; George, clad in his white coat, appears in every group, and invariably he is to be seen standing with his arms folded and his legs stuck out and his face set aggressively— as though determined to merge himself into the general air of combativeness assumed by everybody else in the portrait. But if I say George is not an impartial umpire, it must not be thought he is wickedly unscrupulous. His prejudices are frank and unconcealed; he is partial in his decisions for exactly the same reason that David Smith bowls so fast for Ludbury that his back hurts him all through the following Sunday. George wants Ludbury to win always. Moreover it is my private conviction that George has never correctly read the wording of Rule 3 of the Laws of Cricket as revised by the Marylebone Cricket Club. That rule runs as follows: 'Before the commencement of the match two umpires shall be appointed; one for each end.' Old George, I am certain, when first he read the laws of cricket as a small boy, glanced hastily over the third rule and understood it to signify . . . 'two umpires shall be appointed; one for each side'. It would be of no use attempting to alter George's view of the rule at this time of day; I am afraid he will carry his error to the grave. In Coltswold cricket, of course, each eleven travels with its own umpire. One of these umpires, during a match against Ludbury, once gently remonstrated with George about a strange decision of George's. And George with calm and dignity replied, 'Yew luke after yewr bus'ness and I'll luke after mine.' The implication clearly was that different points of view tend to lead to different judgments.

It is not hard to become a playing member of the Ludbury C.C. Neither birth nor residential qualification is necessary. Any afternoon, if you should happen to be strolling round the ground just before the beginning of a match, the chances are that the Ludbury captain—none other than the Rev. W. G. Soames—will approach you and say, 'Would you care for a game, sir?' If your reply should be, 'I'd be delighted, but the fact is I don't play cricket'—well, the Rev. W. G. Soames is certain to say, 'Oh, that doesn't matter at all; you'll soon pick it up. We've a spare suit of flannels in the pavilion. George! Take this gentleman into the dressing-room and give him Mr. Robinson's trousers. He's not with us today, and this gentleman has kindly agreed to play in his place.' If, on the other hand, you should be in a position to accept the Rev. W. G. Soames's invitation with some confidence, mentioning as you do so the fact that you bowl a pretty off-break and that your batting average is 17.18, the information will be gratefully received and deemed not altogether superfluous. The Rev. W. G. Soames opens Ludbury's batting in company with his gardener, Joseph Huggins. The moment the Rev. Soames breaks his duck he begins to hit; he is an ardent supporter of the movement to 'brighten' cricket and has occasionally written letters to the newspapers on the subject. His favourite stroke is a huge on-drive from, or rather against, a good-length ball on the middle stump. More often than not he is severely bowled, whereupon Joseph Huggins, at the other end of the pitch, turns to the umpire—probably it is George, who as the stumps are sent flying wishes he could restrospectively announce a no-ball—and say, 'George, 'e do be no more patient than you or me.'

Mrs. Renshaw leaves her work with the tea-urn and looks through the little window of her room and watches the cricket whenever the Rev. Soames is batting. And at the fall of his wicket she will go back again to the tea-urn saying, 'It's a great shame they never let him have a nice ball.' The Rev. W. G. Soames contributed last year to the controversy upon Cricket Reform. He wrote a long letter to the newspapers, and in it he delivered himself of this statement: 'As to four stumps, perhaps the opinion of a village club cricketer of thirty years' standing will not be without point. County cricket, sir, is not the whole of the game, and the M.C.C. cannot legislate as though only county cricket existed. In our class of cricket there is no demand at all for four stumps. It not infrequently happens, indeed, that we club cricketers find even three stumps to be one too many. I enclose my card and sign myself, sir, Yours truly, A Country Parson.'

Joseph Huggins does not believe in recklessness; he is something of a stonewaller, even though he does spit on his hands a good deal while he is at the wicket. Huggins is every year at the top of the Ludbury batting, just as David Smith every year is top of the bowling. These two strong men are the team's backbone; the other members, save the captain, vary in skill and identity match by match. 'Birds of passage,' so George rhetorically calls them. The Rev. Soames does his best to bind together his fortuitous material. Now and again he is not successful. In a match the other day a ball was skied in the middle of the pitch by one of Ludbury's opponents. Three Ludbury fieldsmen moved forward, all eager to take an easy catch. With great presence of mind, the Rev. Soames grappled with the dangerous situation. He 'named' the fieldsman most likely to get the ball. 'Thompson,' he cried out, commandingly, masterfully. 'Leave it to Thompson.' Each of the three fieldsmen retired backwards with exemplary obedience, and the ball fell to earth between them. Then the Rev. W. G. Soames bethought himself; there was no Thompson playing for Ludbury this week.

Summer after summer the game goes on down in the Cotswolds. David Smith thunders over the earth and bowls his yorker. A ripple of clapping announces that the fifty is up—for seven wickets—and the boy by the scoreboard sorts out his tins and looks for a Nought and a Seven. In the silences that come over the game you can hear lovely summertime noises, the low hum of a hot June day as it goes towards evening. When the shadows are lengthening and in the slanting light soft sheen falls on everybody's flannels, the match is finished; the cricketers come walking home to the pavilion. David Smith with his sweater hanging about his great shoulders, and last of all old George, wearing his white coat and in his arms all the six stumps gathered together. Very soon the little field is vacant. Footsteps on the wooden front of the pavilion make gentle echoes. A bird runs quickly over the grass, stops quite still for a moment then runs on again. In the high trees the rooks are going to their nests. There is the click of the gate's latch at the corner of the field. Mrs. Renshaw and Miss Renshaw pass through carrying the urn. The Rev. Soames holds open the gate and follows after. But before he departs on his own way home he says: 'Good evening, Mrs. Renshaw; good evening, Miss Renshaw. Thank you so very much. A very enjoyable day, I'm sure, very enjoyable indeed'. Dear cricket of the Cotswolds, would that I were playing you every day—if only to be given the benefit of the doubt by George. 'Not Hout!' he would be sure to say when the bowler hit me on the leg. 'Not quite hout, but nearly.'

THE LEGENDARY RHODES

THE Present is usually impatient when the glories of the Past are dinned in its ears. It takes refuge, naturally enough, in scepticism. Today many a young cricketer is being turned into a doubting Thomas by the persistent glorification of the old masters which goes on week after week, much to the belittlement of his own talents. 'MacLaren?' he exclaims. 'Spooner? No doubt they were good in their own day, but would they be as good now? Cricket is different. Bowling is different. The old batsmen played forward and never covered up with the pads. They'd have a bad time today.' Thus is the protective scepticism perpetuated. 'Tom Richardson? A fast bowler, of course! But would he be able to bowl fast on modern wickets?' And the poor ghost of Richardson chafes in its prison of the immaterial. It cannot revisit the earth to confound incredulity by bowling on contemporary pitches with the strength and velocity which, on the unflawed grounds of Australia, astonished the world many years ago.

One classical bowler, and no more, is left to us, the last of his school. Rhodes is the only surviving exponent of the ancient craft of slow left-handed spin. No shadow of scepticism has yet dared to creep over the setting sun of his renown. No young man has yet dared to say, 'Rhodes? Ah, but he was an old-fashioned slow bowler! He would be helpless on modern wickets. You old 'uns exaggerate his spin. It couldn't possibly happen on a prepared turf. Rhodes must have bowled on some funny wickets. Besides, batting is different—they use the pads more than they did in Rhodes's time. He would never get anybody out now. It's a different game, believe me. Slow bowling, tossed up to the bat? Good gracious! It would be hit all over the field by present-day batsmen!' No; these grudging remarks have not yet been directed at the bowling of Rhodes. For the man is still with us, and every day he announces his mastery. But in a few years, when Rhodes has finished his cricket, is it certain that he will not, with others of the old masters, live to hear his genius challenged by young men who never saw him bowl? And how will it be possible then for him to refute the unbelievers? A cricketer's art is thrown out on the summer air; it enchants us for a while, and then it is gone. Already is the beauty that Ranji spread over our fields a memory, cherished by a few of us here and there. The ballade of Andrew Lang comes sadly to mind.

'Ah, where be Beldham now, and Brett, Barber and Hogsflesh, where be they?' We will be wise to make the most of this Rhodes, while he is here, in action. He was to be seen at Bradford only the other Monday, tossing up the ball in the gentle, insinuating way that he has been tossing it up, man and boy, for thirty years. The same familiar walk to the bowling crease, a few quick but easy steps, a little effortless leap, then the body comes through after a beautiful sidelong swing. No fuss, no waste. Conservation of energy and perpetual motion. And so inscrutable!—poor batsman, what is behind all these curving balls that come to your bat so invitingly, saying 'Hit me, I'm here to be hit'? The curving line of Rhodes's flight—is there anything in cricket, or in any other game, more lovely to see? But the beauty is a spell; the monotonous rhythm of it, as ball after ball comes through the air dropping, dropping, dropping on the same spot at the same pace—take heed, batsman, your senses are being benumbed, minute by minute. The ball does *not* drop on the same spot; it does *not* come through the air at the same pace. It is all a delusion and a snare. One ball pitches well up to the bat: it is played easily, though maybe not for runs, for Rhodes sets his field to an inch. The next ball also is pitched well up—and the next. The batsman is sure of it. Yet somehow he does not seem to think he reached that last one quite so easily as he reached the others! Was it a tiny bit shorter? The batsman takes off his cap at the over's end, wipes his brow, and smiles at Wilfred, who smiles back, but says absolutely nothing.

A matter of skill and science is this slow bowling. Unless it is certain in technique a schoolboy will play it. The fast bowler can get his wickets with long hops, full tosses; the unnerving element of pace helps him. Even your medium-paced bowler owes something to what George Lohmann called 'brute strength'. Slow bowling at its best is all technique and brains. Rhodes has in his life mastered thousands of batsmen by nothing but his strategy and cleverness. When he was young he could make the ball spin like a top, pitch it on the leg stump, and cause it to whip away as though imps were inside. A sticky wicket was needed for the bowling of Rhodes's break-away—and then no stroke in the practice and science of batsmanship could be trusted not to play the spin with the edge. In those days 'c Tunnicliffe, b Rhodes' was a phrase known all over the land. One day, in a hot summer, the weather suddenly changed just as Essex were going down to Bramall Lane to play Yorkshire. Charles McGahey looked over his shoulder at the darkening sun. ' 'Ullo!' said he. ' 'Ullo! Caught—Tunnicliffe, b—Rhodes 0.' And it was so, both innings.

But in the spin of Rhodes, even when he commanded it vitally, did not reside his own secret. Blythe had as much spin as Rhodes. The truth is that no great batsman is likely to be bothered by break, save on unplayable pitches, if he is in no trouble while the ball is coming through the air. Rhodes gets his men out before the ball pitches; spin with him is an accessory after the act of flight—flight which disguises the ball's length, draws the batsman forward when he ought to play back, sends him playing back when he ought to come forward, and generally keeps him in a state of mind so confused that in time he begins to feel it might be a mercy to get out. Against Rhodes, no long innings has ever been played that did not at the end find the batsman intellectually a little worn and weary. In 1903 at Sydney, on a perfect wicket, hard and polished, the might of Australia's batsmanship passed processionally along the hot day— Trumper, Armstrong, Duff, Noble, Hill. Trumper made 185 not out, and Australia's total was nearly 600. Rhodes bowled forty-eight overs for 94 runs and five wickets—one of the great bowling performances of all time. On the smooth Sydney turf he could not, of course, exploit spin. He overthrew some of the most celebrated batsmen that ever lived, on a cast-iron turf, by subtlety in the air. Flight—the curving line, now higher, now lower, tempting, inimical; every ball like every other ball, yet somehow unlike; each over in collusion with the rest, part of a plot; every ball a decoy, a spy sent out to get the lie of the land; some balls simple, some complex, some easy, some difficult; and one of them—ah, which?—the master ball.

The career of Rhodes reads like a romance. He won a name for himself in 1898, when Queen Victoria was on the throne. That season, at the age of twenty, he took 154 wickets at 14 runs each. Two years afterwards his record was 251 wickets in a season, average 15. In 1902 he went in last for England at the Oval, when his country wanted 15 for victory. Hirst, the batsman at the other end, met this young and smooth-cheeked Rhodes and said, 'Wilfred, we'll get these runs in singles.' I like to think that Hirst also said, 'And if tha gets out, Wilfred, Ah'll waarm thi!' Young Rhodes did not get out and England won by one wicket. Rhodes was not supposed to be a batsman then—only the foremost left-handed bowler in the game. But he conceived a strange ambition; he thought that some day he would like to 'go in first for England'. He applied himself diligently to the study of batsmanship, and in time he did go in first for England with Hobbs, against Australia in Australia, and, what is more he contributed his share to the longest first-wicket stand in the history of Test cricket. In 1911 Rhodes scored 2000 runs and took 100 wickets. Then he let his bowling go out of mind a little; he fell wholly in love with making runs and fielding. Yet no England eleven was complete without this same Rhodes, now a great batsman, once a great bowler.

Then came the war, and Yorkshire lost Booth and Drake. In 1919 Rhodes had turned forty, and his bowling days were a distance behind him, an old glorious memory. But now his bowling was needed by Yorkshire again; that was cue enough for Rhodes. He picked up his art of flight just at the point where years before he had put it down—picked it up as though he had never let go of it for a moment. And today, at the age of fifty, he remains the best slow bowler, here, abroad, anywhere. The man's life and deeds take the breath away.

Last summer but one Rhodes played for England and bowled Australia out at the Oval, winning us the Ashes a quarter of a century after he had, a mere boy, batted last for England, on the same ground, at the same hour of the day, England wanting 15 to win and George Hirst waiting for him at the other end. On that August day of 1926 the mellow sunshine of a summer nearly over fell aslant on the ground, touching to dignity the scene of Rhodes's farewell to greatness in Test cricket. We who sat there watching saw the wheel of his career come full circle. Today Rhodes is content to go on confusing the enemies of Yorkshire, quietly, modestly, as a change bowler and a cricketer with a past so full of history's noises that, to those of us who have never known the game without its Rhodes, the sound is like 'the surge and thunder of the Odyssey'.

1928

ROY KILNER
April 1928

IT is sad for a cricketer to die in the fullness of life, but sadder still when a cricketer passes away at the spring of the year. Players of the game will everywhere be sad indeed at the news of Roy Kilner's death in the month of April, just as the call of a new season is gladdening their ears.

To say that Roy Kilner was a popular cricketer is not half enough. It would be a poor sort of man who could not make himself a popular figure with a cricket crowd, for he lives through his summers against the background of the most beloved game of all. It was not only as a clever cricketer that Roy Kilner was liked; the crowd saw more than the successful professional batsman and bowler. They understood that within this rotund and happy shape there resided a deal of honest Yorkshire county. The North Country's humours, its breadth, directness, roughness, and kindliness, were visible wherever Roy Kilner walked. He stood for a rich and substantial part of this England of ours. In Roy Kilner, the average man of the Yorkshire crowd could behold his own self. It is hard to believe we shall never again look upon Roy, with his cap cocked jauntily on his head, a little askew; his wide, bland face; his compact circumference, beautifully rounded at the back; his little pert run to the bowling crease; his flick at the off-side ball with an impudent bat—have all these lovable and human sights gone for ever from a Yorkshire cricket field? It is hard to believe, indeed; it is like being told that some genial Yorkshire breeze has died and will never again blow over the faces of men and refresh them.

In recent years the Yorkshire eleven has been a machine, almost inhumanly working for victory, day after day, grimly, inevitably. You could never fit Roy Kilner into that great machine. He was, of course, as fine a match-winner as anybody else in his eleven, but he was never disciplined by an iron collectivism out of his own original senses. He was constantly a jolly Cavalier amongst a lot of dour Ironsides. Many a time I have seen Roy, in a Lancashire and York-shire match, flashing his bat dangerously at Macdonald's fastest off-side bowling. And at the other end of the wicket I have seen Wilfred Rhodes, or Emmott Robinson, regarding Roy's laughing countenance with the utmost disapproval. Often I have wondered what Emmott was thinking (deep in his heart) about Kilner's behaviour. 'Look at the man! A-tryin' to cut! And Ah've told him till Ah'm tired that the cut never were a business stroke. Hey, Roy! Will t'*never* get any sense!'

With Roy Kilner, as with every true cricketer, the style was the man himself. The rare blend of shrewdness and gusto, of humour and the fighter's spirit, which came out in his batting and bowling— all these qualities were to be felt during a moment's contact with him, in the briefest conversation. Your Yorkshireman is always proud of the stuff of nature out of which he has been put together. Roy Kilner was always himself, whether he happened to be in York-shire, in Middlesex, or in Bombay. He had charm, the most delight-ful ways about him—but there was not a hint of self-conscious manners, acquired secondhand. He was not ashamed of his Yorkshire speech, and what a rich, friendly flavour it had in his mouth! To hear Roy speak of a Lancashire and Yorkshire match was indeed to be warmed with his own country's humour. 'Ay,' he would say, 'it's a reight match, Lancasheer and Yorksheer. Tha knows, t'two teams turns up on Bank Holiday, and we all meets in t'dressin'-room, and we all says "Good mornin'!" to one another. And then we never speaks agean for three days!' A year or two ago I was discussing with Roy the present condition of our country cricket— the absurdly perfect pitches, the huge scoring in Australia, the slow batting, the poor bowling. But Roy was against any alteration in the rules or procedure of the game. 'T' game's all reight,' said he. 'It's

crowd that's wrong—it wants educating up to t'game. Listen to me
—when I were a young lad I goes up to London and there I sees a
play by Shakespeare. And by gum! it did make me tired and weary
wi' yawning. When I gets home I says to mi father, "No more
Shakespeare for me!" But mi father, he says, "Now look 'ere, Roy,
lad; tha's just talking folly. Shakespeare's good enough for me, and
'e's good enough for thee. Tha wants *educating* up to him, that's what
tha wants." ' And Roy closed his delicious homily in these words,
uttered most gravely and sagely: 'And it's same wi' t'crowd and
county cricket. They wants educatin' up to it!' To tell this story is
to feel one's heart running over with affection for Kilner; to hear it,
to read of it, will surely draw cricketers closer and closer to the man's
humanity. Men of humour never ought to die anywhere or anyhow.
And cricketers of the North Country, broad and full of fellow feeling,
ought every one of them to live on and play the game until they are
sick and tired of it. The death of Roy Kilner at the age of thirty-
seven is as outrageous as it is sorrowful.

He was a left-handed batsman who, at his best, changed a solemn
and responsible county ground into the village green. Kilner made
his runs as most of us who love the game would like to make our
runs. He reminded us, often when we needed very much the re-
minder, that the essence of a game is risk. The way that Kilner would
play with the fire of a fast bowler was stimulating. For four or five
balls you would see him withholding his bat from a tempting but
dangerous off-side ball. But as he exercised this discretion, it was
easy to see that it irked his spirit. At last his self-denial would break
down completely; he would let his bat go with a bang, and either
we would see one of the most dazzling cover drives in modern
cricket or we would see Kilner departing from the crease, caught
from a gorgeous and spinning mis-hit. In the latter circumstance
Kilner would be observed to toss back his head as he left the middle.
And also we would see him taking off his gloves, as though saying to
himself, 'Tha art a foo-il, Roy. Got thisel' out agean through thi
impatience. Tha needs to educate *thisel'* up to the game, mi lad!'
But once his eye was in, Kilner's batsmanship was brilliant and
stylish. His cricket came straight from the heart. He made his
mark in county company first as a batsman. After the war he
cultivated his gifts for slow left-hand spin bowling, and quickly
became a master at an art which nowadays seems, like fast
bowling, to be going out of fashion. During the 1924 English tour
in Australia Kilner only once had the luck to get the Australians

71

on a sticky wicket in a Test match. He jumped to the opportunity like a proper Yorkshireman, and spun the woeful batsmen out as quickly as they came in. In recent years he seemed to lose some of this fine spin. He exploited much too frequently the leg-theory trick, bowling over the wicket to a field with only one slip—strategy of a kind that no slow, spinning, left-handed bowler ought to consider for a moment. Possibly Kilner bowled his leg theory at times so that his attack might make a contrast to that of Rhodes. But whatever the idea behind this leg theory, Kilner's bowling did not profit. His natural gifts as a bowler asked for a delivery from round the wicket to a field in which all the slips were there, each ready to snap up the catch from the ball that pitched between the leg and middle stumps and whipped away from the bat. Kilner could bowl this great ball in the true Peel-Briggs-Rhodes tradition; it is a pity he ever allowed himself to become 'educated' up to the modern tricks and 'theories'.

Kilner was a lively fieldsman and an all-rounder in more senses than one. He seemed ever to be 'in the game', doing something for the cause of Yorkshire. He played with gusto; you could not count him amongst those cricketers who are not at all sad when it is a wet morning, and who look forward hopefully to close of play. Kilner only liked rain when it fell in the night—when it wasn't Yorkshire batting. He will be missed on cricket fields the country over. May the earth rest lightly on him.

ARTHUR SHREWSBURY
May 1928

TWENTY-FIVE years ago to this very week Arthur Shrewsbury put an end to his life because he imagined he would never again have the health to play cricket. I saw him only once, and then I was a schoolboy. Probably I played truant—not to look at Shrewsbury, but to watch and pray while Lancashire met Notts at Old Trafford. I remember well the day—a dull morning with clouds gathering. I remember well that I stood for a while outside the sixpenny entrance, looking at the sign which warned me that in the event of bad weather no money would be returned. But the rain did not fall and I saw Shrewsbury. Nevermore did he bat at Old Trafford.

ARTHUR SHREWSBURY

I am afraid that in those far-off years I was too young to appreciate any good cricket that was not performed by a Lancashire man. Youthful enthusiasm does not enable one to see the object (in the other side) as in itself it really is. I was sorry that day when Notts won the toss; I was a bigoted admirer of Albert Ward and MacLaren. When I saw Shrewsbury take his guard and prepare for the attack of Mold, I fancy I put my head against the iron bar that ran round the field on the popular side. And I am sure that I prayed for a swift end to Shrewsbury's innings. It was my practice (narrow and unsportsmanlike partisan that I was, like every other boy) to try to get Providence working hard and carefully on Lancashire's behalf. 'O Lord,' I would pray, 'let Shrewsbury' (or whoever else happened to be batting at the moment) . . . 'let Shrewsbury be bowled middle stump the next over by Mold—middle stump, please, O Lord, the next over.' I took no chances in my prayers; if Providence concentrated on the middle stump, then Providence could scarcely miss hitting one of the the three wickets. I even used to pray for a quick dismissal of Ranji—think of it! Young ignorance, blind to art, lustful for the blood of all enemies of Lancashire. Today I would go through fire and water for an hour of Ranji against Macdonald. My petitions to the gods when Ranji batted at Old Trafford—'Please let Mold knock Ranji's middle stump flying immediately'—were more often than not unheeded; hence the beginning of a period of philosophic doubt in my breast. . . .

Shrewsbury managed to leave an impression on my mind that day, hard though I must have tried not to see his good points. My recollections now are of a very tidy and compact batsman, playing back from his right foot, poised handsomely, his bat like a sensitive thing. Shrewsbury was a serene cricketer. Mr. J. A. H. Catton tells us in a charming essay that Shrewsbury once declared that the greatest gifts of a batsman are 'patience, serenity and happiness'. A beautiful creed for a cricketer! And never did Shrewsbury bat in a style false to that creed. His strongest strokes—and he could drive with power—were somehow tranquil. Even on a sticky wicket—and how vicious turf could be in those days—Shrewsbury seldom was forced into a ruffled attitude, either of mind or of body. He wasted no energy; his every stroke was (as the American metaphysicians would say) a conception objectified. His batting was rational; it perpetually announced the truth and beauty of first principles. And Shrewsbury lived in an age that believed in first principles. While he was expounding first principles on our cricket fields Herbert

Spencer was expounding them elsewhere. Shrewsbury was an eminent Victorian. Cricket, being a great game, is always part of the national environment and cannot help reflecting the changes in habits of thinking and living which occur from time to time. In Shrewsbury's day there was no jazz in the air, no jazz music, no jazz politicians. Hence there were at that time no jazz cricketers. The age which knew Shrewsbury knew Tennyson; the age which has produced the free verse shimmie-shake has also produced Parkin.

Shrewsbury and William Gunn! The modern idea is that these masters were dull. Dull they were, if dullness means equanimity and the mild ease of nineteenth-century England as the Midlands knew it. Day after day the sun went up the sky over Trent Bridge, stood above the place at twelve, passed down the lazy afternoon—and all the time Shrewsbury and Gunn were there at the wicket. The delectable quietness of six o'clock on a bygone summer's day sweetens the imagination even yet—the garish day is gone; it is the hour when shadows fall on the grass. Gone, too, is garish ambition in the hearts of the bowlers. Poor sweaty men, they now understand what a vanity it was they nursed at the fresh of the morning, when they thought that by good bowling they might overthrow Shrewsbury or Gunn, and by grace of Providence the two of them! Here, at the fall of the afternoon, the Nottinghamshire masters remain in untroubled possession. Tap, tap, tap, sound the bats of both—calm noises that go over a field that is softening in mellow sunshine. Right down to close Shrewsbury and Gunn play their stately, old-fashioned, yet immortal cricket:

> There is no hurry in their hands;
> No hurry in their feet.

I do not digress from the subject of Shrewsbury by writing of Gunn. They grew in beauty side by side on the Trent Bridge field. And Trent Bridge, as I have said elsewhere, has always been a Lotus-land for batsmen. But it is unjust to the memory of Shrewsbury to think of him only as a Trent Bridge batsman. He achieved some of his most wonderful innings on wickets of a roughness, nay, a savagery, which would reduce the best batsmen of these days to the helplessness of a schoolboy. In 1887 Shrewsbury actually had an average of 78 for 1653 runs. The next best batsman in that year was Grace, with an average of 54. When we bear in mind the state of the turf on most grounds in 1887 we can only stand astonished at Shrewsbury's performances. An average of 78 would cause a noise in the world even in this epoch of the over-rolled pitch. If Shrewsbury's wicket was hard to take in 1887—when turf was in a state of nature on many grounds; nasty, brutish, horrid, as the philosopher Hobbes might say—then how on earth would bowlers get Shrewsbury out today?

'PLAY UP, SCHOOL!'

I N June weather one's thoughts are not always to be contained within a county cricket ground; they travel, now and again, to the playing fields over the river (you cross by the ferry, but first of all you must call the man, which is done by making a funnel at your mouth with the hands and shouting 'Boat! Bo—at!'). Shastbury's cricket field is the greenest in the world and the most peaceful. It is in the heart of Shropshire, and there is no quieter place under the sun. Here, at last, is a setting for the summer game where no gasometer casts a shadow, where no confident announcements meet your eye about somebody's pale ale. Round the field stand great trees, through which the schoolhouses can just be seen, huddled together. There is the little chapel, too, and after that no other building anywhere, save the pretty pavilion and the wooden scoring-box. Beyond the playing fields stretches the gracious countryside, and in the evenings you will see the sun go down miles and miles away.

Cricket here is the silent game that it ought to be on drowsy days; the game with the softness of summer grass in it. A crack of a bat makes pleasant echoes. In a place where all is still, the slightest movements and sounds become notable—the spacious outstretching of the umpire's arms signalling a wide, the hand raised by the boy in the scoring-box as a sign of response, the rattle of the 'tins' on the grass as the scorer looks for a 5 and a 0, to 'register the half-century', as the newspapers put it; the thud of long-field's feet as he chases a boundary hit. A match at Shastbury goes on in an air so calm that a footstep on the walk near the sight-screen will disturb it. Perhaps it is old Quinn on the way to his lesson—for a great joy in the cricket at Shastbury is that it is played with everybody at work in school, for the best part of the day—everybody, of course, save the school XI and the twelfth man, who does the scoring. The Rev. P. Quinn, a tremendous Greek scholar, is also a cricketer—once, in the

'seventies, he bowled 'W. G.' with a lob—and on his way to the
11.45 lesson he will stay his progress towards the Schoolhouse and
take a glance at the game. I have seen him loiter, walk on, and then
loiter again; I have seen him look back at the field over his shoulder
as he turned the corner of the chapel leading to his classroom. One
morning I saw him disappear slowly round that corner and, a
second later, come back for just one more look at the match. It was
perhaps on this same morning that I heard the Rev. Quinn say
(aloud to himself, and he did not guess he was overheard), while he
watched the cricket, 'Lord, *what* a stroke!'

Cricket to the sound of somebody clipping a hedge on a June
morning; cricket to the sound of a bird singing or of a dog barking
a long way distant—think of it, dwellers on crowded country
grounds, where turnstiles make a clatter and voices cry out the day
long 'Sixth edition' or 'Card and the analis'! It was well past high
noon, on any match-day, before the field at Shastbury lost the still-
ness in which all the murmur of summertime can be heard. Then
morning school would break out and fellows would unfold their rugs
on the bank at the boundary's edge and sit on them. Thus would
the game for a while have a 'crowd'; and here and there a player
would feel a little self-conscious. But with lunch taken (O the shadi-
ness of the pavilion and the plenteous table and the gleaming
tumblers and the snow-white napkins all in a row!), school carried
everybody but the cricketers away, and the match went on, as it
did in the morning, to none but summer's noises.

In those days, whenever I came to Old Trafford, I was astonished
to discover that the match 'piece' there was small and cramped. At
Shastbury the field will hold fifteen games any Saturday afternoon,
and there is not too much congestion, though, of course, a player in
one match may occasionally get mixed up with the match proceeding
alongside his own. Old William was Shastbury's 'pro'; he had
played for his county and for his country in his time, and even yet
his length was perfect in the nets. I shall hear for ever his 'Come
for'ard, sir; get your left leg to it, sir.' Good old William!—how you
did drone it out—'Come for'ard, sir!'—through many a golden
evening. Did you always understand the theory of it; did it not rather
fall from your lips like some ancient rubric? In your wise old heart,
I doubt whether there was much trust in instruction at cricket. 'It's
natur' as does it,' William told me once. 'Nobody coached me, an'
Ah were playin' for England when Ah were twenty-three.' His
character had an amplitude that transcended his job at Shastbury;

nowadays I remember him not as a cricketer but as a profound philosopher. There was the strain of religion, too, in his speech. If ever he chanced to be discussing some future event at which he wished to be present he would say: 'Ah s'all be there if God spares me.' Even if the event was taking place the next morning William would say, 'God willin', Ah s'all go.' The point I would wish to stress about this philosophic sense in William of his own mortality is that he was built so sturdily and healthfully that Providence could only have laid him low suddenly by means of a miracle worked on a large scale.

One summer I shared a bedroom with William in his lodgings. At dawn I sometimes awoke and in the half-light I would see him lying there on his bed, flat on his back, with his arms folded on his breast—a position of much stateliness. Outside in the sunrise the air was rich with the song of birds, and the scent of lime trees came through our window. And on certain of these mornings at cock-crow I would hear William speak words into the bedroom. He took it for granted that I was awake; never did he look for, or heed, a reply. On many a morning, I reckon, he must have spoken while I was asleep. And this was the strain always—'Hey! listen to them birds. Singin' as though they was goin' to burst. Hey! all natur's up and doing'; the lowest of God's cre'tur's is out and workin'. And here are we, a-lyin' in bed, with the sun shinin' and every beast of the field busy. Here are we idlin' the day away, a-lyin' in bed, shamin' natur', wastin' God's sunshine in sleep!' With fervour would he utter these words; but four hours later, at eight o'clock, when the smell of bacon was everywhere, and the little streets outside were rattling with the market's traffic—William would still be lying in state on his bed, enunciating his philosophy of idleness and denouncing the Sluggard.

It is sad to think that William is no longer at Shastbury, that he is now become too old for the game and has been compelled to go back into the factory he left, when a boy, to play for Nottinghamshire and for England. But he will have good memories to dwell upon in his sunless old age. He will not only think of his brilliant days at Adelaide and at Lord's; never will he forget net practice at Shastbury, with the 'cotton' tree hard by dropping its blossom on the grass. He will have in mind to the end of his time the sound of 'Play up, School!' shouted by young voices from the soft bank running round the playing field; he will think again and again of how the two of us would set out on summer afternoons for the ground over the ferry, and of how we would stand on the brow by the market-place and see the winding street going down to the river that flashed through the trees like a silver chain. And countless June evenings will be in his mind—evenings on which he tended the grass in the falling sun, the water from his hose making a delicious noise on the turf, sometimes a bird hopping boldly near him, looking for worms. All these thoughts will sustain William's old age; to have lived at Shastbury and known cricket there, is to have lived for a while in a little heaven down here below.

AN INNINGS OF HAMMOND

May 1927

OFTEN have I been told by my readers that my praises of modern batsmanship are doled out parsimoniously. Sometimes, indeed, I have thought so myself. In imagination I see myself walking about our cricket fields like a Diogenes looking with a sceptical lamp for a really great batsman. Frankly, I cannot get enthusiastic about the cricket of a Sandham, a Hearne, a Sutcliffe. I was not brought up amongst cricketers who got their runs by waiting for a very bad ball, then hitting it to the boundary— after lunch. Here is my idea of a great batsman: he must obviously enjoy his own play; he must be courageous and skilful in the face of a fine attack and in a bad hour for his side. He must not bow to circumstances, but must take them in his own hands and bend a situation to his will. Above all, his cricket must delight us by its beauty, power, resource, individuality. The score-board can never tell you half the truth about a great batsman. I am prepared to argue, indeed, that when a Trumper, a Hutchings, a J. T. Tyldesley, a MacLaren, is at the wicket, the true lover of the game often forgets the existence of the score-board. He sees the moving figures on it only with the physical, the outward eye; in his soul he lives in a world which transcends the partisan interest of a match. The great batsman lifts us out of our utilitarian selves; we admire his work for its beauty, not merely for its value in runs. When an artist-batsman is at the wicket we many times may feel in our bosoms a strange conflict of desires and reactions; if we happen to be Lancashire men and our county is playing Gloucestershire, we want Hammond to get out quickly, for the sake of our team's chances in the championship. But all the while that our clannish ambition is wishful for Hammond's downfall, some other part of us, deep in our nature, is praying that Hammond may be spared to go on and on along his knightly ways. The other day at Old Trafford only Hammond stood between Lancashire and victory. And after Hammond had hit thirty superb runs in a few minutes a man in the crowd said, 'I hopes as 'e gets a couple of hundred.' 'What about Lancashire?' I asked. 'Oh,' replied he, 'Lancashire be——!' Yet he was a true man of the county, and, in his normal moments, hungry for Lancashire victories and jealous of Yorkshire. Hammond's wonderful innings at Old Trafford expelled from all of us, Lancashire to the bone though we were, the lust for points and sovereignty.

Remember Macartney's innings in the Test match at Leeds of 1926. Every Englishman present that morning was keen to see Australia beaten. For years had English cricket been in the wilderness. Well, Macartney gave a chance when his score was only two; at lunch he had made a hundred and was not out. In the interval I heard stalwart Englishman after stalwart Englishman say: 'Thank the Lord Carr dropped that catch, else we'd never have seen this innings!'

Such is the power of the artist-batsman; his spells descend on everybody, and even the savage competitive breast is stilled. Of how many present-day batsmen may we say that they possess this power? Hobbs, sometimes; Woolley, frequently. And Macartney and Hammond always. There is nothing in English cricket of the moment more beautiful to look at than an innings by Hammond. It need not necessarily be a long innings. Watch any average 'All-England' batsman of our period, watch him all day while he makes 200, and at the end of it you will still be arguing whether he will compare well with, say, R. H. Spooner and R. E. Foster. But watch Hammond for half an hour, even if he is slightly below his best form; he will convince you that in his own way he is a batsman not less handsome in skill, not less individual in style, than any of the great batsmen of the past. There is no going beyond perfection, and Hammond's back strokes are not less than perfect. A good test of any innings that you may see may be made in this way: try to imagine an improvement upon it, along the lines of the particular style in which it has actually been played. If you see an innings by, say, Hendren, and you are unable to conceive better batsmanship in that particular style, then you must conclude that Hendren has given you a glimpse of perfection. To say the truth, I have never seen an innings by Hendren or Sandham or Ernest Tyldesley or Sutcliffe which has not immediately passed out of my mind the minute I have thought of an innings by J. T. Tyldesley, Tom Hayward, J. T. Brown and R. H. Spooner. The mind is unable to grasp at the notion of a better batsman in the forcing style than Hobbs at his finest—and by that I mean the Hobbs of the pre-war days. Likewise, the imagination boggles at the notion of a better driving innings against fast bowling, than Hammond's 178 at Manchester in May 1927. The mingled strength and sweetness of his cover shots I cannot hope to describe in words. If I sit down, close my eyes and think of all the glorious batsmanship I have ever seen—even then the bloom and power of Hammond's innings remain warmly and incomparably in my mind. The possibilities of this boy Hammond are beyond the scope of estimation; I tremble with delight at the very thought of the grandeur he will spread over our cricket fields when he has come to maturity. He is, in his own way, another Trumper in the making. His innings against Lancashire satisfied every reasonable ideal of the great batsman. He came to the wicket when his side was almost beaten, when Macdonald was bowling his best and fastest. He did not bow humbly to circumstances; he did not hunch himself before the stumps and let the ball do its will against a meek bat. He lifted up all of his height, he lifted up a lion heart—and attacked. In an hour the Lancashire bowling was routed, and as I have suggested, the Lancashire crowd was sent half crazy by the beauty and bravery of the cricket.

A Hammond in the field provides criticism with a criterion, a standard. Let us keep this swan in mind and we shall not mistake a common, if ambitious, goose. It may be argued that a Hammond can only happen once in a score of years. It may even seem so nowadays. But great though Hammond is already, in his own way, he would not have stood almost by himself twenty years ago. All of these following cricketers might have been seen in one and the same match during 1905; R. E. Foster, R. H. Spooner, F. S. Jackson, A. C. MacLaren, C. B. Fry, H. K. Foster, A. O. Jones, Hayward, Tyldesley, Hirst and G. L. Jessop. Hammond would have shone a bright light in this company. But he would have been simply one star in a constellation.

PARKIN—THE CARD

IF cricketers' memories are not short they will agree that the game has seldom known a much better right-hand bowler than Parkin, and never a man of more intriguing 'personality'— hateful but useful word. The course of genius never did run smooth; Parkin—a genius of cricket if ever one has lived—always possessed the defects of his qualities. But none of us, surely, is going to harp on these defects at this time of day. If we are not rank churls, we will think of Parkin's many excellencies. Is there anywhere a lover of cricket who, with his hand on his heart, is likely to deny that he owes to Parkin many a thrill of admiration and many a happy laugh?

Let us be content to keep in memory Parkin at his best. We shall see him for many years to come 'with the mind's eye'—see him walking to his bowling-place erect as a Grenadier, head tossed back jauntily, his black hair gleaming in the sun, elbows up—the image all over of snapdragon, angular alacrity! He turns suddenly on his heel, eager to attack. Down dips his head gracefully; then he runs in a lovely rhythmical curve to the wicket; his arms describe a wide cartwheel circle; the ball 'fizzes' from his long, supple fingers—and we behold the finest break-back of modern cricket as it uproots a stump. Or maybe the spinning ball thuds against obstructing pads, whereat we hear for a certainty the most spirited and resonant appeal of modern cricket—an appeal which is as much a statement of fact as it is a request for information. Old Trafford, if you wish never to fall into acrid age and lose all the fun and tolerance of youth, remember well the way Parkin came out to bat, delighted boys cheering him on. The ground is agog as Parkin takes his guard, not too scrupulously, for he ventures a joke with the stumper as he marks his block. The first ball he gets—crack! and suddenly a palpitating scutter and stampede. If Richard Tyldesley is the batsman at the other end a frantic 'No!' is roared out; and laughter holds its sides. I have seen tears of merriment on the cheeks of hard-headed men of Manchester in those unstaled times when first Parkin's motley flashed its gay colour across the dull background of Lancashire cricket. Mind you, Parkin's buffoonery usually mingled sense and nonsense in proportion, as good buffoonery always must, according to George Meredith. Old Trafford cannot have forgotten how Parkin's folly

won a match against Leicestershire a year or two ago, after gravity
and discretion had done no better service than to render a drawn
match almost a certainty. Twenty minutes remained for cricket and
forty or fifty runs were needed. The decorous straight bat had
dropped Lancashire 'behind the clock'. Parkin came in and immediately took decorum by the ears. He darted in and out of his crease;
his bat whirled in windmill fashion; in the most literal sense of the
term he raised a dust. Before his advent the Leicestershire bowlers
and fielders had been 'on top', working together with match-winning
precision. Five minutes after the advent of Parkin, those same
Leicestershire bowlers and fieldsmen were a disorganized rabble and
the game a mad sequence of blind, frantic shots at the stumps, lucky
but profitable snicks, thumping drives, helter-skelter dashes up,
down and across the pitch. Lancashire won on time; Parkin did not,
if I remember rightly, make many runs with the bat, but the over-
throws and byes were his very own. His antics, coming as they did in
a moment of crisis, put the Leicestershire men into a maze of
bewilderment. A high easy catch was hit to Coe. Poor Sam, agitated
by Parkin's scutterings as the ball hung in the air, walked round in a
distraught circle—I believe the ball dropped behind him when at last
it came to earth. A famous victory indeed—one which left Old
Trafford limp with excitement and laughter.

Yet this 'motley Parkin'—the title is his own—is the same
cricketer who has imparted to bowling a spin so elaborate that without exaggeration we can say that his art is best discussed in terms of
scientific formulae. No other cricketer since the war has shown us
an attack with Parkin's unique admixture of beautiful curve through
the air, venomous break and acute angle from the turf. And Parkin's
art has been the more precious because it came to us in a period
badly off indeed for masters of spin. There is little of finger spin
about the bowling of Tate and Macaulay; A. M. Noble, in his book,
deplores the passing of the right-handed medium spin bowler—how
glad the eyes of the subtlest Australian captains would have been to
look upon Parkin on a sticky wicket! A cricketer's greatness is frequently to be measured by the influence his work has on the technique of the game. Parkin was not the first cricketer to exploit a leg
field by means of off-breaks pitched on the wicket. But Parkin's 'leg
theory' was so cleverly worked between 1919 and 1924 that other
bowlers quickly paid Parkin the sincerest form of flattery. Parkin
was the main cause of the on-side field common in these days—a
field that has put all save the best batsmen into chains. But many of

Parkin's imitators have not used the 'leg trap' with his intelligence, nor for the reason which forced him to the use of it. Parkin on a convenient pitch gave the ball so wide a spin that batsmen would have had liberty to indulge in pad play if special measures had not been taken to prevent them. By going 'round the wicket' Parkin got the angle of break at his end, as cricketers say—pitched on the stumps and thus compelled a use of the bat. Many a catch achieved at forward short-leg by Richard Tyldesley from Parkin's attack was a blind hit at a spinning ball that would have uprooted the leg wicket. Parkin never exploited 'leg theory' bowling with that lack of imagination which marks his disciples—those who bowl on a batsman's legs without spin, trusting to a batsman's stupidity and to safe fieldsmen in the net spread on the leg side. Parkin's theory of the on-side trap was positive, not negative, cricket; the batsmen were driven into the trap; Parkin never was content to wait for victims of absent-mindedness. At his best all the tricks of the trade were in his possession—fast balls, slow balls, googlies, swingers, break-backs and flight variations.

Parkin's cricket was full of the spirit of the age—which, of course, is an age of jazz. In the artist's sense of the word, he was a grotesque; energy in his work broke the bounds of conventional forms. His slow ball, in the days when he bowled it well, could be called a very gargoyle of a ball, a twisting grin of a ball. An unintelligent criticism of Parkin is that he 'played to the gallery', the implication being that he was not sincere in all his antic humours. But Parkin—and anybody who has studied the man will readily agree with this—was incapable of assuming a pose not genuinely his own; he was, indeed, too much the egoist to simulate any trait in nature that he did not feel born of his blood. It was his very frankness, his unwavering faith in Parkin, in season and out of season, that occasionally sent him running headlong into the properties. He won a lot of handsome names—*l'enfant terrible* of cricket, the Artful Dodger, the Merry Andrew, the Jack Ketch of cricket. He deserved them all, and, because of that, he never lacked judges. 'With what great cause was he ever identified?' ask the guardians of law and order, even as they asked the same question about Denry Machin. We can surely respond with the answer that was triumphantly given on behalf of 'The Card': 'Why, with the great cause of cheering us all up!'

WHAT'S IN A NAME?

MR. E. V. LUCAS has somewhere written a charming essay on cricketers' names, and such is my annoyance at not having thought of the theme first that (without Mr. Lucas's permission) I now borrow it and use it myself. Why should I not? In music, composers have never had scruples against stealing subjects from one another for their variations. Besides, many years ago, long before Mr. Lucas's writings on cricket came pleasantly into my life, I pondered frequently the question of the poetic justness of the names of cricketers. I used to choose my 'favourite' batsmen on the strength of an agreeable name, much as ladies pick a winner at Ascot. I was, even while a schoolboy, as convinced as Mr. Shandy would have been that a cricketer's surname possessed an enormous influence one way or another upon his skill, nay upon his very destiny. When Hobbs first played for Surrey I would have none of him. 'No man ever has or ever will do good with a name like that,' I said, adding, 'Hobbes, maybe, but not Hobbs.' My Shandean theory was, of course, rather shocked by the quick movement of Hobbs to fame; I consoled myself with the reflection that there must be exceptions to every rule.

One afternoon I remember running out of school to get the latest news of the Lancashire match. In those years Lancashire cricket meant more to me, perhaps, than anything else on earth. One afternoon I escaped from school eager about Lancashire, who were meeting Worcestershire—a rare side that year, with the Fosters, Ted Arnold, Burrows and Wilson. I bought a newspaper and turned to the scores on the middle page inside. I never could as a boy—and sometimes cannot yet—muster up courage enough to plunge headlong to the 'stop-press'; news had to come to my apprehensive young mind gradually. Inside the paper, which I opened cautiously, I learned that Worcestershire were 67 for 6 and all the Fosters out. These tidings of joy sent me confidently to the 'stop-press'. And there, what did my incredulous eyes read? 'Worcestershire 152 for 6, Gaukrodger not out 82.' I decided on the spot that (*a*) this was outrageous and absurd, that (*b*) Gaukrodger was an impossible name for a cricketer, and that (*c*) with such a name he ought never in this world to have been permitted to score 19, let alone 91. From that afternoon, until Gaukrodger passed into honourable retirement, I

84

regarded him (or rather his name—which amounted to the same thing) with open derision. 'Gaukrodger!' I would murmur. And to this present time I have remained unshaken in the view that 'Gaukrodger' was a heathenish name for a cricketer; I am glad he never played for England.

There is, I am aware, a sophistical argument which tries to persuade us that only by force of mechanical association do we begin to regard a great man's name as part and parcel of all that we feel about his personality and genius. I admit this notion can gather support from the way the ridiculous monosyllable 'Hobbs' has, with the passing of time, come to sound in many ears like a very trumpet of greatness. But my strong opinion is this: Hobbs has conquered in spite of his name. It would have crippled many a smaller man. 'What about Trumper?' asks the scoffer. 'How can you fit in a name like that with the destiny of a glorious cricketer?' And again do I freely confess that at first glance 'Trumper' seems a name not at all likely to guide anybody towards sweetness and light. But Trumper's Christian name was Victor; the poetry in 'Victor' neutralized the (let us say) prose in 'Trumper'; had Trumper been named Obadiah he could scarcely have scored a century for Australia against England before lunch—as Trumper rapturously did at Old Trafford in 1902.

The crowd in the shilling seats will bear me out that there's much power for good or for evil in a cricketer's name. Consider how the crowd instinctively felt, when Hendren began his county cricket, that the man's Christian name was Elias was all wrong—not only that, but a positive danger to his future. The crowd looked at Hendren's face, his gigantic smile; also at his admirable batting. Then they pronounced to themselves 'Elias'. And they looked at Hendren once more and, to a man, they agreed that that 'Elias' was not true . . . They called him 'Patsy'—even as they called Augustus Lilley 'Dick'.

Mr. Warner has invented a sort of rainy-day pastime for cricketers; you to pick a 'World XI' to play a side from Mars. I always select my 'World XI' on the principle that handsome name is a harbinger of handsome achievement. And herewith I publish my 'World XI'—every man chosen with no reference at all to form, but simply because he carries a name which, if not actually poetic, has suggestions which are far from those of unlovely prose:

Grace
Shrewsbury
Darling
Noble
Warwick Armstrong
Knight (A. E. or D. J.)
Lilley
Rhodes
Flowers
Mead (W., of Essex)
Blythe.

Perhaps I ought to go a little into my choice of 'Rhodes'. It is not exactly musical in sound, or, *as* a word, poetic or picturesque. But it is redolent of the ancient Ægean, the Dorian Hexapolis, and the Colossus of Chares. Besides, I am prepared to go to any extreme of subterfuge and sophistry to get Wilfred into my 'World XI'. 'Tennyson' is a name of handsomer aspect at first glance than 'Rhodes'—which really is a hideous word, if only we could look at it with fresh eyes. But as a cricketer Tennyson

> . . . altogether lacks the abilities
> That Rhodes is dress'd in.

Against my XI of delectable names I would like to see opposed the following team, which might be called 'The Onomatopoeics':

Hobbs
Fry
Studd, C. T.
Gunn (W.)
Brown (J. T.)
Hirst
Trumble
Boyle
Briggs
Sugg
   and (of course)
Gaukrodger.

My XI's inevitable victory would demonstrate once and for all that there is plenty of virtue in a name—amongst cricketers, at any rate. Could Grace conceivably have been Grace, known as W. G. Blenkinsop?

HOBBS IN THE NETS

NOT long ago I had the good fortune to see Hobbs at practice. He used a beautiful white bat, and as he made stroke after stroke he would glance solicitously at the face of his blade as though he were reluctant to do it hurt. The noise made by his hits was music to every cricketer present—a clean, solid noise, with no overtones. One could imagine, and envy, the thrill of delight that passed through Hobbs as he made these strokes—delight running its current from the bat's end up the arms, down the spine, and all over the body. Batsmen in other nets ceased their ineffectualities as Hobbs practised; they ceased them for very shame and also because the art of Hobbs held them in thrall.

Hobbs himself was not in serious vein. He was merely improvising like the pianist who lets his fingers move irresponsibly and experimentally over the keyboard; like the artist who in a 'rough study' will indulge in bold 'chancy' sweeps of the crayon. But it is during these improvisatory moments that we sometimes get a peep that takes us deeper into the mind and character of an artist than his finished work permits. The finished work often gives you the artist 'dressed up for the occasion', so to speak. He is, of course, himself in a finished work, but plus something conditioned by his medium and his public. It is by means of his improvisations that the artist can break free from the tyranny of his medium.

A quarter of an hour of Hobbs in the nets revealed to us a Hobbs above that ruthless law which, by the grim paradox of all art, is the source of perfection and the death of it. Here was a Hobbs free to use his bat as waywardly as he chose, and every stroke he made was made to serve no ends other than the artist's. The strokes were worth nothing in runs—no Surrey axe had to be ground in the nets. They were strokes thrown away on the air, squandered by our greatest batsman in a moment that found him free to the uttermost. In a quarter of an hour only three balls passed Hobbs's bat. The practice almost guaranteed that this summer will find him as masterful as ever.

From behind the net the technique of Hobbs is, so to speak, seen under a magnifying lens. Or it is as though one were looking at a painting with one's eyes almost glued to the canvas. You can see that now more of energy, even of roughness, goes into Hobbs's cricket than is apparent when watching him from a distance. He grips his bat in the middle of the handle as he waits for the ball, but frequently when he plays back the right hand drops almost to the bottom of the handle. This denotes strong right forearm leverage in Hobbs's defensive strokes. Immediately the bowler begins his run Hobbs seems to have some instinct of what manner of ball is on the way; rarely does he move his feet to an incorrect position. His footwork is so quick that even from behind the nets it is not always possible to follow its movement in detail.

And he covers a lot of ground—forward and backward. No wonder it is almost impossible to pitch a length to Hobbs when he is at his best. His style, like the style of the master of every art, and of every fine art, seems to sum up all that has gone before in the development of his technique. Hobbs's batsmanship has enough in it of the straight bat and the forward left foot to link it up with the batsmanship of Grace and the other old masters. Yet his on-side strokes, which he makes from a full-fronted stance, are sufficiently modern. The glorious truth is that many an honourable sowing by cricketers of the past comes to a fine flower in the batsmanship of Hobbs.

A FIGHT TO A FINISH

Trent Bridge, August 1928

WE have this afternoon been given compensation for the long dreary hours on Wednesday, when wet clouds hid the sun and the cricketers' brief butterfly season seemed over already. Today the warm light of summer has made us all happy and young again, and splendid cricket has happened on this most ancient and historic cricket field. The pitch was protected from Wednesday's rain, but when the covers were moved away this morning it is likely that some moisture remained secreted in the turf. The ball frequently kept low and seemed to skid from the earth with that acceleration of speed which means all the difference between a stroke in time and a stroke too late. In no sense, however, was the wicket difficult—W. G. Grace would have pressed his thumb into the grass and murmured, 'A hundred for me.'

Larwood gave the game a breath-snatching prelude: galloping over the earth like a young horse, he bowled down four Kent wickets in less than half an hour. Kent were six when Hardinge sought to stop a very fast ball which possibly nipped back an inch: Hardinge played on, and his cross bat, the consequence of a discreetly retiring right foot, was not worthy of a cricketer of Hardinge's scientific upbringing. With Kent's total nine Ashdown's off stump was sent round and round. Ashdown's stroke was done by reflex action: he flicked his bat just as a man flicks his head as he hears a wasp buzzing about him. Kent were fifteen when, in three balls, Larwood crashed through the bats of Ames and Deed. A ball that rose no higher after pitching than the middle of the stumps utterly baffled Ames, and the next ball but one nipped back and knocked the centre wicket of Deed out of the ground. Larwood's analysis hereabout was:

Overs	Maidens	Run	Wickets
3·3	2	1	4

The collapse was a clear case of feeble batting against bowling very fast from the pitch, hurled down with youth's own temper and vitality. The Kent batsmen contributed to their own misfortunes by letting their bats move away and aslant from the line of the ball. For, though Larwood occasionally bowled a break-back directed by his body swing, the line of his flight was straight in to the bat. Never did he exploit an out-swinger, and his length was not short. Clearly, then, the Kent batsmen who allowed their right feet to stray from the line of the ball, and by doing so let their bats play across—these batsmen were not acting according to the gospel of Lord Harris. You need the full width of the blade to stop Larwood at his fastest.

The moment Bryan came in we were able to see Larwood's bowling in a new and cultivated light. Bryan played forward beautifully, his bat moving with its full front down the ball's line. His forward shoulder was over the ball when his bat met it, and Larwood immediately began to look a very fine but not unplayable fast bowler. The ease and confidence of Bryan's batting demonstrated the essential straightforwardness of Larwood's attack. Bryan, being a left-hander, would have suffered a painful experience if Larwood really had been bowling a break-back with anything like an acute angle. Bryan made only seven, but he helped Woolley to add thirty for the fifth wicket in just over half an hour. Bryan's little innings was full of cricket sense. He is one of the very best left-handed batsmen of our day, and if I were a member of the Selection Committee I would argue for his place in the England eleven—as batsman and possibly as captain of the side.

Woolley came in at the fall of Kent's first wicket, was unbeaten at the end, and scored 66 out of 109 in two hours. With his innings worth only 18 he was missed from a graceful leg hit: at 22 he gave another chance, a hit to mid-off. This chance was low to the earth, Woolley probably mistiming his drive because the ball lifted a little after pitching. These two mistakes did not for a moment give us a suggestion that Woolley was playing anything but great and beautiful cricket. His strokes were of the utmost ease, and calm even in the face of Larwood's hurricane. He turned the ball to leg with an incline of the body and a sweep of the bat which were courtly. A high drive over mid-off's head saw his body upright yet in effortless poise; a leg hit from Barratt was musical in its rhythmical energy. He rose tall as a Grenadier and flicked a rising ball over the slips, his bat describing a quite negligent movement. Larwood beat him and missed his wickets by inches when Woolley's innings had lasted but a few minutes; had he failed, Kent must surely have been all out for a ridiculous amount, and our memories of the season when the days of winter come would not be able to dwell—as now they will dwell—on a flower of batsmanship, one that grew proudly out of the barren earth of a Kent innings of 118. Here is the sequence in which Kent's wickets were tumbled down:

1	2	3	4	5	6	7	8	9	10
9	9	15	15	45	48	54	93	114	118

Wright and Woolley made Kent's eighth wicket put on 39; the difference between Wright and Woolley as batsmen is the difference between nature and art, instinct and culture. Barratt bowled well, keeping that very nasty length which is just too short for a forward stroke. Moreover, he frequently caused the ball to run away from the bat. One of his in-swingers to Bryan's left-handed bat rose awkwardly, and Lilley, the wicket-keeper, stopped it well on the leg-side. Woolley's cricket was highly appreciated by a crowd that could afford to be affable and generous. He is still the world's greatest left-handed batsman. To leave so glorious a cricketer out of the England eleven is rather like leaving Keats out of an anthology of English poetry. In every innings of Woolley sweetness cometh out of strength.

Notts batted at a quarter to three in torrents of sunshine. It was an afternoon that quickened one's love not only of cricket but also of summer and England. The watcher of the game sat at ease feeling the sunlight on his face. This is the game that suffers a chill in its very heart whenever the day is gloomy. It is the summer game, and as we watch it under a blue sky we can feel it is part of summer's passing show of rich nature and loveliness. In the silences that come over a cricket match from time to time on an August afternoon the lazy air breeds reverie, and we think of all the country's quiet and gracious places—the Cotswolds, Old Cockington Forge and the Wiltshire Downs. For cricket somehow holds the English secret; it belongs to summer in this land not less than our great trees and our beneficent countryside.

George Gunn and Whysall scored 34 for the first wicket, while Ashdown and Wright exploited the new ball and its supposed swerving properties. Then the spin bowlers came on, and with the total still 34 Marriott beautifully yorked Gunn, and Ames stumped Whysall off Freeman with great speed and a commendable lack of bodily fuss or tenor vocalism. Walker and Payton then added 38 by good cricket. The Kent score was passed when three wickets were down, whereupon Notts tried to force the game with all the spirit and lust for conquest which must be expected from a team led by A. W. Carr. He himself set an invigorating example, and though his innings was not long it was lion-hearted, despite a few vicissitudes in the face of Freeman's break. Fine catching was substantially the cause of Notts losing eight wickets for 163.

Now followed some magnificent hitting by Larwood and Staples which made the Trent Bridge welkin to ring. In some thirty minutes 68 runs were hit—nay, let us use honest English and say clouted— right and left. Larwood smote two sixes, Staples five boundaries. Here were the animal spirits of cricket running loose.

Notts are going for a victory outright in two days. Nothing is wrong with the game, played as it was this afternoon by both sides, men of Kent and Notts alike. Walker for more than two hours displayed a neat and scrupulous technique. Freeman's spin was clever without being waspish, and to the student of the game Marriott's variation of pace and spin were a constant joy to watch, whether he was getting wickets or getting hit.

SECOND DAY

The cricket at Trent Bridge today has been played in the finest spirit by both teams. Nothing is wrong with the game, given cricketers of heart and imagination as well as skill. On an afternoon of delicious sunshine we have seen Notts all out for victory, and we have seen Kent take up the challenge of Carr like the cavalier county we have always known Kent to be. Carr, although leading by not more than 111, closed his innings straightway and sent Kent to the wicket in the fresh of the morning. This was a declaration of the right temper. Let us hope to see other county captains emulating Carr's gusto.

Kent lost Bryan's wicket with only 27 scored, and though they now were needing 84 to save defeat by an innings, Woolley and Ashdown proceeded to try to turn the wheel of the match round at the rate of 100 runs an hour. Ashdown began with three fours in the morning's first two overs—two cuts and a glorious cover-drive. Bryan was caught at the wicket from a capital ball of Barratt which whipped away from the bat at the last fraction of time after pitching on the blind length. Woolley hit his first ball as though Kent's score were 650 for two, and Carr fielded it brilliantly and saved the four. Ashdown went his dashing way, cutting and off-driving with all of Jim Seymour's skill and daring. Now and again fortune smiled on his hazards through the slips, but he gave no actual chance. In half an hour Kent were 50 and nine boundaries had been hit. In swift succession Ashdown made a cover drive and two slashing cuts from A. Staples—brilliant and impudent strokes. Woolley, as negligent and inscrutable as ever, toyed with the vehement Notts attack: in little more than a quarter of an hour he made 30, letting us see four ravishing hits to the rails. In the morning's first hour Kent flashed 94 runs over the field: the batting challenged the sun's splendour.

Ashdown reached his 50 in an hour, then danced ahead of Woolley, his bat crackling like a jolly fire. Ashdown and Woolley in an hour scored 109. The lead of Notts was cancelled in 75 minutes, and at one o'clock Carr began to wear a thoughtful look; another hour of Woolley and Ashdown would give Kent a chance of going for a win. Watching this beautiful cricket I got the impression that Ashdown and Woolley had both forgotten that there were three stumps behind their bats needing an occasional thought. Woolley and Ashdown played defensively only as a last resort and with obvious reluctance. Defensive strokes were invariably singles. When Kent's total was 90 we had revelled in the sight of fourteen boundaries. I doubt whether Old Trafford will see fourteen boundaries in the next three days. This gallant stand by Woolley and Ashdown was ended tragically; Woolley drove a ball hard to Carr at cover, and Ashdown ran eagerly and too impetuously down the pitch. Carr fielded magnificently, and Ashdown's wicket was broken before he could turn on his heels and get home again. The score was now 148

for two. Woolley and Ashdown had added 121 in 70 minutes. Ashdown's innings did honour to cricket; there is no higher praise for
him than that.

Woolley went on playing a match-winning game, and just before
lunch he fell to a deep-field catch most judiciously performed by
Whysall in front of the pavilion. From one point of view Woolley was
indiscreet in making this hit so soon after Ashdown's dismissal, and
so close to the lunch interval. But Woolley's genius is above the
criticism of the ca' canny: others abide the championship question;
he is free. Woolley made his 66 in 80 minutes. After lunch Hardinge
was bowled by a fine ball which swung in with Voce's arm. Ames
batted stoutly for 70 minutes, for Kent had by this time realized that
the job of saving a match must not any longer be mixed up with the
job of winning one. A grand slip catch by Staples got rid of Ames,
and another swift slip catch by the same fine fieldsman dismissed
Deed. A half-hour of stern resistance by Legge and Longfield
threatened to frustrate Carr after all, for the time of day hereabout
was half-past three, and Kent, with four wickets in hand, were more
than 100 ahead. The obstinacy of Legge was scotched by Carr himself: he caught the Kent captain at short leg with a thrilling speed
and opportunism. Whereupon young Voce began to bowl straight
instead of swinging the ball to the batsman's body, and the Kent tail
end crumpled up. At a quarter to four the side were all out, and
Notts wanted 157 runs, and there were two hours and a quarter left
for cricket. Clearly the running-out of Ashdown was the turning-
point. Kent's efforts to play defensively after lunch were not impressive, but there is likely always to be more rejoicing in the cricketer's
heaven over a Kent defeat in today's spirit than over all the dismal
championship points ever won.

Again the D'Artagnan spirit was shown when Notts batted a
second time. Gunn and Whysall played with bats that parried and
thrust like the quick steel of swordsmen, and Notts actually hit
158 runs in 95 minutes. A ten wickets' victory seemed certain, but
Whysall was out with nine runs still to get. He batted with a stimulating blend of power and precision.

The match, one of the best I have ever seen, was appropriately
crowned or garlanded by a hundred from George Gunn—sheer wit
of batsmanship, flicked over the brilliant grass in ninety minutes. He
drove to the off with a blade that seemed less to strike the ball than
to perform magical sweeps and 'passes'—'fluence', as they say in the
crowd. His cuts to third man were done in his own charmingly

coxcomb manner. He achieved strokes entirely belonging to himself, connived at the wrist's ends, and so rapid were they that the eye could not follow the technique of it all. At one moment Gunn is as classical in poise as the great William Gunn himself; then he will show you a capricious inverting of the old ways of doing things; he will cut from the middle stump—and a yorker at that! Gunn got his second fifty this afternoon in just over half an hour: what a game this cricket is when great and not small batsmen take it in hand!

The match was indeed a constant joy for the lover of real cricket. In a couple of days we had on a splendid wicket a finish to a contest between two strong counties. In these two days wickets were always falling, yet nearly 800 runs were scored. Today we saw the making of 425. Cricketers of Lancashire and Yorkshire on Saturday morning will do well to study these facts. The Notts attack, when Ashdown and Woolley tried to turn the game for Kent, was not less deadly than it was on Saturday last against Lancashire. Good bowling can be hit, but the batsmen need mind and energy for the job. This is no plea for elemental slogging. Woolley and Ashdown, of course, played finished cricket—as pretty to the sight as it was thrilling to the blood. Nothing is the matter with the game—excepting the mental and physical indolence of some of its modern exponents. It may be argued by dour men of the north that as Ashdown and Woolley were unable to save Kent from disaster, the dashing play they exploited stands condemned. But it was the running-out of Ashdown that caused the downfall of Kent, not anything in the actual batsmanship displayed by Ashdown and Woolley. Another hour of this partnership would have seen Notts fighting against Freeman with little but a draw to play for.

Carr's captaincy today was an inspiration to every man in the Notts team. He visualized victory the moment he reached the ground. If it is a fair question—would Lancashire or Yorkshire have closed an innings on the morning of the last day when in possession of an advantage of merely 111? Carr's management of his attack was as thoughtful as MacLaren's. He invariably had on the very bowler most likely to search out a given batsman's weak spot. A fast bowler was in action whenever a Kent cricketer reached the wicket. Woolley, who likes the ball to come through straight, usually found himself confronted by Sam Staples, who bowled spin and flighted the ball cleverly. Staples thoroughly deserved Woolley's wicket, for he angled after it perseveringly. Carr dominated his side all the time, he could see he was holding the reins,

KENT

First Innings		Second Innings	
Hardinge, b Larwood	4	b Voce	12
Ashdown, b Larwood	1	run out	84
Woolley, not out	66	c Whysall, b Staples (S.)	66
Ames, b Larwood	1	c Staples (S.), b Barratt	24
J. A. Deed, b Larwood	0	c Staples (S.), b Larwood	6
J. L. Bryan, lbw, b Staples (S.)	7	c Lilley, b Barratt	10
G. B. Legge, b Barratt	3	c Carr, b Voce	11
T. C. Longfield, c Lilley, b Barratt	4	not out	29
Freeman, b Staples (S.)	8	b Voce	2
Wright, b Barratt	15	b Voce	0
C. S. Marriott, b Barratt	0	b Larwood	3
B 4, lb 5	9	B 8, lb 8, w 4	20
Total	118	Total	267

NOTTS

First Innings		Second Innings	
Gunn, b Marriott	16	not out	100
Whysall, st Ames, b Freeman	15	c Bryan, b Woolley	46
Walker, c and b Freeman	56		
A. W. Carr, c Woolley, b Freeman	19	not out	9
Payton, c Legge, b Wright	30		
Lilley, lbw, b Freeman	1		
Staples (A.), c Legge, b Freeman	16		
Barratt, c Legge, b Marriott	5		
Larwood, not out	36		
Staples (S.), not out	30		
B 2, lb 1, nb 2	5	B 2, lb 1	3
Total (for eight wickets)	*229	Total (for one wicket)	158

* Innings declared

BOWLING ANALYSIS
KENT—First Innings

	O.	M.	R.	W.		O.	M.	R.	W.
Larwood	12	2	28	4	Staples (S.)	11	0	28	2
Barratt	18	2	47	4	Voce	1	0	6	0

Second Innings

	O.	M.	R.	W.		O.	M.	R.	W.
Larwood	16.2	2	62	2	Staples (S.)	19	4	47	1
Barratt	13	2	58	2	Staples (A.)	7	0	35	0
Voce	14	3	45	4					

Voce bowled four wides

NOTTS—First Innings

	O.	M.	R.	W.		O.	M.	R.	W.
Wright	15	3	31	1	Freeman	33	9	98	5
Ashdown	6	0	20	0	Marriott	24	5	75	2

Marriott bowled two no-balls

95

Second Innings

Ashdown	4	0	10	0	Longfield	2	0	15	0
Freeman	14	2	51	0	Woolley	2.4	0	28	1
Marriott	8	2	31	0	Wright	7	1	20	0

now pulling this one, now pulling that. The Australians would hail either Carr or Fender as a captain by more or less divine right.

It was a memorable match throughout; I shall think gratefully of its spirit, its endeavour and its achievements—during those 'dour' periods which are certain to happen at Old Trafford within the next few days. Trent Bridge in August's mellow light, fearless play, the gauntlet thrown down and picked up with chivalry; cleverness and spirit, craft and imagination; English sun and air and lovely poise of men in white flannels—the game at its bravest and most beautiful! This is the end of every cricketer's desire.

MACDONALD v. KENT
Old Trafford, August 1928

THERE was real cricket in this match at Old Trafford—the most beautiful of our fast bowlers attacking the most beautiful of our batsmen, and the champion county face to face with their most dangerous rivals, all on an afternoon of fresh wind and sun, an afternoon which passed down to the sunset with Hallows batting in the slanting light like Woolley's own brother. The wicket was fast enough for Macdonald to cause the ball to rear awkwardly, but he alone amongst living bowlers could have done that much; it was a good wicket, and nothing less, especially when Hardinge and Ashdown began the Kent innings. During the luncheon interval a shower of rain fell and delayed the resumption for twenty minutes, but the collapse which set in after the fall of Kent's fourth wicket was clearly the consequence of a batting technique quite unaccustomed to the practice of fast bowling.

Kent's side possessed a long 'tail'; Freeman came in sixth wicket down, and at the sight of him Sammy Woods would most certainly have said something about the hutch having been well and truly opened. It is a pity Chapman was not playing; his county needed him, and he at the moment cannot afford to neglect chances of getting experience in big games against severe bowling. Woolley saved the Kent innings from ruin; he, being a cricketer who learned

MACDONALD *v.* KENT
KENT
First Innings

Hardinge, c Duckworth, b Macdonald	8
Ashdown, c Duckworth, b Macdonald	17
Woolley, c Iddon, b Macdonald	151
Ames, b Macdonald	48
J. L. Bryan, lbw, b Sibbles	28
C. H. Knott, b Macdonald	0
G. B. Legge, b Sibbles	8
Freeman, b Macdonald	4
B. Howlett, c Watson, b Sibbles	0
Wright, c Barnes, b Macdonald	1
C. S. Marriott, not out	0
B 5, lb 7	12
	—
Total	277

LANCASHIRE
First Innings

Watson, not out	36
Hallows, not out	61
Nb 1	1
	—
Total (for 0)	98

Tyldesley (E.), Makepeace, Iddon, Hopwood, J. R. Barnes, Sibbles, Duckworth, Tyldesley (R.), and Macdonald to bat.

BOWLING ANALYSIS
KENT—First Innings

	O.	M.	R.	W.		O.	M.	R.	W.
Macdonald	25.1	4	101	7	Iddon	8	1	34	0
Sibbles	25	1	59	3	Watson	9	0	10	0
Hopwood	9	1	34	0	Tyldesley (R.)	8	1	27	0

his game before 1919, understands how to counter a quick ball; moreover, his height enables him to get on top of even Macdonald's most alarming bumper. He played one of the most beautiful innings Old Trafford has seen in several summers; his poise and reach stole a yard of pace from Macdonald, and he made runs with ease from bowling that most batsmen would have gladly 'let alone', as cricketers say.

Macdonald's first ball, sent down at half-past eleven, flew ominously upwards after hitting the earth half way along the pitch. Hardinge did not exactly revel in the fast bowling; he flashed his bat to it, possibly without knowing what he was 'at' to an inch. In Macdonald's second over he edged a possible chance to Sibbles at second

97

slip; then he snicked a four to leg, and it is possible that Ashdown at the other end was aware it was a four a little in advance of Hardinge's own realization of the fact. From the last ball of Macdonald's third over Hardinge was caught at the wicket; he made an instinctive act of protection with his bat, much as a man flicks his hand as he hears a wasp buzzing about his head. Kent were 14 for one, and Woolley walked his easy, unhurried way to the wicket. He opened with a cut from Macdonald which was not entirely masterful; he then cut the fast bowling superbly three or four times through the slips to the boundary, rising to his full inches, graceful as a tall, slender tree, his bat all curves. Ashdown hit a four from Sibbles's first over—a dashing off-drive. He also snicked Macdonald to leg like a cricketer blindfolded. He was caught at the wicket from Macdonald at 43 and was perhaps unlucky, for his stroke was not speculative and the ball did not kick. He brought his bat down in the right way, but seemed to mistime the pace from the pitch. Ames, who came next, was completely beaten by Macdonald with his score 6; the next ball he edged to the slips, and had A. O. Jones been one of them—any one of them —Ames would have been out. Duckworth was in quicksilver vein just now—indeed, the cricket in all parts of the field was red-hot from the great flame of Macdonald's attack. Ames drove Macdonald to the off for three—a pretty stroke. But our eyes were all for Woolley and Macdonald.

Here was a sight for the gods of the game who sit aloft and watch whenever greatness is in action on the green earth below. Macdonald, running his silent way over the grass, his aspect sinister but princely, a Lucifer of his craft, dealing out fire and evil to all batsmen. And at the wicket's other end we saw Woolley, calm and chaste, his bat exorcizing for the while the demon out of Macdonald. It must have been thrilling to see Spofforth bowling at Grace, Lockwood bowling at Ranjitsinhji. But let us be just to our own day's glories; Macdonald bowling at Woolley was a sight not less grand than any ever seen on a cricket field; the mirrors of the cricketers' heaven will reflect it for ever.

Ames settled down, and when Macdonald had gone out of action temporarily for a rest he drove Richard Tyldesley strongly to the on immediately after Tyldesley had wheeled up his very slow ball, his cerebral one. Tyldesley's slow leg-breaks, of course, came at an easy angle to Woolley, and successive balls were put to the boundary with a lack of effort that would have seemed contemptuous from a batsman of less than Woolley's inscrutability. Woolley's face is a mask;

he seems unaware of the joyousness of his own cricket; his bat makes its rippling music, but it is as though it were all done by a player who cannot hear what he plays.

When Macdonald did not bowl, Lancashire's attack was not difficult. Woolley drove Hopwood over the on-boundary for six, and Ames off-drove Iddon for four and also achieved a handsome square-leg hit. Ames proved himself a batsman who is not afraid to use his feet to slow ball; he watches the bowler carefully, and belongs to the realistic, as distinguished from the idealistic, side of Kent cricket. Woolley reached his 50 out of 91 in an hour and a quarter, and at lunch Kent were 149 for two wickets. After a swift shower that left the field sparkling, the match went on at twenty-five minutes to three. Ames cut Macdonald with a swordsman's stroke. Then he was hit on the hand by a ball that sped from the turf viciously. The mishap no doubt disturbed Ames's confidence; next ball he was clean bowled, his middle stump flying out of the earth stupendously. Ames and Woolley scored 128 for the third wicket in 95 minutes, and Ames's portion was conscientious 48. Bryan, also a left-handed batsman, defended while Woolley went along his felicitous way. There was, of course, sheer force in this cutting, pulling and driving, but we watchers could scarcely believe it; his cricket seemed to us to to be at one with the afternoon's soft air and gleaming sunshine. A forcing stroke off his pads to the square-leg boundary from Macdonald snatched the onlooker's breath away; it was made across the line of a very fast ball; Woolley gently moved to the side of it, on the daintiest feet, and timed the stroke to the last second's last fraction. He off-drove Macdonald for four, and reached his hundred in two hours and ten minutes. He lapsed from grace when he mis-hit a ball high to long-off. He sweetly swung his bat at a half-volley from Iddon, and lo! it was a sixer to the on, rather straight. He also hit a six from Hopwood in the same direction—without the slightest departure from his eternal poise of ease and unconcern. Bryan's steady bat was a sort of figured-bass accompaniment in this allegro of Woolley.

The fourth Kent wicket was worth 91; it fell at 262, when Woolley lost his wicket. Iddon was moved round on the leg-side, and Woolley hit a ball from Macdonald, challenging all the fieldsmen in the world that ever had hands and quick eyes. Iddon held the catch cleverly, and as Woolley left the wicket the summer's sun seemed to go out of the sky. He batted for three hours and five minutes, hit three sixes and sixteen fours, and let us all understand yet again that he is the greatest artist-batsman in the game at the present time. An England eleven without Woolley is, of course, a nonsensical conception. He ought to be sent to Australia if only to remind everybody there that once on a time English cricket was, as they used to say at Hambledon, an elegant game, the game of all the graces.

Knott could not 'connect' with Macdonald once, though he tried a variety of strokes. He was bowled at 264. At the same total Bryan was leg-before-wicket; he had not been seen at his best, for though his innings had plenty of cricket sense, he did not bring into play his true range of strokes, but overdid the current trick of moving across the wicket with his legs. Macdonald sent Freeman's bail flying to the boundary's edge; he let panic loose in the Kent ranks. Sibbles bowled well now and came in for one or two easy wickets. Kent, at one period, were 262 for four; they were all out for 277. The innings, on the whole, was not worthy of a team aspiring for championship honours. Gaiety and style are desirable in cricket at all times, but these attributes must take their rise from a technique. When all has been said that can be said about 'grim Lancashire batting', the fact has to be admitted that in Lancashire we do possess a number of batsmen who deserve the name technicians, craftsmen who do not fall into the grosser errors of batsmanship. Macdonald took Kent's first five wickets; he was at his finest and most thrilling. I doubt if he ever bowled faster for Armstrong in 1921.

Lancashire in seventy minutes played Kent at their own game, gave us all of the Kent sweetness and light, and added to it a technique—at both ends of the pitch. Hallows reached 50 in under an hour; his strokes were delicious drives, leg hits, and cuts. Watson, too, was a match-winning batsman. This was Lancashire cricket at its happiest and most skilful. The pace was swift, yet safe as houses. All through the season I have insisted that Lancashire batsmen have occasionally done themselves injustice by exploiting a game untrue to their proper gifts. The afternoon's closing hour made a good end to a day that went far indeed to justify Lancashire's place at the head of all counties. The captaincy of Barnes was admirable, in its control of both the field and the bowling.

The second day was cold, with exasperating showers coming from time to time, breaking the game's rhythm. Watson and Hallows batted well until nearly half-past twelve, when the first of a sequence of 'cloudbursts' drove everybody indoors, save the hardy spirits of the popular side and the ladies' pavilion. Play was resumed for but a few minutes at one o'clock, and Watson was caught on the leg-side.

100

Hallows and Watson, in two hours and ten minutes, scored 155 for the first Lancashire wicket; their play on Thursday morning scarcely lived up to the rosy promise of Wednesday evening. Watson gave a chance at the wicket and was without forcing hits, save a solitary off-drive for three. Hallows drove straight and powerfully at the morning's outset for four from Freeman; then he had some slight trouble with the googly, and when he was 91 he popped a ball dangerously towards mid-wicket. He arrived at his hundred after less than two hours and a quarter of delectable cricket.

Not until half-past three did the match settle down again. Then we saw Ernest Tyldesley in a rather tentative vein for a while against Freeman, giving birth to hope and expectation in the Kent slips. But he quickly found his proper form; two beautiful drives off Freeman were sure signs that he was ready to play the right game for Lancashire, which, of course, was to get all the points possible out of the engagement before the rain came uncompromisingly.

At tea Lancashire were 235 for 1, and Ernest Tyldesley had made 43 to Hallow's 27 in the hour between 3.30 and 4.30. After tea heavy clouds again rolled up the sky, and Lancashire attacked the Kent bowlers like skilful, sensible and opportunist cricketers. Both Hallows and Tyldesley were on toes for the loose ball. In half an hour 50 were cut and driven. Tyldesley's stroke-play was as clean and strong as it was rapid. He jumped to the pitch of Freeman decisively, and Hallows drove with his own air of negligence, almost concealing from us his energy and effort. One or two of Ernest Tyldesley's cuts were the hammer-blows of his own immortal brother.

The first innings' spoils were acquired at a quarter-past five; Tyldesley had before that time reached his 50 in seventy-five minutes. Lancashire rounded the 300 mark at twenty-five minutes to six, and the innings was now some four hours old. Hallows was at this point 162 and Ernest Tyldesley 83. Kent's attack on the easy turf was not likely to give good batsmen food for thought, though Marriott tried cleverly to send problems of flight through the air. But the Kent bowling is terribly dependent on Freeman, who was not suited by yesterday's conditions. A delightful ball from Marriott, which broke away after pitching straight, baffled Ernest Tyldesley when his score was 95. In an hour after tea Ernest Tyldesley made 52 and Hallows 31; Hallows seemed a little tired, and perhaps that was the reason why Lancashire's pace at both ends of the wicket was not quite fast enough, considering the fairly easy opportunities which were present for the smiting of match-winning runs, though Wright worked hard to keep the ball just too short for a forcing hit.

Tyldesley got his hundred in two hours and a quarter, his share of 178 made so far for the second wicket. His cricket was on the whole admirable in spirit and technique alike; no cricketer can give to power more than Tyldesley's courtliness of manner. Once he has played himself in, he seems incapable of a tasteless stroke; his play is thoroughly civilized and sums up the best principles in the ancient and modern schools of batsmanship. He can drive forward with the best; he also understands the defensive specific of these days—the passive bat, which yields at the right angle and renders spin dead at 'the moment of impact'.

At five minutes past six Lancashire were 350; another fifty had been added in half an hour. This was the conquering tempo—and its invigorating pace was considerably helped by some doubtful work in the Kent field. His century behind him, Tyldesley hit at everything and sliced a ball from Ashdown over the slips dangerously but gallantly. Lancashire's colours were being nailed to the mast with cracking blows now, and the crowd roared home every run. At 362 Hallows's superb innings came to an end; he was lbw to Freeman, just as this bowler of slow spinning stuff had at last been compelled to open out his field. Hallows batted four hours and three-quarters, and he hit twenty boundaries. Hallows and Tyldesley scored 207 in two hours and a half. Makepeace was sent in at the afternoon's fall; some of us would have preferred to see a quick scorer taking his place.

THIRD DAY

Lancashire defeated Kent in this glorious match by an innings and 88 runs, after losing only five wickets in a first innings which was declared closed at the grand total of 478. It was the summer's most famous victory; it was achieved by real cricket, cricket of royal temper and skill. Lancashire's claims to the championship for the third year in succession are now above suspicion. The Kent second innings was smashed on a beautiful wicket in round about two hours and a quarter. It was a typical modern turf, one of the artificially prepared kind on which, so we are told in these times, Tom Richardson himself would be powerless.

On this same pitch, a batsman's vision of heaven, Macdonald held the Kent batsmen, all save Woolley, in the hollow of his hand.

Yesterday he took eight wickets for 53, and in the match his spoils in full were 15 for 154. He was Lancashire's great axe—no, the metaphor is too brutal for bowler of Macdonald's circling and sinuous grace; he was, let us say, Lancashire's flashing spear-point. He exposed mediocrity in the batsmen who came before him; Kent, against the commonplace, medium-paced swerve bowling fashionable just now, are a side of mighty hunters of runs before the Lord; in the face of a fast bowler only Woolley could show a technique; the rest were either strokeless or worse, timid-footed novices holding out beseeching bats like so many club cricketers. Batsmen used to crash to ruin against Richardson and Lockwood in the ancient days, but I fancy they did die the death showing some sort of stroke that was honoured in the art of batsmanship. Give me a Macdonald and I will prove on the best wicket that no alteration is required in the laws of cricket, rendering batsmen more vulnerable. Three times in a fortnight have I seen Kent wickets mown down at pleasure by a fast bowler; shades of Kenneth Hutchings and C. J. Burnup! On the form of the last few weeks Kent are not a championship side; a charming manner is, of course, desirable in cricketers; not less desirable is an all-round technique of batsmanship, comprising defence and offence whatever the bowling, fast or slow. Yesterday Kent's last six wickets fell for 22; on Wednesday Kent's last six wickets fell for 15. Shades of Marsham and R. N. R. Blaker! The other week Macdonald smashed the Surrey eleven on a perfect Oval pitch, and now he has as masterfully destroyed Kent on the best turf in England. Is it certain, after all, that English batting is cleverer against fast bowling than it was in 1921, when Macdonald and Gregory swept over our cricket fields in a ruthless Attila ride? Mr. Warner's answer to this question would be interesting. And Macdonald's would be more interesting still.

For an hour in the morning Lancashire forced the game and scored 87 at the cost of three more wickets—the losing of which was, of course, neither here nor there, since the Lancashire innings was going to be brought to an end one way or other well in front of lunch. Ernest Tyldesley and Makepeace hit at everything at all reachable; Makepeace even banged straight for four a shortish ball from Wright, and he swung his bat with a violence that in his normal moods he would probably regard with an emphatic disapproval. Like the great player he is, Makepeace can adapt himself to extreme ends; his swashbuckling innings against Notts a year or two ago comes to mind. It is conceivable that Makepeace looks back upon that terrific display of hitting as the one reprehensible episode in an otherwise unimpeachable career.

Tyldesley got out in the right spirit—stumped! Makepeace also threw his wicket away, going for the runs; he was thrown out rather unluckily. In forty minutes he scored 36 yesterday, exploiting a real batsman's range of hits with colossal energy and arrogance. Hopwood also showed signs of a punitive bat, but Barnes got most of the bowling, even though he could do little with it except stop it. The Lancashire declaration left Kent with 201 to save the innings defeat. Lancashire had to get Kent out within four hours and forty minutes.

In thirty-five minutes before lunch Kent scored 37 for the loss of Ashdown. Macdonald's very first ball was like the grim sounding of Kent's doom motif. It crashed half way along the pitch and then hurled itself high over the heads of the batsmen and Duckworth. Whence does Macdonald draw his terrible strength and velocity? His run to the wicket is so easy, so silent. He does not thunder over the earth like Gregory—like a bull at a gate. No, he runs along a sinister curve, lithe as a panther, his whole body moving like visible, dangerous music. A more beautiful action than Macdonald's was never seen on a cricket field, or a more inimical. The man's whole being tells of the sinister destructive forces of nature—he is a satanic bowler, menacing but princely. Yesterday he was at his best; he like a comet burned, and from his wheeling arm shot pestilence and war. His attack mingled in proportion the strength of the lion and the subtlety of the serpent. He husbanded his forces craftily; for Woolley he slackened his pace, reserving the thunderbolts for the frail. He bowled unchanged, never resting once from lunch until the end. When Bryan opposed him with a defence of some science he exploited medium-paced off-spin, but once, when Bryan would not go for a run—which would have given Macdonald a 'rabbit' to shoot at—he sent down, next ball, a streak of lightning that left Bryan standing and missed the off wicket by inches. Hardinge again was as a sightless man before Macdonald; Ashdown, like a pretty butterfly, fluttered again and again into the flame. He had a charmed life. From successive balls of Macdonald he was missed by Duckworth and Richard Tyldesley. Ashdown also gave a chance to Duckworth from Sibbles with his score only 12; he also hit high to the off-side from Sibbles, and Macdonald jumped up and nearly achieved a magnificent catch. The crowd got very restive at the sight of Lancashire's fielding blunders; Macdonald regarded them with a superb disdain and indifference. Just on lunch Ashdown sliced once too often; Barnes held the catch and tossed up the ball in a glee that clearly was born of relief.

After the interval Woolley played Macdonald in the old style, putting the full face of the bat to the ball. He cut in his prettiest and most negligent way. But Hardinge, at 44, was again caught at the wicket, making a flick with a horizontal bat, the light of speculation in his eyes as he did so. Ames cut Macdonald square for four in dashing style; he is a good batsman. He was third out at twenty minutes to three, when Kent were 63; he fell to a catch at the wicket from a good-length ball of Sibbles that made pace from the ground. Woolley went along his own effortless way; he even hit Macdonald to leg in the air. He knows not the meaning of crisis; cricket is always the carefree meadow game with a beautiful name when Woolley plays. At five minutes past three he tried to cut an out-swinger from Macdonald, and was triumphantly caught at second slip by Sibbles.

This was the end. Knott once more tried to make his bat 'connect' with Macdonald's pace; four times he cleaved the sunny air, much to the crowd's amusement. He was applauded when at last he hit, or rather stopped, a ball. Duckworth brilliantly caught him, falling over to the leg-side yet holding the prize, and somehow contriving at the same time to crow like a chanticleer. A smashing break-back upset the wicket of Legge at 105, and in the same over Macdonald comprehensively bowled Freeman. Then Iddon bowled Howlett, whereupon Macdonald swept Wright and Marriott from the scene with the lordly gesture of Charles Hawtrey's piratical Captain Applejohn —'Out of my way, scum!' Here is the sad sequence of the Kent innings:

1	2	3	4	5	6	7	8	9	10
37	44	63	91	95	105	105	108	113	113

Macdonald's steel deserved foemen in stronger armour. He, of course, won the match; on the flawless wicket every other bowler who took part in the game was helpless. Lockwood could not have let us see a greater attack. Bowling of Macdonald's skill and dreadful beautiful energy ennobles the game; the spark of it belongs to life immortal and it kindles imagination's fires in all men who look on. When Macdonald ran to the wicket yesterday Old Trafford held its breath; you could have heard a pin drop. The greatest bowler of our day!

KENT

First Innings		Second Innings	
Hardinge, c Duckworth, b Macdonald	8	c Duckworth, b Macdonald	17
Ashdown, c Duckworth, b Macdonald	17	c Barnes, b Macdonald	17
Woolley, c Iddon, b Macdonald	151	c Sibbles, b Macdonald	31
Ames, b Macdonald	48	c Duckworth, b Sibbles	14
J. L. Bryan, lbw, b Sibbles	28	not out	16
C. H. Knott, b Macdonald	0	c Duckworth, b Macdonald	3
G. B. Legge, b Sibbles	8	b Macdonald	4
Freeman, b Macdonald	4	b Macdonald	0
B. Howlett, c Watson, b Sibbles	0	b Iddon	0
Wright, c Barnes, b Macdonald	1	c Iddon, b Macdonald	1
C. S. Marriott, not out	0	c Iddon, b Macdonald	0
B 5, lb 7	12	B 7, lb 3	10
Total	277	Total	113

LANCASHIRE

First Innings

Watson, c Legge, b Wright	56
Hallows, lbw, b Freeman	184
Tyldesley (E.), st Ames, b Freeman	159
Makepeace, run out	46
Iddon, st Ames, b Freeman	0
Hopwood, not out	13
J. R. Barnes, not out	12
B 2, lb 5, nb 1	8
Total (for five wickets)	*478

* Innings declared.

BOWLING ANALYSIS

KENT—First Innings

	O.	M.	R.	W.		O.	M.	R.	W.
Macdonald	25.1	4	101	7	Iddon	8	1	34	0
Sibbles	25	1	59	3	Watson	9	0	10	0
Hopwood	9	1	34	0	Tyldesley (R.)	10	1	27	0

Second Innings

	O.	M.	R.	W.		O.	M.	R.	W.
Macdonald	22.2	6	53	8	Iddon	6	1	17	1
Sibbles	16	3	33	1					

LANCASHIRE—First Innings

	O.	M.	R.	W.		O.	M.	R.	W.
Wright	36	7	118	1	Howlett	14	0	52	0
Ashdown	21	1	89	0	Marriott	21	4	74	0
Freeman	42	6	137	3					

Howlett bowled one no-ball.

GOOD DAYS

'PATSY'

E was baptized Elias and the crowds would have none of it; they were right, too, for he is Patsy not only by name but by nature. His smile says Patsy; sometimes it is so enormous that it hides the little man; one fine day he will be given out smile before wicket. He represents democracy at Lord's in the same way that Lord Aberdare and his forward drive represented the aristocracy of the pavilion and the Long Room. He is the idol of the Tavern—that rich part of Lord's where East End is West End and West End is East. Sir James Barrie watches cricket near the Tavern. 'It's surprising,' he told me once, 'how many people you meet near the Tavern who know you. Only the other day a man in a cap came up to me and slapped me on the shoulder and said, " 'Ello, George." ' I have seen men leave their drinks at the bar of the Tavern when Patsy has just come in to bat. I don't know where he played his cricket as a boy, but I like to think it was on a rough common amongst dirty-faced happy urchins, the wicket-keeper using a coat, one bat for the lot of them. To this day Patsy always runs his first run hugging his bat in his two arms as though afraid to let it go from his possession. To give your bat up was out when I was very young. And Patsy has never grown up, and never will.

The skill of the specialist often keeps us at a distance. We bow before the majesty of Hobbs's flawless machine, but we do not feel we can ever understand it or become part of it. So with the cricket of a C. B. Fry or an Arthur Shrewsbury; we feel the presence of the straight bat of the much too virtuous life. It is the cross bat that is the sign of the cricketer beloved by the multitude; one touch of original error makes us kin. Besides, no cricketer is able to make great strokes with a straight bat, which is the supporting crutch of mediocrity. The cut and the hook cannot be performed save by a cross bat, and no batsman is great if he is not master of these two strokes. Hendren's bat is as straight as Macartney's was, or Johnny Tyldesley's, or David Denton's—and no straighter.

His batting is far more than grammatical. You can achieve good grammar and yet remain inarticulate. Hendren's strokes are idiomatic; they have about them the smack of the place in which he was born and bred. An innings by Hendren is alive, because the energy that goes into it is Patsy's energy. He has in all his career made not one artificial stroke. Sometimes he plays forward dubiously at spin bowling (on other days he jumps out on quick feet and flogs it far and wide); the timidity he exhibits then is a throw-back to the self-taug. little hero who years ago was the father of the man. He has never been able quite to believe in the greatness and the glory he has achieved; perhaps, he seems to say to us sometimes, it is all a dream and I am poor little Patsy yet, intended by Providence to go birds'-nesting all my life, not to play for England under the terribly austere eyes of the pavilion at Lord's, but to scamper about Turnham Green on summer evenings.

Hendren has known what it is to score 3000 runs in a season and stand on the top of English averages with the wonderful figures of 77. But conquest and mastery do not stale his heart, do not imprison him in a ring of routine. He simply cannot take achievement for granted. All boys who play cricket are anxious to break their ducks every time they go out to bat, and they all fear that they won't. Patsy is like that to this day—this is his secret that makes us love him. He has never become blasé through success. Nobody runs a first run with Patsy's open delight and thankfulness; how his feet twinkle across the wicket! He is even afraid they'll run him out. You never will see Hendren opening his score by means of a casual but thoroughly assured push to mid-off, and a leisurely jaunt along the pitch; that is Hobb's supreme way of announcing that he has begun; Hendren, I am prepared to swear, looks upon Hobbs with the awed adoration of a lad of fourteen. Some day Patsy will be seen outside the Oval waiting diffidently for the cricketers to come out, autograph-book in his hands.

I am perhaps making too much of his lovable humours. He is really one of the most pugnacious batsmen of all time, a terror to bowlers. Adversity toughened him, for Patsy has been through the mill. In 1921 circumstances nearly broke his heart. He starved in the midst of plenty. Day after day runs burgeoned from his bat's end, save on the very days he most dearly needed them, the days of the Test matches. He went to Nottingham, county honours thick upon him. And one of the most ferocious break-backs ever bowled knocked his leg-stump flying—'Hendren b Gregory 0.' A fortnight later, at Lord's, Patsy went to the wicket with his bat still red-hot from a dazzling century the day before. And another break-back fired him out—'Hendren b Macdonald 0.' Hendren played no more for England that year, but he waxed fat on runs in county cricket. He visited Australia with Douglas's eleven and with Gilligan's eleven, and he many times was fortune's fool, in luck one day when his side were doing well, but bankrupt for a mere 20 when England were wanting only 50 in a second innings for victory. Poor Patsy, how he suffered—and how he made the rest of us suffer! I remember the Second Test match in the 1925 Australian season, at Melbourne. England lost by 81 runs; they were winning towards close of play of the sixth afternoon. Patsy came in to bat at five o'clock or thereabouts. It was in his power to win the match, and perhaps the rubber. He got as far as 18—then Gregory bowled him. How we chastised him by word of mouth on that cold winter morning when we heard the news! 'Let his name be anathema!'

Often in this our life do we begin by cursing men and end by loving them. A sense of the common fallibility of all flesh makes us kin. No man is lovable who is invincible. Patsy has crowded his days with glorious deeds, yet tomorrow, as he goes forth to bat against Australia, every one of us will know that he is setting out on another adventure, and that our wishes and affection must be with him for a while, until he has crashed a four past mid-on. We really ought not to feel diffident about him, and he ought really not to feel diffident about himself. His technique is magnificent; his strokes are many and powerful. But his nature is not grim and hard; that is why we call him Patsy and not Elias. See him fielding near the wicket (a few years ago he was one of our swiftest outfields, but now he is more than forty years old). He bends forwards with his hands on his knees and his anatomy sticking out comically. If he mis-fields a ball he becomes momentarily forlorn, his whole body wilts. When he catches a great catch he is the happiest man alive. I shall never forget the way he finished off the Test match at Lord's the other week; he dashed in from silly mid-off, and held the ball, falling over and round and round like a clown in the circus. A day or two afterwards, at Lord's, he chased a hit to the boundary, and a little girl retrieved the ball. Patsy made a motion with his right arm, representing a throw. He was getting in touch with the little girl, showing her how to send the ball back to him. That was Patsy all over; is it a wonder that people are fond of him, here and in Australia and everywhere?

FRANK WOOLLEY

DURING the quarter of a century which is the length of Woolley's career so far, the game has gone through many changes. Bowling has had its fashions. Fast break-backs; slow and medium spin, now from the off, now from the leg; swerve and googly; this theory and the other—Woolley has had acquaintance with the lot of them. And while other batsmen have compromised some virtue of their style so that they might do the proper and expedient thing, Woolley has gone his ways undisturbed, as though unaware of the ambuscades about him. Other and more suspicious men have looked ahead. 'Ah!' they have told themselves, 'here are gins and snares of a strange new invention. Here are googlies and swerves. I must borrow the latest specifics. Fatal to trust to the ancient counters. The straight bat, the clean drive—why, these would lead me to disaster were I to use them to stop the modern bowling. I must hold my bat down, watch the ball all the way, keep my legs in front. Yes, I must be modern in the presence of the modern bowling.'

Since 1919 few batsmen have dared to drive a cricket ball hard and straight; fewer still have dared to cut past point. They have, most of them, got back on their wickets, watched the spin and the swerve to the last fraction of a second. The delayed stroke, supposedly safe, is bound to be cribbed and confined, unfree and unbeautiful. Even Hobbs has suffered a change in his play; his bat no longer moves where the master would have it go; it has for years now been weighted by circumspection, a doubting, empirical bat. Woolley on the eve of his forty-seventh birthday made runs as felicitously as he first made them for us nearly thirty years ago. Never has he compelled a crowd to ask whether cricket is as good as it used to be; never has he made the pavilion clock seem to go round with slow, tedius fingers. No other cricketer living has served the meadow game as happily and as faithfully as Woolley has done, summer after summer. No other living cricketer has moved cricket crowds to the happiness which has been felt whenever and wherever Woolley has batted, north, south, east, or west, green and pleasant Mote Park or grim and sulphurous Bramall Lane.

Cricket belongs entirely to summer every time that Woolley bats an innings. His cricket is compounded of soft airs and fresh flavours.

The bloom of the year is on it, making for sweetness. And the very brevity of summer is in it too, making for loveliness. Woolley, so the statisticians tell us, often plays a long innings. But Time's a cheat, as the old song sings. Fleeter he seems in his stay than in his flight. The brevity in Woolley's batting is a thing of pulse or spirit, not to be checked by clocks, but only to be apprehended by imagination. He is always about to lose his wicket; his runs are thin-spun. His bat is charmed, and most of us, being reasonable, do not believe in charms. There is a miracle happening on every cricket field when Woolley stays in two or three hours; an innings by him is almost too unsubstantial for this world. His cricket has no bastions; it is poised precariously—at any rate, that is how the rational mind perceives it. But, for that matter, all the loveliness of the world seems no more lasting than the dew on the grass, seems no more than the perfume and suppliance of a minute. Yet the miracle of renewal goes on, and all the east winds in the world may blow in vain. So with Woolley's cricket; the lease of it is in the hands of the special Providence which looks after the things that will not look after themselves.

His batsmanship, like all fine art, can be enjoyed by everybody, because it is fresh and natural, and, at bottom, as simple as it is modest. Other cricketers need sophistication to praise them. Their point of view must be understood. The state of the game, or the wicket, has to be looked into. 'I simply must play so-and-so,' 'Why, look at the bowling!—you cannot play a long-lengthed hit against that kind of spin.' 'The pitch is getting drier; the ball's turning.' We have to attend to these esoteric points before we can get to the quality of the latest innings by Bloggs of Blankshire—one hundred and six in four hours and a quarter, without a chance, without a risk. No child, knowing nothing of cricket but bat and ball, could understand the game as Bloggs plays it. But innocence itself will open eyes of understanding when they look upon an innings by Woolley. Here, indeed, is true, unspoiled cricket; bat and ball, indeed, and little else, save the touch of an artist—a cricketer who is as much a weaver of beauty's spells as any Kreisler that has ever lived.

The score-board does not get anywhere near the secret of Woolley. It can tell us only about Bloggs; for him runs and results are the one justification. To add up the runs made by Woolley—why, it is as though you were to add up the crotchets and quavers written by Mozart. An innings by Woolley begins from the raw material of cricket, and goes far beyond. We remember it long after we have forgotten the competitive occasion which prompted the making of it;

111

it remains in the mind; an evocative memory which stirs in us a sense of a bygone day's poise and fragrance, of a mood and a delectable shape seen quickly, but for good and all. Some of Woolley's innings stay with us until they become like poetry which can be told over again and again; we see the shapeliness of his cricket with our minds and we feel its beauty with our hearts. I can think of cricket by Woolley which has inexplicably found me murmuring to myself (that I might get the best out of it)

> Lovely are the curves of the white owl sweeping,
> Wavy in the dusk lit by one large star.

I admit, O reader, that an innings by Woolley has nothing to do with owls and dusk and starlight. I am trying to describe an experience of the fancy; I am talking of cadences, of dying falls common to all the beauty of the world. My argument, in a word, is concerned not with Woolley the Kent cricketer, but with that essence of his batsmanship which will live on, after his cricket is done with, after his runs and his averages have been totted up and found much the same as those of many other players. He has made music for cricket in all places—muted music, for never is Woolley's cricket assertive, strident. He is the soul of courtesy, of proportion, as he drives his boundaries. He will hit a bowler for four fours in an over and not give him reason to feel bruised or affronted. It is all done so quietly, so modestly. The game's hard combativeness is put out of sight, out of all one's senses, when Woolley bats. Even the bowlers may well be deceived, and think that they are not Woolley's adversaries at all, but, at his own sweet pleasure, his fellows-in-bliss, glad followers of him along an enchanted way.

MEASURE FOR MEASURE

CRICKET more than any other game is inclined towards sentimentalism and cant. The players of cricket have been arranged and displayed in a white and shining hagiology. At fellowship beanfeasts given from time to time by Buffaloes, Rotarians and so forth, there is usually a speech in which a reference is made to 'playing cricket'; the term is supposed to stand for all that is fair and holy and English. Other games, we must assume, are by their nature more prone than cricket to mortal error and weakness.

This ethical grandeur came to cricket during the nineteenth century, what time W. G. Grace was matching his wits against those of the equally artful A. N. Hornby. The game had been cradled at sweet and innocent Hambledon, where the beer was good and the stakes worth playing for. In the 'eighties, just as the little angel's wings were sprouting, the Test matches between England and Australian began. Cricket henceforward shone with the splendour of the one true faith. And the heathens (footballers, jockeys, golfers and dart-throwers) were shamed and put in their places. Grace and Murdoch and Briggs and Billy Barnes—they all wore the white flannels of a blameless life. The world wondered why umpires were necessary at all.

It is astonishing how long the humbug of cricket has lasted—this unction which, if it really were given a chance to ooze and spread amongst cricketers, would ruin the rigour of the game. Fortunately, it was only part of what G. K. Chesterton has called the 'Victorian compromise'; it has been like the shiny tail of the period, a symbol and not a deed. Today the complacent gloss has more or less gone; cricket is openly played as a sport for men and not for cherubim. The shrewd gumption of Yorkshiremen prefers a lusty 'Howzat!' to the best hymn. And for years the Australians have brought an astringent Realpolitik to the game. Let me tell a beautiful story, which has a 'moral' of its own.

Years ago an Australian team won the rubber in this country mainly by means of fast bowling which was not particular whether it occasionally whizzed past an English batsman's head. At the season's end, with the shouting and the tumult over, this victorious Australian team were engaged in a harmless holiday match at a South Country festival. The atmosphere of the match was generally urbane; nothing was at stake in the calm September air, as moment by moment the leaves fell from the trees and the harvest home was celebrated and the sun waned. Two Australian batsmen sought to put humour into the game by the jolly practice of stealing short runs. They would merely block the ball and then scamper across the wicket. At last one of the English bowlers decided to stop this pretty comedy. He bowled a ball which was patted half way down the pitch. Quick as lightning the English bowler darted to pick it up, eager to run the batsmen out. And he and the batsmen reached the same spot at the same moment. The Englishman was about to pick up the ball and aim at the vacated wicket when he felt a severe blow on his right arm. It was dealt by the bat of the Australian. With his arm momentarily paralysed, the bowler watched the batsman walk leisurely home to the safety of his crease. At the end of the over the Australian said to the English bowler in accents of perfect love, 'I say, Arthur, I hope you don't think that was done on purpose?' The Englishman simply replied, 'Get on with the game, old chap.' The sequel occurred at the luncheon interval, when one of the Australians approached the English bowler and said, 'I say, Arthur, I don't think old —— ought to have given you that crack; it wasn't the game, Arthur. After all, this isn't a Test match' . . . Let us have the humour of life and down with the namby-pambies.

Until recently the English teams which have visited Australia have tended to overdo the gesture of gentlemanly compliance, forgetting that the enemy of grand contention is lack of realistic vision. A number of English captains of cricket have wasted their public school amenities on heroes whose greatness has come out of a hearty appreciation of things as they are. A national game simply will not be confined in cotton wool. The rigour of battle is spoiled if a cricketer is not prepared to take as much as he is prepared to give. When you shake hands with the iron glove it is an insult to the man who wears it if your own glove is made of delicate wash-leather. The Australian plays cricket to win; he has usually left it to Mr. Warner to make the Empire-binding speeches. One summer we decided in this simple old land to put an end to all that. We decided to have for our captain a man who had a rare capacity for unsentimental leadership. Jardine will go down in the history of the game as one of the strongest and sternest and most realistic of all English captains. He has no moonshine in his make-up; he is a Scot, and is in the habit of counting the change given him in any match, whether against Australians, Lancastrians, Yorkshiremen, or the blue-blood of Middlesex at Lord's. He is armed with common sense and irony. His batting lets you know what his conception of cricket is like. He takes nothing for granted, not even a long-hop. If it is necessary for victory's sake for him to bat an hour and make no runs—very well, then, Jardine will enjoy the grind of it all; the crowd can perish of boredom. He has remained master of himself against all the roaring of the 'Hill' at Sydney; I have, indeed, felt sorry for the 'Hill', poor souls, with their howls and contumely splitting the heavens in vain while Jardine has gone his way ruthlessly.

We need not discuss the body-bowling affair except to say that none but a man of remarkable character could have stuck to his guns with Jardine's cool purpose, in the face of a whole country's rage and indignation. It is easy to court popularity nowadays, so much so that we have come to the state in which the worst thing that can be said of anybody is that he is popular. The sure sign of greatness is an ability to stand alone, to accept as inevitable the feeling that people are saying things behind your back which they would not dream of saying to your face. For my part I admire Jardine beyond words. I dislike his view of cricket. I believe that the qualities of character he possesses would suit better a leader of armies than a leader of cricketers. None the less, I see in Jardine a personal force in a period which finds the game woefully short of personality. I would not willingly sit out an innings by Jardine, but I would go a long way to see him stand four-square to the raving winds of the mob. His influence on modern cricket has been sanitary; he has cleared away cant. To the Australians he has returned tit for tat; it is a pity his chief opponent was not Warwick Armstrong.

If Jardine lacks humour, well, we must understand that we cannot have humour and unswerving purpose at one and the same time. A sense of humour would have made Napoleon at the Bridge of Lodi realize 'it wasn't worth it'. Cricket ought no doubt to be the 'meadow game with the pleasant name'. But in Test matches it is nothing of the kind. And so long as the world wants Test cricket, let us emulate the Australians and have no shilly-shallying. Australia being Australia, and the 'Hill' being the 'Hill'—*il faut cultiver notre* Jardine.

BRADMAN, 1930

THE power of genius in cricket is not to be measured by the scoreboard, and not even by the clock. A Trumper, a Spooner, will reveal art and energy in one or two personal strokes or by some all-pervading yet indefinable poise and flavour. At Leeds Bradman announced his right to mastership in a few swift moments. He made 72 runs during his first hour at the wicket, giving to us every bit of cricket except the leg glance. But long before he had got near the end of his innings he was repeating himself; it was as though the sheer finish of technique was a prison for his spirit. He could not make a hazardous flight; he reminded me of the trapeze performer who one night decided to commit suicide by flinging himself headlong to the stage, but could not achieve the error because his skill had become infallible, a routined and mechanical habit not at the beck and call of anything so volatile as human will or impulse. When Bradman passed 200 at Leeds I felt that my interest in his play might break out anew at the sight of one miscalculated stroke. But none was to be seen. His cricket went along its manifold ways with a security which denied its own brilliance. Every fine point of batsmanship was to be admired, strokes powerful and swift and accurate and handsome; variety of craft controlled by singleness of mind and purpose. Bradman was as determined to take no risks as he was to hit boundaries from every ball the least loose—his technique is so extensive and practised that he can get runs at the rate of fifty an hour without once needing to venture romantically into the realms of the speculative or the empirical. The bowler who had to tackle Victor Trumper was able to keep his spirit more or less hopeful by some philosophy such as this: 'Victor is moving at top speed. Well, I'm bound sooner or later to send along a really good ball. Victor will flash at it in his ecstasy—and I'll have him.' The bowler toiling at Bradman cannot support himself by a like optimism. For hours he will see his ordinary balls hit for fours along the grass; then his good one will wheel from his arm, by the law of averages which causes every bowler to achieve one moment of excellence in every hour. But is Bradman ever likely to be so blinded by the radiance of his own visions that he will throw back his head at the good ball, confuse it with the others, and lose his wicket through a royal expense of spirit? Not he; he sees the dangerous ball with eyes as suspicious as those of a Makepeace. Down over his bat goes his head; the blade becomes a broad protective shield—and probably two pads will lend a strong second line of defence. It is not a paradox to imagine some bowler saying to Bradman, with strict justice, after Bradman has punished five fours in one over and cannily stopped the sixth ball: 'For the Lord's sake, Don, do give a fellow a chance and have a hit at her!'

The genius of this remarkable boy consists in the complete summary he gives us of the technique of batsmanship. In every art or vocation there appears from time to time an incredible exponent who in himself sums up all the skill and experience that have gone before him. It is not true that Bradman has inaugurated a new era in batsmanship; he is substantially orthodox in technique. Nearly all his strokes at Leeds could very well have been used as illustrations to C. B. Fry's thoroughly scientific and pragmatic book on batsmanship. But Bradman shows us excellences which in the past we have had to seek in different players; nobody else has achieved Bradman's synthesis. It is, of course, a synthesis which owes much to the fact that Bradman stays at the wicket longer than most of the brilliant stroke-players of old ever dreamed of staying. Perhaps he is marked off from the greatness of his predecessors not so much by technique as by temperament. It is hard to believe in the possibility of a more masterful stroke-player than Trumper was, or Hobbs in his heyday. But when Trumper and Hobbs were great batsmen it was customary for cricketers to try to get out when their scores went beyond, say, 150. How many times has Hobbs thrown his wicket away after reaching his century? Bradman brings to an extensive technique the modern outlook on cricket, a hundred runs is nothing to him; he conceives his innings in terms which go far beyond Trumper's or Macartney's most avaricious dreams. He has demonstrated that a batsman can hit forty-two boundaries in a day without once giving the outfielders hope of a catch; he has kindled grand bonfires of batsmanship for us. But never once has he burned his own fingers while lighting them.

When I think of an innings by Macartney, I do not think entirely of cricket. My impression of Macartney's batting are mixed up with impressions of Figaro, Rossini's Figaro, a gay trafficker with fortune, but a man of the world; hard as iron though nimble of wit; an opportunist wearing a romantic feather in his cap. And when I think of an innings by Trumper I see in imagination the unfurling of a banner. Not by Bradman is the fancy made to roam; he is, for me, a batsman living, moving, and having his being wholly in cricket. His batsmanship delights one's knowledge of the game; his every stroke is a dazzling and precious stone in the game's crown. But I do not find his cricket making me think of other and less tangible things; the stuff of his batsmanship is skill, not sensibility. In all the affairs of the human imagination there must be an enigma somewhere, some magical touch that nobody can understand and explain. You could never account for Macartney, Ranjitsinhji, Spooner, Trumper, in terms of even a marvellous technique. Bradman, as I see and react to him, is technique *in excelsis*. I could write a text-book on him with comprehensive and thoroughly enlightening diagrams. Could anybody have written a text-book saying anything that mattered about the batting of Johnny Tyldesley?

The really astonishing fact about Bradman is that a boy should play as he does—with the sophistication of an old hand and brain. Who has ever before heard of a young man, gifted with quick feet and eyes, with mercurial spirits and all the rapid and powerful strokes of cricket—who has ever heard of a young man so gifted and yet one who never indulged in an extravagant hit high into the air? Until a year or two ago Bradman had seen little or no first-class cricket. Yet here is he today, bringing to youth's natural relish for lusty play with a cricket bat a technical polish and discretion worthy of a Tom Hayward. A mis-hit by Bradman—when he is dashing along at fifty runs an hour—surprises us even as a mis-hit by Hayward did when he was in his most academic vein. How came this Bradman to expel from him all the greenness and impetuosity of youth while retaining the strength and alacrity of youth? How did he come to acquire, without experience, all the ripeness of the orthodox—the range and adaptability of other men's accumulated years of practice in the best schools of batsmanship? The cricket of Trumper at the age of twenty-one could not be accounted for, but we were content to accept it in terms of spontaneous genius. Besides, there was always the rapture and insecurity of the young man in Trumper. But while we can account for Bradman's batting by reason of its science and orthodoxy, we are unable quite to accept it—it is too old for Bradman's years and slight experience. The genius who thrills us is always unique but seldom abnormal. If Bradman develops his skill still further—and at his age he ought to have whole worlds to conquer yet—he will in the end find himself considered not so much a master batsman as a phenomenon of cricket.

As I say, the remarkable fact about Bradman's batsmanship is its steady observance of the unities. At Leeds he was credited with the invention of a new kind of hook. But there was no scope at Leeds for any sort of hook, ancient or modern. The ball never rose stump high on the first day; how can any batsman hook a ball that does not rise at a sharp angle from the ground? I have never yet seen Bradman perform the hook stroke, but I have seen him pull often enough. The pull, indeed, is one of his most efficient hits; it is timed to perfection, and the sound of it is as sweet as a nut. (This essay, the reader will bear in mind, was written of the Bradman who first astonished us in 1930.)

At Leeds more than half of his forty-six fours were drives in front of the wicket. His drive and cut, indeed, were much more frequently to be seen than his pull and leg hit. The secret of his stroke-power lies in his ability to move quickly backwards or forwards, making the length short or over-pitched. The area of the wicket wherein a ball can be pitched that is a good length to Bradman is considerably narrower than that which is defended by all our county batsmen, Woolley excepted. He judges the direction of the attack rapidly; never is he to be seen lunging forward, stretched speculatively out: never does he fall into that 'two-minded' state which compels a batsman to make 'A-shaped bridges down the wicket feeling awry in the air for the ball', to quote C. B. Fry. Bradman clinches Fry's celebrated Fallacy of Reach: 'The Fallacy of Reach is fatal to true cricket. None but a giant by advancing the left foot and pushing out down the wicket can reach within feet of the pitch of a good-length slow ball or within yards of the pitch of a good-length fast ball. Why, the very thing the bowler wants one to do, what he works to make one do, is to feel forward at the pitch of his bowling.' Bradman plays back or else goes the whole way of the forcing stroke on punitive decisive feet. When he is as a last resort compelled to play forward, he actually goes back on his wicket to do so, and his legs are behind the bat, and his eyes are on the ball. So strong is his back play, and so quick his eyes and feet, that it is fatal to bowl a short length to him. Yet, so far, that is the mistake the English bowlers have made against Bradman. Frankly they have not 'stood up' to his punishment. Flattered by everyday batsmanship (right foot footed behind the crease), English bowling has wilted at the sight of a bat that is busy and resolute; hence an attempt to take refuge in short bowling, a safe enough dodge in front of a cricketer who cannot cut. Bradman has thriven on bowling which he has been at liberty to see all the way, to see pitch yards in front of him. If he has a weak point, Robins, by accident or design, found it out occasionally at Trent Bridge. Every time (which was not often) that Robins sent a well-flighted ball to Bradman, pitched on the middle stump and spinning away, Bradman was observed to be thinking hard, entirely on the defensive. It is not, of course, for the pavilion critic to presume to know the way that Bradman can be got out cheaply. But it is surely not presumptuous for anybody to suggest that the short-pitched ball is about the last of all to send to a batsman with Bradman's voracious appetite for fours and his range of hits.

He has all the qualities of batsmanship: footwork, wrists, economy of power, the great strokes of the game, each thoroughly under control. What, then, is the matter with him that we hesitate to call him a master of style, an artist who delights us, and not only a craftsman we are bound to admire without reserve? Is it that he is too mechanically faultless for sport's sake? A number of Bradmans

would quickly put an end to the glorious uncertainty of cricket. A
number of Macartneys would inspire the game to hazardous heights
more exhilarating than ever . . . But this is a strain of criticism that
is comically churlish. Here have we been for years praying for a
a return of batsmanship to its old versatility and aggression; we have
been desperate for the quick scorer who could hit fours without
causing the game to lapse into the indiscriminate clouting of the
village green. In short, we have been crying out for batsmanship
that would combine technique and energy in proportion. And now
that a Bradman has come to us, capable of 300 runs in a single day
of a Test match, some of us are calling him a Lindrum of cricket.
It is a hard world to please. Perhaps by making a duck some day,
Bradman will oblige those of his critics who believe with Lord
Bacon that there should always be some strangeness, something
unexpected, mingled with art and beauty.

CONSTANTINE

GENIUS is originality, and in cricket the man is a genius
who does a thing superbly, masterfully, and entirely in a
way of his own. His play must make us cry out, 'Nobody
else could do it!' We must feel and know that without it the game
would be short of some quality or power necessary to the fulfilment
of all its delightful parts and possibilities.

We cannot think of cricket save in terms of W. G. Grace, Ranji,
MacLaren, Hobbs, Woolley, to name a few of the indispensable
names. These men helped to make cricket—which is a living growth
not an abstraction. Cricket, considered purely as a game in the
abstract, is any engagement between two teams using bats, wickets
and a ball for the implements. The cricket we love as a people the
wide world over is the sum-total of all the personal skill and
character which have been put into it by great men who have played
it and who, by giving to the technique and form some turn or push
of their own, have kept developments alive and in touch with the
people, decade after decade. W. G. Grace not only demonstrated the
art of placing the ball and how to play forward and back in one
comprehensive system of footwork; also he was an eminent Victorian and the embodiment of Gloucestershire. Ranjitsinhji not only
demonstrated the leg glance; he also expressed the genius of his race.

Hirst was one of the original great swervers, but he swerved with a Yorkshire accent. In the age of jazz and Irving Berlin, Parkin became the first jazz cricketer; his slow ball was a syncopation in flight.

The most original cricketer of recent times is Constantine. Nothing so original, indeed, has been witnessed on a cricket field in our time. It is not enough to say that he hits the ball hard and often, with strokes which defy analysis; Jessop did all that, incomparably. No; Constantine's originality is a vital and full expression of the West Indian temperament, a temperament which has never before been able to find complete articulation in a West Indian cricketer, because it takes some time for any activity of life to reach that stage of evolution which produces the representative man and master. There have been, of course, West Indian cricketers with as much as Constantine's skill. Challenor was a great batsman, but he was not essentially West Indian in style or temperament. When we see Constantine bat or bowl or field, we know at once that he is not an English player, not an Australian player, not a South African player: we know that his cuts and drives, his whirling fast balls, his leapings and clutching and dartings in the slips are racial; we know they are the consequences of impulses born in the blood, heated by sun, and influenced by an environment and a way of life much more natural than ours—impulses not common to the psychology of the over-civilized quarters of the world. When Constantine plays cricket the whole man plays, not just the professional cricketer part of him. There is nothing in the world for him, when he bats, save a ball to be hit—and a boundary to hit it over. When he bowls, the world is three wickets, there to be sent spinning gloriously. Cricket, indeed, is Constantine's element; to say that he plays cricket, or takes part in it, is to say that a fish goes swimming. Constantine is cricket, West Indian cricket, just as Grace was English cricket. The branches are the tree; the players are the game.

Constantine performs strokes not set down in the Englishman's or the Australian's repertory. He breaks all the laws, save his own laws. Sometimes, when he allows spirit to run away with him, he lets energy come out crudely, instead of in significant form. In a Test match once at Lord's, he lost his wicket by heaving a ball 'down square-leg's throat'; the hit was not more Constantine's than it was any slogger's enjoying the humour of the village green. But next day he was an artist, a master of the grotesque. He hit a ball for six to leg so fine that you were ready to vow that it went over the wicket-keeper's head. The ball was past him when he smote, as though by

121

an afterthought, incredibly late. Constantine's strokes are always made late: he must have marvellous eyes. He does not lift up his bat high behind him as the ball is coming; a high back-lift means that a batsman is feeling he must give himself plenty of time. Constantine waits until the ball is on him; then, swift as lightning and swifter, he cracks his bat like a whip, using forearms which are as flexible as they are powerful.

No man living or dead has hit a ball to the boundary with more than the strength and the velocity of Constantine. The strokes leave the field standing, and they make the sound of triumphant aggression. He can cut from the middle stump, clean down to third-man, with a stab that momentarily takes away the eyesight of the slips. He will lie back on his right foot and crash the ball past mid-on—a good-length ball too—with an energy that threatens broken legs. The field anywhere when Constantine is batting seems to be in danger of serious hurt any minute. He causes the largest cricket ground to look small; when he is riding his hurricane, eleven men are not half enough in the field. His strokes are not blind; he knows what he is doing, and the penetrative strength of his bat reduces the swiftest runner to a misplaced block of wood.

Because he was born to be a representative West Indian cricketer, he is a fast bowler. All West Indians who come to the game try to bowl fast as a matter of course; to train a West Indian slow bowler you must begin with his grandfather. Constantine runs to the wicket for dear life, a bouncing, galloping sort of run; then he leans sideways, and without a jump, brings over his arm high. He is a hostile bowler. Every fast bowler should be hostile. Constantine expects to take a wicket every ball; at the end of each fruitless over he looks puzzled, and takes his cap from the umpire with his head down, lost in thought as he considers the mystery of frustration. When the ball leaves his arm the swift line of flight seems somehow part of his run up to the wicket; Constantine's bowling, the line and direction of it, always strikes me as a visible flashing current of the man's life-force. The pace, indeed, apparently pulls his body after it; his run follows the ball, and you can never see exactly where it ends and where exactly Constantine ceases to be a bowler and becomes a fieldsman, quick as a cat after a mouse for a catch from his own attack. Constantine has brought off many a 'c and b' which has beggared explanation and description. Apparently he has the power to be in two places at the same time.

Years ago at Lord's, in the first Test match ever played with the

West Indians in this country, Larwood began the second day batting against Constantine. A ball of terrific pace jumped straight up, and Larwood, shielding his breast, popped the ball in front of him. None of us thought the stroke was really a chance; we saw the ball in the air and said to ourselves, 'If only the wicket-keeper had been closer up; if only point had been not quite so deep . . .' But lo and behold! Constantine came down the pitch in two animal leaps, and he fell in front of the block-hole, missing the chance only by inches. The catch would have been the most unexpected ever made in cricket's history, surely. The effort left us all breathless; Larwood stood there the picture of astonishment, wondering 'where Constantine had come from'. The movements of Constantine in the field are strange, almost primitive, in their pouncing voracity and unconscious beauty, a dynamic beauty, not one of smooth curves and relaxations. He does not run after a ball hit through the slips; he springs after it, swoops on it rather than picks it up. There are no bones in his body, only great charges and flows of energy. You cannot see some of his slip-fielding, so rapid is his action. You hear the bat's crack, and then you hear the ball crashing the stumps. He can catch anything. Constantine ought to have first refusal of all chances hit to any part of the field. Only one thing can he not do; he cannot save the over-throws which sometimes happen from his own returns.

A genius and a representative man. He has made his unique con-tribution to the style and technique of the game. He has at the same time told the tale of his people. At Lord's, that same day while Constantine was batting, a number of his compatriots wept for joy and shook hands in brotherly union. Constantine was their prophet; they saw in his genius some power all their own, a power ageless, never to be put down, and free and splendid.

'MERCUTIO'

HE was Mercutio amongst batsmen; every ball was an affront to him, especially a good ball. Once, in a Test match at Lord's, he stood back on his right foot, lifted his left, seemed to wrench all his inches upward—and he was not a tall man—to crash a ball that rose breast-high, savagely. The stroke was wonderful, creative. Next day I congratulated Macartney on the hit, and he said, 'It was either four or out. When I saw the ball coming it was wobbling in the air; then it swooped down, and I said "One of us is for it." ' That was Macartney all over; he never declined a challenge, not he! He himself was the great thrower-down of gauntlets, the slapper of cheeks, with his cuts from the middle stump, his pulls on fast wickets from straight balls. He had (like Mercutio) no use for the man who fought by the book of arithmetic. Macartney's every innings was Queen Mab's scherzo, a flight fantastic, with nimble strokes of quick cross-lightning. His bat was here, there and everywhere, never still for a moment. It flickered and played round his wrists. His footwork was so rapid that eyesight could not follow his movements, his dartings and pouncings. No such thing as a good-length ball existed while Macartney batted. If his genius was ready for great deeds, the rest was irrelevant. Barnes himself could not keep Macartney quiet. His strokes were shooting stars. I once tried to make a diagram of his hits in an incredible innings played at Trent Bridge against Nottinghamshire; I broke my pencil endeavouring to express on paper the forked explosive energy of his cricket that day. It was the occasion when he scored 345 in three hours and fifty-five minutes; heavens, did it really happen, or did we dream it? After Macartney reached 200 in something like the time the average player needs to score seventy, he waved his bat towards the pavilion, and signalled. 'What do you want, Charles,' asked A. W. Carr: 'a drink?' 'No', replied Macartney; 'I want a heavier bat; I'm going to have a "dip".' One of the Nottinghamshire bowlers, overhearing the conversation, nearly fainted.

Three Australian batsmen (but never an English) have scored centuries in Test matches before lunch: Victor Trumper, Macartney and Bradman, each in this country, too. (So much for the Jardinian theory of the survival of the slowest.) When Macartney became one of the immortal three, at Leeds in 1926, he was missed in the slips when his score was only two by A. W. Carr, who had put Australia in to bat on a soft wicket. Two and a half hours after the occurrence of this frustration of England's chances, Macartney came back to the pavilion, and the multitude acclaimed him to a man, gratefully, loudly. Nobody said, 'Ah, but he ought to have been out for two'; nobody mentioned Carr's blunder. For nearly three hours every man, woman, and child had been sitting there, willing prisoners to the spell woven by Macartney. When at last he broke his wand, it was with sorrow we came out of the enchantment and realized it had all been merely cricket, not music and twanging instruments, not the

124

woods of Westermain, not the everlasting enfranchisement of mortal spirit; only bat and ball at Headingley. Such is genius.

Macartney's batsmanship was always personal art, as much so as if he had composed allegros or had woven the Bayeux tapestry; there was always chivalry in his cricket, a prancing sort of heroism. He lifted cricket far above the narrow circumstances of partisan interest; the dauntlessness of his play, the manliness, the brave beauty and original skill, bring tears to my eyes yet. And he was but one knight in the memorable hosts—Trumper, Clem Hill, Darling, Tyldesley, MacLaren, Spooner, R. E. Foster, Hutchings, Woolley, Hobbs. And now we are told that Test matches must be stopped because they breed bad sport, ill-feeling. When I think of Test matches of old between England and Australia, I see a glorious frieze of gallant deeds. Do you tell me that distance lends enchantment to the view, that I am glorifying in retrospect a past which was really just like the present? But Macartney retired from cricket only the other day; his contemporaries were Gregory, Macdonald, Woolley and Hobbs at their best, George Gunn, J. W. H. T. Douglas, Parkin, Mailey, Rhodes—all of them artists, original and independent spirits, all playing together. It is because of these men, or men of their breed, that cricket became the national game of England and Australia; because of these men the great pavilion at Lord's was built, emblem of greatness, like Wotan's Valhalla; because of these spirits and the great company of them, Francis Thompson wrote poetry about cricket; and countless men not especially interested in sport grew to love the game, finding in it a spur to pride and imagination. Lord's pavilion would never have been built and Francis Thompson would never had gone to Lord's, if cricket had always been played 'for results'.

The war interrupted the tradition that nurtured a Macartney. A game is exactly what is made of it by the character of the men playing it. New laws, new ways of preparing wickets, new schemes of reckoning championships—these external things do not matter. The style is the man himself. You could not in any circumstances have had dull cricket with Macartney. Dullness at cricket comes out of the souls of the players. On and off the field Macartney was the same vital man; his jaw was strong, his mouth firm and humorous; and out of his eyes shone temperament that was accustomed to being expressed. No inhibitions in Macartney, either as man or as cricketer. See him at breakfast before a Test match, as I once did; he was tremendously alive. 'Marmalade? yes; some more toast.

Good wicket today; plenty of runs. Sure.' You felt sorry for the bowler already. And what a sense of the occasion he had! He was always at his best at Lord's. It was there he hit Barnes for six, and made ninety-nine against him on a doubtful wicket.

In the September of 1926 I went to Scarborough; I knew it was to be the last time I would see him play, ever. I asked him to give me a farewell innings. He did not disappoint. To the end of my life I shall remember how the softening autumn sunshine touched his cricket that day. He did not seek to astonish me by the old audacious hits; he knew I had seen all those tricks often enough. He played a modest game, noble in poise, sad in its sense of a leave-taking. He drove a four past cover-point, then he was bowled trying to cut—the old Adam simply had to come out once more. I saw him walk from the field, walk back to the pavilion. That was my last sight of Macartney; and the like of him will not be seen again by anybody.

YORKSHIRE

A FEW summers ago I arrived at Bradford an hour or two late for the first day of a match between Yorkshire and Middlesex; I got mixed up with a train connection round about the wilds of Low Moor. As soon as I reached the field my eyes went straight to Emmott Robinson, like the eyes of the lover to the beloved. At once I saw that something was wrong with the man. Middlesex were batting, and the score-board said 128 for two. 'What's been doing?' I asked a man in the crowd, using the vernacular. 'Nowt,' he said, 'nowt but slow play—and Emmott missed Hearne when he was fower.' Hearne was now 57 not out; Emmott Robinson walked across the wicket between overs with his head down. He was a man who took Yorkshire cricket seriously. That day at Bradford he did not look up until, at four o'clock, he bowled Hearne all over his stumps. Just before he achieved this desire he appealed for leg-before-wicket against Hearne, appealed with all his heart and soul and lungs. I happened to be watching the game from behind the bowler, with glasses fixed on Hearne. I saw that Hearne's legs were not quite in front, and involuntarily I murmured, 'Not out.' Immediately I felt that somebody was observing me. I turned round and saw a typical Yorkshireman eyeing me from my feet to my head. 'And what's the matter with thee?' he asked.

All Yorkshiremen are like that at cricket, and Robinson summed them all up in himself. When Yorkshire were playing Lancashire at Old Trafford a season or two ago they somehow found themselves in a dreadful hole on the third afternoon. With only a draw to play for, they had lost five wickets at half-past three; they were hundreds of runs behind. In came Robinson, and he fought the good fight. For two hours and more he defended, bat and pads and all. Ten minutes before the close of play, when Yorkshire had but two wickets in hand, Robinson died the hero's death—lbw. He waited a while after he saw the umpire's finger go up, waited on the off-chance that some mistake had been made. Then he proceeded to depart. You could not say he was not going, was not definitely moving in Time and Space from one point to another. The retreat was masterful; it was a strategic withdrawal. Alas! the scheme miscarried, through the incredible impulsiveness of Waddington, who rushed to the wicket, ran yards down the pitch and was stumped. Lancashire won first innings points with two minutes to spare.

Months afterwards, in the depth of winter, I was in Yorkshire at a dinner. Who should be sitting next to me but Emmott Robinson? (He ordered a cup of tea after the dinner, saying that he thought coffee 'were no good' for anybody after a meal.) I had forgotten the match at Old Trafford, and Waddington's rashness. But the wound was still bleeding for Emmott. 'Think of it,' he said. 'Gettin' stumped wi' t'match in that state.' He paused, and then, looking at me terribly, he said, 'I'd 'a' died first before they stumped me.' He meant it; Emmott meant everything he ever said about cricket, or did about cricket, in all his life. He once told me how Derbyshire were put out by Yorkshire at Chesterfield for 86. 'But,' he added, 'they should never 'a' got them. Townsend were missed before he scored. They should never 'a' got them.' He was referring to a match that had taken place six years ago. 'Never mind, Emmott,' I said, in the hope of consoling him, 'it all happened a long time ago.' He smote the table with his fist. 'It's no matter,' he answered, 'they should never 'a' got them!' He will die in that belief.

No cricketer has played the game with more than Robinson's grand passion. He was one of the richest characters in the game's great seasonal comedy. He bowled the finest out-swinger of his period; he could use the new ball with more venom than any other bowler. He loved what he called a 'green wicket', and at the beginning of a match it was a joy to see him inspecting the turf, pressing his fingers in it, feeling it and talking of 't'texture' like a shrewd buyer of cloth testing material. He could tell you exactly what the wicket would be doing at half-past four. Yorkshire once batted the whole of the first day against Surrey and made 400 for six. On the Sunday the weather broke. Yorkshire continued their innings on the Monday while the wicket was slow and gradually becoming difficult. Everybody was asking when Yorkshire were going to declare. I watched the morning's first hour in the Yorkshire dressing-room, and Emmott and Major Lupton and I sat and talked. The game at this stage was not particularly interesting and we talked of many things. Suddenly a ball jumped up; Emmott was in the middle of a sentence. 'Aye, and I told him'—then the ball jumped— 'I told him (call 'em in, Major), I told him . . .' Robinson missed nothing.

He was not in technique a cricketer of extraordinary gifts, but by taking thought he added yards to his stature. He bowled as though nothing in the world existed at the moment but the batsman at the wicket's other end; he would gather up all his loose energy and hurl himself at Makepeace as though at an object detestable. I remember how once he defeated Makepeace's bat with a glorious swinger, and appealed for leg-before. It was the last ball of the over, and when the umpire said 'Not out,' Robinson stood still, not comprehending, baffled at the inadequacy of justice in the world. So upset was he that he ran to his wrong place in the field. Against Worcestershire on a certain occasion he decided to field 'silly-point' for M. K. Foster, who was in form and hitting the ball hard. 'If I were you,' said Foster solicitously, 'I'd move back a little, Emmott.' And Emmott simply remained where he was and said, 'Get on with thi lakin', Mr. Foster.'

Cricket was Emmott Robinson's mission; Yorkshire was his religion. Only once did he ever forget himself. He was saving a match with Rhodes, and against Lancashire, of all counties. Over after over Robinson stonewalled. Suddenly, for no reason whatever, he made a magnificent late cut towards third man off Richard Tyldesley. He was so taken out of himself by the brilliance of the stroke that he stood there, transfixed. And when at last he returned from the world of aesthetic contemplation to the world of things as they are, Wilfred Rhodes was on his doorstep. Emmott was run out by the length of the pitch. No doubt he has not forgiven himself to this day, and no doubt he never will. He and Rhodes were the brains of the great Yorkshire team of their conquering period. I can see the two of them now, watching Roy Kilner flashing his bat at Macdonald's pace. Roy Kilner was incorrigible; the Yorkshire grimness could not be taught him. Humour would creep in with Kilner, even on an August Bank Holiday at Sheffield. I can see him trying to cut Macdonald, with his cap all a-cock over his eye. 'Hey, look at him!' said Emmott to Wilfred. 'He'll never get sense, never get sense.'

Robinson seemed to be made out of the stuff of Yorkshire county; I imagine that the Lord one day gathered together a heap of Yorkshire clay and breathed into it and said, 'Emmott Robinson, go on and bowl at the pavilion end for Yorkshire.' He looked the old soldier, with his lined face and fine grey hairs. He shambled about the field with his trousers loose. You were getting ready to see them fall down altogether when he would remember them in time. His feet were noble. And thrive he did though bandy. I loved the man, and the crowd loved him, because he did his job with all his heart. His cricket was of a kind that could never be estimated by all the averages, by statistics; it was an activity that came out of his own being. Of ordinary cricketers there is little to be said when they are not doing well; on such occasions we overlook them. Robinson was always in the game passionately; indeed, it was in moments of frustration that he was at his most impressive. He had an eloquent droop of the body in his hours of impotence. You see, he expected to take a wicket every ball. Lancashire and Yorkshire matches, and perverse umpires, silvered his head. Often have I looked at his fine keen face and loved the lines in it, graven by experience. He enriched the nature of cricket, put into it the humours of the soil, invested it with character. Like Tom Emmett, he belongs to Yorkshire for all time.

BLYTHE OF KENT

BLYTHE OF KENT—what a name, how perfect for the prettiest slow left-handed bowler of his, or surely any other, period! His great days happened at the same time as the great days of Rhodes, but Rhodes was always a classic. The eternal wheel of his action expressed nothing of the game's caprice and love of young life; Rhodes's bowling wore always the Yorkshire aspect of disguised and aged menace. When Rhodes deceived a batsman with the ball that went straight through he merely said 'How is it?' to the umpire, and then, hearing a decision in his favour, he would receive back the ball from the wicket and toss it from hand to hand, as though nothing had happened that was not in the day's work.

Blythe was all nervous sensibility; his guile was a woman's, you might say a pretty lady's; the guile of Rhodes was masculine, the old soldier's. Remember the little chassée which Blythe made with his feet just before his left arm swung over from the right trousers-pocket, behind the back. It was almost timid. Rhodes wore his victims out by a terrible policy of persistence; the ball dropped, over after over, on the perfect length—water wearing out the rock of even Quaife's patience. Blythe's bowling seldom curved through the air with the fulsome deceit of Rhodes's flight, a wicked, dishonest flight if ever there was one! Blythe's flight and curve were modest, a little short if anything, pitching in front of the batsman's very eyes. He did not fling his allurements about shamelessly. His trick was sharp and sudden spin; the batsman was overwhelmed by a ball which flashed from the leg to the off stump, a ball that had come straight down to the earth, inviting, almost with a blush, the compliment of an elegant forward stroke.

There has never in our time been a slow bowler with more than Blythe's skill on hard wickets. I have seen him, in dry weather on a good turf, sending down his delicately spun overs to a field with two slips in it, even with J. T. Tyldesley using wonderful footwork. The low trajectory of Blythe's attack prevented the drive; it was hard to run out to him. And in those legendary days batsmen did run out of their creases and attempt to knock slow bowlers out of countenance. It was a familiar phrase then 'c Denton, b Rhodes',—quite as familiar as 'c Tunnicliffe, b Rhodes'. And Denton fielded in the deep.

Blythe's spin and length were the stumper's and slips' delight. The first time I ever went to Old Trafford I heard a terrific shriek as I entered the gates. Thinking in my boy's ignorance of the ways of county cricketers, that somebody had been killed, I rushed to the seats, heart in mouth. I was told that the noise had been Huish appealing for a catch at the wicket from a ball bowled by Blythe. I imagine that none but a most quick-minded stumper could have served Blythe's purpose. For he spun the ball with more alacrity, and with a sharper rise, than any other bowler I have seen. Huish was always taking Blythe's catches off the bat, an inch from the off bail; and the noise of the smack which the ball made as it sped into

Huish's gloves, and the noise of Huish's accompanying roar, are things I shall hear in imagination whenever I go to Canterbury or Tonbridge. There is a world of difference between the slow bowler whose catches at the wicket are a foot away from the stumps, and the slow bowler whose catches are near the batsman's wrists and the consequence of a stroke made late, by sheer reflex action. On a sticky wicket Blythe was unplayable; there was no getting to the half-volley and, by the grace of fortune, enjoying a few fours off the edge of the bat. His length, as I say, defied a drive; it forced the batsman to play just when the break was taking effect like a knife, and coming up from the earth at an angle which turned scientific stroke-play into vanity.

Blythe, while he spread about the batsman's ears—or wrists—these buzzing wasps of spin, was himself the least menacing of men. It was as though his happy heart knew not what sinfulness his fingers were doing. I have seen him bowl A. C. MacLaren with the loveliest spinner in creation—from leg to off in a trice, and a round button of turf splashing through the air. And I have seen him begin to walk down the wicket involuntarily, as though to apologize to the most majestic of batsmen. Once, at Canterbury, R. H. Spooner, on a flawless wicket, hit Blythe unmercifully through the covers and at last pulled him square for six. And Blythe applauded and cried out, 'Oh, Mr. Spooner, I'd give all my bowling to bat like that!' Charming, pale-faced Blythe, slender and given to fits, because his nerves were sticking out, so to say. He used to play the violin and make music even as the old cricketers of Hambledon did. In the ancient chronicles you will read descriptions of players in some such phraseology as this: 'A good bat, sound in defence. Bowls well, down the brow of the hill; is a sharp long-stop, and sings in a pleasant tenor voice.' I never heard Blythe performing on his fiddle; but I am told his left-hand technique and finger-work were supple; well can I believe it.

When I was very young and Blythe was one of my heroes I did not know that he came from Deptford and was a gorgeous Cockney. My lad's imagination made romance around his name—Colin Blythe. I invented a story about him; he was out of a public-school tale, and the villain had (temporarily, of course) swindled him of his inheritance. One day I saw Blythe walking round a cricket field, and I followed him about. I never dreamed of asking for an autograph; I simply wanted to hear him speak. He was talking and laughing with a player of the Kent side, Seymour, who used to hold, and sometimes miss, his slip catches. And I heard Blythe say: 'I'll 'it yer on top o' the nose in a minute.' It was a shock, because a boy's romanticism is always snobbish. Kent found Blythe playing cricket on a piece of waste land in a grimy part of his county; Kent is not all lanes and hop gardens. Colin Blythe came out of a slum, and became the darling of Canterbury Week, with all its fashion and fine ladies. And I was not the only one to follow Blythe about on cricket fields in those days. Sometimes a thin, tall, gawky, nervous youth would be seen walking in Blythe's footsteps, watching him all the time, worshipping him. This boy was Woolley, who later was to become a glorious batsman and Blythe's own shadow as a spin bowler. Blythe and Woolley, loveliest of names, loveliest of cricketers.

War broke out when Blythe was in his maturity. There had been days when this delicate artist was too ill, too sadly overstrung to bowl and win honours for England in Test matches. But he lost his life fighting for England, one of the first to join up. A shell made by somebody who had never known cricket and directed by eyes that had never seen a Kent field, fell on Blythe and killed him. On any of those quiet, distant, delicious afternoons at Canterbury, when Blythe bowled his gentle spin and the summer blossomed all around, could even the ironic gods have discerned the course of events which was to take Blythe over the seas and leave him there part of the foreign dust?

GEORGE GUNN

GEORGE GUNN was one of the characters of cricket, a rare 'original', to use the old term. We cannot discuss his style of play, his technique, in the abstract, as a thing separable from the man himself in all his humours. For our delight, George Gunn could do things which with other men would have seemed foolish and vain. We must try to remember him always in terms of his personal touch; we must get him permanently into a scene, frame him like a picture. I see him now, and for ever, as I once saw him on a hot July day at Trent Bridge when Macdonald was great and formidable. Along the earth ran Macdonald silently, curving his sinuous beautiful wrist. George Gunn walked down the pitch to the fastest balls, and played them away from intimate singles, with time to spare. Suddenly Macdonald dropped one short; it flew upwards savagely. And George Gunn calmly reached it with his bat as it was flashing near his head; he hit the ball straight to the earth, 'swatted' it like a man killing a disagreeable wasp. The ball spun round and round on the grass at George Gunn's feet. When the whirling motions had ceased, and the ball was quite still, George Gunn gently patted it down the wicket back to the bowler, who, had he been anybody but Macdonald, would have dropped with surprise.

Another picture—and if it is not true it ought to be; it certainly observes the highest order of truth, which is truth of character. A sweltering day at Edgbaston; a lovely stretch of turf on which a novice at batting was at liberty to make runs for the asking. George Gunn came in with Whysall to begin the Nottinghamshire innings. He wore a white panama hat for the occasion. In a quarter of an hour he scored twenty runs by impertinent little cuts from Howell through the crowded slips. He pulled a noble break-back off his middle stump for four. Then, without a warning sign, he daintly returned a half-volley to the bowler, a gift direct into the hand. When he returned to the pavilion his captain said: 'Good heavens, George, what were you doing to get out to a ball like that?' And George Gunn replied: 'Too hot, sir.'

A year or two before the war, Nottinghamshire had to tackle a huge score by Yorkshire. They had nothing to hope for or play for but a draw. George Gunn batted six hours and scored a hundred runs not out. The Yorkshire bowlers waxed sarcastic at George Gunn's slowness. Nottinghamshire followed on; the score-sheet of their second innings can be seen in Mr. A. W. Shelton's fine collection of relics and memorials in the Trent Bridge pavilion. Nobody in Nottinghamshire's second innings made double figures, the final score was Nottinghamshire some 138 for five; George Gunn's share was 108 not out, cut and driven and coaxed and cajoled in less than two hours.

He was the wittiest batsman that ever lived; his bat was a swift rapier used not for warfare but just to tickle the ribs. He played the game for fancy's sake; he never knew where the imp of his genius was going to take him. He could stonewall, but with what a relish of the irony of it!—because he knew that he could as easily be hitting boundaries. And he knew that the bowlers knew. Often he allowed a wretched long-hop to bowl his wicket down; he would pick up the fallen stump, and put it back into its hole, and give it a helpful knock on the top with his bat before departing to the pavilion. But as often would he send the finest ball of the match to the rails by a stroke as impudent as a coxcomb. At Old Trafford a year or two ago he won a match by himself against Macdonald on a fiery pitch. The other Nottinghamshire batsmen ducked their heads helplessly, and suffered many bruises. George Gunn was not touched once by Macdonald's flashing pace; either he journeyed forth from his crease and pushed a ball forward as it bounced on the half-volley, or he waited far back on his stumps until the ball was passing him shoulder high, when he flicked it between the slips to an inch. Sibbles sent him an over-tossed length; he drove it to the on, lazily, at arm's length so to say—a reclining stroke. He did not run, because he expected the ball to go over the boundary; but it stopped an inch or two within the field. Sibbles's next ball was entirely different in pitch and direction, but George Gunn drove it to the on exactly to the same place where the other hit had travelled. This time, though, the ball was four all the way. I have seen him tease one of the finest fieldsmen in the world for hours, playing a ball a yard or so to the right of him, then to the left of him, then in front of him, then suddenly knocking the man almost off his feet by a cover-drive so splendid that it opened classical doors on the game, and let us see the image of William Gunn himself. George Gunn could invest himself in armour as well as in motley.

Years ago he happened to be in Australia for his health when the England eleven were beaten in a Test match by a new and devastating googly bowler. George Gunn was asked to play in the subsequent Test match. He scattered the googly bowler's attack to the winds; he pounced on the spin, and drove far and wide; then, when the googly bowler dropped the inevitable short length, George Gunn cut it to ribbons, as the saying goes. He scored a hundred, and exposed the limitations of the new terror, and when he came back to the pavilion he threw his bat with a thud on to a locker and, indicating the googly man with a jerk of the thumb through the window, he said: 'He's a Saturday afternoon bowler, that's what he is, Saturday afternoon!' There was no good or bad bowling for George Gunn; it all depended on his mood.

I fancy he arranged his centuries as he arranged all his pleasures, on the spur of the moment, according to whether he felt like it. Once he argued to me in his own humorous accents, that 'what cricket needed nowadays was brighter batting'. The public, it seemed, deserved some consideration. After delivering this homily, George

Gunn proceeded (at Bradford) to bat for four hours for 48. I have no doubt he did it on purpose, knowing that I would see the joke. His mastery over all sorts of bowling was remarkable; never did he seem to be attending to any tune not his own. His range of strokes apparently included them all, ancient and modern, with, of course, variations of his own thrown in to lend savour. His bat might well have been an extension of his right arm, with the funny-bone in it. It was a tactile bat, a bat that seemed to 'feel', to vibrate to, every stroke. George Gunn's cricket possessed a quality, a sensibility, which I can only call 'touch'. Even an ordinary forward defensive push by George Gunn caused you to get a sense that some current of his personality had run down the bat's handle, through the blade, into the ball. He had a lovable way of tapping a ball through the slips as he was beginning his run for the single. And as he sauntered along the pitch he would pat the turf with his bat.

He was a man who enjoyed the flavours and significances of things private and intimate. There was always a little comedy, or rather a conceit, going on in George Gunn's cricket. His strokes were quips and paradoxes and wise saws. Because there was sense in the chaff continually. George Gunn's style at bottom was classical in its soundness and beauty; no handsomer cover-drives and cuts than his were seen in his day. He learned to play cricket in its greatest period; and at the age of fifty he was, with Hobbs and Woolley, one of the complete batsmen of our own period. He was an instinctive cricketer: he was related to the immortal William Gunn, and did not know how he came into his heritage; he was born a great batsman. I have never heard him indulge in theories about batsmanship. I can imagine that if anybody talked to him about the science of the game, he would answer much as my Uncle Toby answered old Shandy (I quote from memory, and make the necessary adaptation): 'And have you never considered the theory of cause and effect in these things? 'No more than my horse!' O rare George Gunn, the game is poorer now that, at last, the comedy of your long career is finished.

GRIMMETT

H E is an unobtrusive little man, with a face that says nothing to you at all; seldom is he heard by the crowd when he appeals for leg-before-wicket. He walks about the field on dainty feet which step as though with the soft fastidiousness of a cat treading a wet pavement. He is a master of surreptitious arts; he hides his skill, and sometimes, when he is on guard at cover, he seems to hide himself. He knows a trick of getting himself unobserved, and he darts forward to run a man out like somebody emerging from an ambush.

'Gamp is my name and Gamp my natur'.' That is a dark metaphysical saying; the meaning cannot be put into words, but none the less we can grasp it by the instinct for eternal substances. It is like that with Grimmett; the name penetrates to the quiddity, like 'curl', 'twist', 'slithery'; his name is onomatopoeic. I love to see him bowl a man out behind his back, so to say—round the legs; the ball gently touches the stumps and removes perhaps one bail. The humorous cunning of it reminds me that the Artful Dodger used to walk stealthily behind his master and extract the handkerchief from the coat-tails without Fagin's ever noticing it. Compare Grimmett with the wonderful leg-spin bowler he succeeded in the Australian eleven, Arthur Mailey. An Australian once said to me: 'Mailey bowled the googly stuff like a millionaire; Clarrie bowls it like a miser.' Mailey tossed up his spin with all the blandness in the world; his full-tosses were like a generous sort of fattening diet—before the killing and the roasting. Mailey did his mischief by daylight. Grimmett goes to work with a dark lantern; his boots are rubbered. Mailey's wickets were like a practised and jolly angler's 'catch'; Grimmett's wickets are definitely 'swag'. When he goes off the field he has had seven for 57, I can see the bag he is carrying over his shoulder.

He is the greatest right-handed spin-bowler of our period. The comparison with Mailey was employed to stress not resemblance but difference; Grimmett is less a googly than a leg-break bowler. He used the 'wrong 'un' sparsely; he is content to thrive on the ball which breaks away and leaves the bat; that is the best of all balls. A straight ball, wickedly masked, is Grimmett's foil to the leg-break. He makes a virtue of a low arm; his flight keeps so close to the earth that only a batsman quick of foot can jump to the pitch of it. And then must he beware of Oldfield, the wicket-keeper who stumps you with courtesy; he does not make a noise to the umpire, but almost bows you from the wicket. Or he is like a perfect dentist who says when your heart is in your mouth: 'It's all over; I've already got it out; here it is.' To play forward to Grimmett, to miss the spin, and then to find yourself stumped by Oldfield—why it is like an amputation done under an anaesthetic.

Moments come to all of us when we are uplifted beyond the ordinary; we become touched with grace for a while; we become vessels of inspiration. Felicity descended on Grimmett at Trent Bridge in June 1930, on the first day of the Test match. I have never seen cleverer bowling on a good wicket against great players. Hammond was batting; he made two of his own great forcing off-side hits, off the back foot. These strokes told us that Hammond was in form. Grimmett bowled him a straight ball which sped sinfully from the beautiful turf. Hammond lbw to Grimmett. Next came Woolley. Left-handed batsmen love leg-spin bowlers; the break turns the ball inwards to the middle of the bat. But Grimmett did not send a leg-break to Woolley; he sent the googly, whipping away. Woolley's forward stroke was seduced by the fulsome length. Woolley was stumped by Oldfield. A few minutes afterwards Grimmett drew Hendren a yard out of his crease like a mesmerist; then, having got Hendren where he wanted him, not far enough down the pitch, but yet too far, he bowled him. Grimmett will remember in his old age how he spun and 'floated' the ball that day; by the chimney corner he will babble of the way he turned batsman's smooth lawn into a 'sticky dog'. By sheer craftsmanship he overthrew three great batsmen; nothing to intimidate, no brute force (as George Lohmann called fast bowling of sorts); nothing but a slow spinning ball bowled by a little man with an arm as low as my grandfather's.

The first sight of Grimmett bowling arouses mild laughter. His action recalls the ancient round-arm worthies, or it recalls cricket on the sands with a walking-stick for the wicket and a father of six playing for the first time for years. A few steps, a shuffle, and Grimmett's arm seems to creak. But watch his wrist and his fingers; they are sinuous and beautiful. The wrist twirls and swivels; the fingers seem to adore and caress the ball, with the touch of a parent. Grimmett's fingers are always light and wonderfully tactile; when he passes the salt at dinner he imparts the ' 'fluence'.

He is, I believe, a sign-writer by profession. Can't you see his right wrist at work, sweeping the brush along the ornamentation? Can't you see the fingers intimately putting the finishing flick to a full-stop? Or can't you see the skeleton at work, finding the way through the locked door of Sutcliffe's bat? He is, as I say, a master of surreptitious arts. His countenance expresses no joy when he confounds his opponents. But I imagine that long after close of play, as he lies in bed and thinks about it, he laughs far into the night. That apparent half-volley which Walters tried to drive; that obvious long-hop that Hendren tried to hook. Confidence tricks! O my lungs and liver, the wickedness of the world!

He seldom gets a man caught in the deep field. That is an open and a brazen way to rifle the English house. Better by far a swift catch at first slip, or at the wicket; best of all lbw; nobody knows anything about it away from the scene of the burglary. He is a great character, not only a great bowler. Sometimes he fancies himself as a batsman. He thrusts his left foot across and drives. Or he waits for it and cuts elegantly. Occasionally he plays late and sees his stumps all awry. Then, and only then, does he wear his heart on his sleeve. Everybody cherishes private ambitions; we all wish to be what we are not. Dan Leno sighed to play Hamlet; Henry Irving enjoyed himself best when he sat on his top-hat and pretended to be Jingle in a farce derived from *Pickwick*. Grimmett made fifty in a Test match at Nottingham in June; perhaps in his old age he will remember Trent Bridge not for his great bowling of 1930, but for his preposterously stylish and first-class half-century of 1934. The rest of the world will dwell for ever on his spin, learned in Australia, where a slow bowler must do his own work and not depend on nature and friendly wickets. For my part I shall think of him always as I saw him at Worcester in May, taking the county's last wicket and winning the game. A catch was missed from him, and in the same over another lofty chance was skied near cover. Grimmett would trust nobody but Grimmett this time; he ran after the ball himself, and when he caught it he put it in his pocket and glided from the field, concealed entirely amongst ten other victorious Australians.

RANJITSINHJI

CRICKETERS will never see the like of Ranjitsinhji; he was entirely original, and there is nothing in all the history and development of batsmanship with which we can compare him. His style was a remarkable instance of the way a man can express personal genius in a game—nay, not only a personal genius but the genius of a whole race. For Ranjitsinhji's cricket was of his own country; when he batted a strange light was seen for the first time on English fields, a light out of the East. It was lovely magic, and not prepared for by anything that had happened in cricket, before Ranji came to us.

In the 'nineties the game was absolutely English: it was even Victorian. W. G. Grace for years had stamped on cricket the English mark and the mark of the period. It was the age of simple first principles, of the stout respectability of straight bat and good-length ball; the flavours everywhere were John Bull's. And then suddenly this visitation of dusky, supple legerdemain happened; a man was seen playing cricket as nobody born in England could possibly had played it. The honest length ball was not met by the honest straight bat, but there was a flick of the wrist, and lo! the straight ball was charmed away to the leg boundary. And nobody quite saw or understood how it all happened. Bowlers stood transfixed, and possibly they crossed themselves. I once asked Ted Wainwright, the Yorkshire cricketer, what he thought of Ranji, and Wainwright said, 'Ranji, he never made a Christian stroke in his life.' Why should he have done? The style is the man, and Ranji belonged to the land of Hazlitt's Indian jugglers, where beauty is subtle and not plain and unambiguous.

Marvellous game of cricket that can give us a W. G. Grace, English as a Gloucestershire tree, and George Hirst, Yorkshire as a broad moor, and Ranji as true to his racial psychology as any of them!

The game has known no greater spectacle than that of C. B. Fry and Ranji as they made a great stand for Sussex. I notice that Mr. J. A. Spender has described the Ranji-Fry combination as 'the perfect display of the first-wicket stand'. But Ranji never went in first with Fry; he always batted second wicket down, and thereby hangs a tale—and again the teller of it is Ted Wainwright. 'Ranji and Fry,' he would murmur as memory moved in him, 'every year it were the same owd story. We used to go down to Brighton with the sun shining and the ground hard as iron. And Sussex allus won the toss. And we all went on the field and started bowlin', and, sure enough, we'd get Vine out and the score-board would say Sussex 20 for one. And then George Hirst would get Killick out quick, and we all on us said, "Come on, Yorkshire, we're going grand; Sussex 31 for two!" ' Wainwright paused here in his narrative, and after a while he added, 'But, bless you, we knowed there were nowt in it. Close of play, Sussex three 'undred and ninety for two, and the same owd tale ever year.'

Bowlers have never known a problem so heart-breaking as the

problem of Fry and Ranji on a perfect Brighton wicket. Happy the man who today can close his eyes and see again the vision of Ranji, his rippling shirt of silk, his bat like a yielding cane making swift movements which circled round those incomparable wrists. He saw the ball quicker than any other batsman; he made his strokes later, so late, indeed, that Lockwood almost saw his great break-back crashing on the leg stump while Ranji remained there at his crease, apparently immobile. Then, at the last fraction of the last second, Ranji's body leaned gently over his front leg, the bat glinted in the sun, and we saw Lockwood throw up his hands to heaven as the ball went to the boundary, exquisitely fine to leg, with the speed of thought. This leg glance was Ranji's own stroke, but it is a mistake to say he could not drive. Usually he was too indolent for forcible methods, but none the less his front-of-the-wicket play could reach unparalleled range and precision; and his cut was a dazzling lance of batsmanship.

He caused a revolution in the game: he demonstrated the folly of the old lunge forward to a ball seductive in length. Ranji's principle was to play back or to drive, and his many imitators contrived in the course of years to evolve the hateful two-eyed stance from Ranji's art, which, of course, was not for ordinary mortals to imitate. He is today a legend. Modern lovers of the game, jealous of their own heroes, will no doubt tell us that Ranji, like all the old masters, was a creation of our fancy in a world old-fashioned and young. We who saw him will keep silence as the sceptics commit their blasphemy. We have seen what we have seen. We can feel the spell yet, we can go back in our minds to hot days in an England of forgotten peace and plenty, days when Ranji did not so much bat for us as enchant us, bowlers and all, in a way all his own, so that when at last he got out we were as though suddenly wakened from a dream. It was more than a cricketer and more than a game that did it for us.

BATSMANSHIP OF MANNERS

IN the summer of 1899 a schoolboy walked to the wicket at Lord's to begin a Lancashire innings against Middlesex; with him was Albert Ward. He was a graceful young cricketer, and a little tuft of hair stood up on the crown of his head. His flannels seemed soft and billowy. This boy—his name R. H. Spooner—was making his first appearance in county cricket in his summer holidays, fresh from Marlborough. It would be hard to imagine a severer ordeal for anybody, a trial in the sacrosanct air of Lord's, the searching eyes of the pavilion on you, MacLaren your captain, and one of the bowlers against you Albert Trott at his best, spinning and curving and dipping the ball astonishingly.

R. H. Spooner that day made 83, an innings full of strokes that seemed to ripple over the grass, light and lovely as sunshine. Straight from the playing fields of Marlborough he came and con-quered—nay, the word conquered is too hard and aggressive for Spooner; he charmed and won our heart and the hearts of all his opponents. 'It were a pleasure to bowl to Maister Spooner,' said an old player to me the other day; 'his batting were as nice as he were hisself.' Yes, it was nice; it was the batsmanship of manners. Spooner told us in every one of his drives past cover that he did not come from the hinterland of Lancashire, where cobbled streets sound with the noise of clogs and industry; he played always as though on the elegant lawns of Aigburth; his cricket was 'county' in the social sense of the term. This flavour of equability took the grimness out of a Lancashire and Yorkshire match even; I once saw him score 200 against Hirst, Rhodes and Haigh, at Bank Holiday time, and he transformed Old Trafford to Canterbury. I'll swear that on that day long ago there were tents and bunting in the breeze of Manchester while Spooner's bat flicked and flashed from morning till evening.

He was the most lyrical of cricketers, and for that reason he had no need to play a long innings to tell us his secret. The only differ-ence between 30 by Spooner and 150 was a matter of external and unessential form or duration; the spirit moved from the very beginning. A rondo by Mozart is just as complete and true as a symphony by him. One daffodil is as precious and delectable as a hundred daffodils. And a single stroke by Spooner had likewise a quality absolute, beyond the need of mensuration or any mathe-matical means of valuation whatever. It you consider Spooner's average for the whole of his career it will tell you nothing of con-sequence about his cricket; as well count the words in a poem or the notes in an allegro.

I must suppose that he hit the ball hard, because I remember seeing fieldsmen blowing their hands after they had stopped a stroke by Spooner. And once I sat on the shilling side when Parker, of Gloucestershire, bowled his first ball in county cricket: Spooner

141

pulled it clean over the rails, and it crashed amongst the dust and cinders like an exploding shell. Yet my impression today is that Spooner's cricket was all bouquet; I think of it as I think of a rose, because of the perfume, not because of the substantial stuff which went to its making. Never did I see Spooner strike an ugly position, either at the wicket or in the field, where at cover he was the picture of swift, diving elegance.

If I called his batsmanship that of manners, I do not mean it was ever affected: every innings by Spooner was natural and modest, like the man himself. The poise was a consequence of an instinctive balance of cultured technical parts. What's bred in the bone comes out in an innings; I never saw Spooner bat without seeing, as a background for his skill and beauty, the fields of Marlborough, and all the quiet summertime amenities of school cricket. He was my favourite player when I was a boy—he and Victor Trumper. And with a boy's illogicality I at one and the same time thought him wonderful and yet always in need of my prayers. All the time I watched him—and often I played truant to do so—I said in my heart, 'Please, Lord, don't let Reggie get out; let him score a century.' Sometimes I was more moderate: 'Please, Lord, let Reggie make 95.' I called him 'Reggie' even in my petitions to Providence. Like every delightful cricketer, he seemed at any moment ready to get out; no great batsman has ever been content to keep strictly within the scope of the things that can be done safely. I remember once seeing Spooner begin an innings against Hirst. All round his legs was the notorious Hirst 'trap'—four fieldsmen holding out avaricious hands. And Hirst swerved the ball terrifically across from Spooner's off stump. And time after time did Spooner flick the swinging ball at his wrists' end through the leg-trap—each stroke a brave and lovely butterfly going into the flame.

Yet he was a sound as well as a brilliant batsman. There is a stupid legend about the batsmen of old. Because they made runs handsomely it is thought in certain places that they were constantly thrusting out the left leg and leaving their stumps exposed to the breaking ball. Not long ago a cricketer actually said to me, 'Yes, Spooner was splendid to watch, but he couldn't abide the googly.' And I said, 'God forgive you for blasphemy.' In September 1912 Spooner made a century against South Africa, and amongst the bowlers were Pegler, Faulkner and Schwarz. These men have never had superiors as masters of the googly; they were as clever at spinning the ball as anybody today. Spooner played them carefully

—with his bat, not with his pads. He was superb in his back strokes; he could hit a four from a defensive position. The second line of defence—which is the pads—was known well enough to the batsmen of the Golden Age: Arthur Shrewsbury organized it scientifically. But it was a second and not a first line of defence; Spooner never put his bat ignominiously over his shoulder to any ball and stuck out his legs crudely and ungraciously. The fact that he could achieve a great innings as a boy against Albert Trott is ample retort to the absurd notion that he was ever at a loss against swerve or spin. No bowler who ever lived could give to a cricket ball more than Trott's curve and break.

Spooner and MacLaren—has a county possessed two batsmen who could begin an innings with more than their appeal to the imagination? They were as the King and the Prince, or as the eagle and the flashing swallow. Spooner was one of the cricketers who, when I was very young, made me fall in love with the game; I think of his batting now, in middle age, with gratitude. The delight of it all went into my mind, I hope, to stay there, with all the delight that life has given me in various shapes, aspects and essences. When the form has gone—for it is material and accidental, and therefore perishable—the spirit remains. And Spooner's cricket in spirit was kin with sweet music, and the wind that makes long grasses wave, and the singing of Elisabeth Schumann in Johann Strauss, and the poetry of Herrick. Why do we deny the art of a cricketer, and rank it lower than a vocalist's or a fiddler's? It anybody tells me that R. H. Spooner did not compel a pleasure as aesthetic as any compelled by the most celebrated Italian tenor that ever lived I will write him down a purist and an ass.

THE NOBLEST ROMAN

THERE never was a cricketer with more than the grandeur of A. C. MacLaren. When I think of his play now, years after it all happened, the emotions that stir in me afresh, and all my impressions of it, are mingled with emotions and impressions I have had from other and greater arts than bat and ball.

MacLaren's cricket was a classical education because of its magnificent outlines, and yet, at the same time, it possessed the colour and hint of danger which tell of the romantic attitude. His poise and the mould of his technique, as he made his runs, were clear and firm, almost serene; but in his more commanding strokes there was an energy that seemed ever to be reaching outward, beyond the academically proscribed scope of the game, an energy which signified a man very lordly, a man born to rule, to dictate and to wear the imperial robe.

Magnificence was enthroned at the wicket when MacLaren took his stand there and surveyed the field with a comprehensive eye. I thrill to this day at the very thought of his perpetual aspect of mastery. He was an England captain by divine right; every cricketer who came into his company—great players like Ranjitsinhji, Fry, Hirst, Lockwood and Shrewsbury—knew at once that this man was their master and that he would brook no denial. He was never in all his career seen to assume an awkward mien or make a common gesture. He could cause you to behold visions of empire upon empire, Amurath succeeding unto Amurath, simply by standing in the field at the beginning of an innings and ordering his men into near and far places by royal waves of his hand. Always was Mac-Laren a being of consequence; if he missed a catch in the slips he gave us no sign of futility, only one of kingly frustration. He was a beautiful slip fieldsman, and the little pluck of his trousers with his fingers as he bent down was aristocratic and true to life. When he held a low quick catch from Brearley he would throw up the ball with a great sweep of the arm; it was a gesture of majestic finality.

There was the same air of personal prerogative even at those times when MacLaren was bowled for none. I see him yet, playing forward to Hargreave, of Warwickshire, missing the ball, and having his off bail gently removed—so gently, as though the essential supremacy of him were not a fit subject for violent disturbance. Most portentously MacLaren would achieve a nought; the pavilion sat in silence as he returned from the wicket, bat under his arm while he unfastened his gloves. There we sat, not feeling the sense of a cricketer cheaply dismissed, but of power 'dispossessed, chucked-down'. He remained, no matter what the score-board pretended to declare, '. . . above the rest. In shape and gesture proudly eminent'.

He was a batsman of sculpturesque rhythm in his driving to the on. He seemed always erect, bat on high. When he made runs with Spooner at the other end, we could understand the difference between sonorous blank verse and melodious lyric poetry. Spooner rippled the grass with a bat all light curves, easeful and unself-conscious; but in MacLaren's strokes we heard the roll of deliberate measures, a rhetoric not a little arrogant. I shall never cease to be moved by the recollection of MacLaren hooking a short ball of great pace from Lockwood one day; it was, for Lockwood, a bad ball, a long-hop; it rose at MacLaren's head with dreadful velocity. Mac-Laren stood straight up and swept his bat across the line of the flight and hit round to leg, as though over his shoulder, to the boundary. Do I say 'hit'? Nay, he dismissed the ball from his presence.

MacLaren had a fine disdain for all bowling which deviated from excellence. He batted on his own terms; he would not compromise at the behest of anybody, let his name be Lockwood, Noble, Trumble, or Hirst. MacLaren scorned to wait for the easy ball. He was one of the strongest batsmen that ever lived at forcing away good-length bowling in front of the wicket. His defensive play was as positive and as dominant as his forward drives. He made strokes, true strokes, all the time, each of them informed by an idea; he was indeed a most political batsman who could not abide stalemate. Every innings by MacLaren was strategical, a captain's innings. At Sydney many years ago, when an England innings began, MacLaren, after taking his guard against the fast bowler Ernest Jones, saw that Darling had sent four men on the leg side to block the hook-stroke. Now this was one of MacLaren's prolific hits, and he realized that if those four fieldsmen remained in their on-side cordon his batting would be robbed of value, and his innings an enchained one. So MacLaren, in Jones's first over, drove two fours, both straight past the bowler, daring and powerful. Whereat Darling had to open out the field; the leg-trap[1] was partially dismantled; MacLaren's two drives, off Jones at his fastest, were superb gambles—and they came off. That was the way of the man, ready at all times to risk a hazard for the sake of an ambitious plan. In a long innings MacLaren seemed to take both ends of the wicket into his province; if a player had just come out to bat MacLaren would take charge of the bowling if it was deadly. He was able to place the ball with the accuracy of 'W. G.' himself, so that he could get a single off the last ball of the over. Thus would he give an exhibition to the new man in of how to play the attack. And if a right-handed off-break bowler happened to be viciously on the job, MacLaren would see to it that any left-handed partner of his was kept away from the spin which is the most difficult of all spins to left-handed batsmen.

[1] This was written long before the Australians objected to 'body-line'. *Verb. sap.*

In the field, as captain, he perceived the moves of the game before they were beyond the conceptual point; he was like a chess-player. 'In every match,' he once said to me, 'there comes a moment when the tide turns one way or the other; every captain should be on the look out for that moment.' He seldom set a purely defensive field, and on a good wicket he would purposely leave a batsman's favourite stroke uncovered, and then tell his bowlers to encourage the stroke, but with artful variations. He was fond of arguing that if a batsman's favourite stroke is blocked he will not take the risk of it. Too many of our contemporary captains play for safety and set the field merely to prevent runs. Yet, despite all his fine brain, MacLaren did not often lead England to victory against Australia. He had the misfortune to run into Australian cricket at its greatest; also, he sometimes seemed to risk danger for sheer pride in an idea, or because his nature would not permit him to lie low and wait for his opponent to fall into error. But MacLaren's blunders, when they occurred, were not small blunders; he achieved catastrophic miscalculations; he went along the primrose path to the everlasting bonfire.

I hope I have not suggested, in this attempt to get on to paper some notion of MacLaren's grandeur of manner and of egoism, that he was, as a batsman, in any way unsound or reckless. His cricket was based on science; he was a sound player first and last. But his mind and imagination did not readily obey the patient logic of science, with its niggling sequence of cause and effect, and its prosaic prohibitions. MacLaren had a haughty spirit and a fine scorn.

He was the noblest Roman of them all. The last impression in my memory of him is the best. I saw him batting in a match just before the war; he was coming to the end of his sway as a great batsman. And on a bad wicket he was knocked about by a vile fast bowler, hit all over the body. And every now and then one of the old imperious strokes shot grandeur over the field. There he stood, a fallible MacLaren, riddled through and through, but glorious still. I though of Turner's 'Fighting Temeraire', as MacLaren batted a scarred innings that day, and at last returned to the pavilion with the sky of his career red with a sun that was going down.

THE UMPIRE

May 1934

CRICKET has begun; the umpires have walked to the
wicket, and they have adjusted the stumps with the precision of great masters of geometry. Probably they have
bowled a ball up and down the pitch to one another, just to let the
crowd understand that they, too, have in their time been mighty
hunters before the Lord. And the cry of 'Play!' has been uttered
decisively and authoritatively.

The umpire is the law of cricket personified, image of the noble
constitution of the best of games. He can make or mar the match for
us. A bad umpire means bad-tempered cricketers, and, therefore,
bad play. Yet how little notice we take of the umpire, once we have
seen him step into his onerous office. It is only when he commits a
blunder that we realize he is there. Often is the phrase 'A bad
decision' heard amongst cricketers, but how seldom any of us talk
about and praise a good decision!

The umpire at cricket is like the geyser in the bathroom; we cannot do without it, yet we notice it only when it is out of order. The
solemn truth is that the umpire is the most important man on the
field; he is like the conductor of an orchestra. If first slip misses a
catch, the error involves only a personal fallibility; we say 'Hard
luck!' and first slip begins again. If the umpire falters, everybody in
the game is drawn into the range of mortal frailty; we do not say
'Hard luck!' to the miserable man in the white coat; we even add to
our gloating over his fallibility the imputation of stupidity or of
malice prepense. If a batsman misses a half-volley and is bowled,
the crowd laughs or, at the worst, call the guilty one an ass. But the
umpire who errs as obviously as that is likely to be regarded as unfit
for his job. His fallibility can be reported at Lord's; nobody reports
to Lord's the cricketer who in the excitement of the moment runs his
partner out.

All day long, ball after ball, the umpire must keep his mind
intensely on the game. The players are free to enjoy relaxations.
Some of them indulge in a good sleep while their side is batting.
When rain falls and stops play, the cricketers can forget the match
for a while. The umpire enjoys no release from responsibility; until
the match is over, or until weather causes an abandonment, he is

obliged to watch, watch, watch—either the play or the pitch or the groundsman. The amount of concentration he is expected to perform every day is almost an abuse of human endurance. What a great country this would be if every man, whatever his station, concentrated half as much on the smallest detail of his work as an umpire it compelled to do, from high noon to dewy evening of a cricket match!

The umpires are the Dogberry's of the game. We see them as essentially comic characters. Whenever a batsman swipes to leg, and hits the umpire in the small of the back, how the crowd roars! If the wind blows the hat off the umpire's head, laughter holds sides. The reason for the humour which comes out of the activities of the umpires is a matter of deep psychology. For the simple fact is that no man can sustain with dignity the semblance of infallible judgment. Man is born to sin and error; and when he wears the robes of virtue and wisdom and law and infallibility all rolled into one, the gods infect us with their merriment.

'How's that?' shrieked the whole field when a batsman was brilliantly thrown out. 'Wait a minute,' answered the umpire. 'Who did it?'

It is, of course, to country cricket that we must look for the really comical Dogberry of the crease. I remember Old George, in the days when we used to go on a jolly tour through Shropshire. The custom was for each side to bring its own umpire, and at the beginning of every match old George made a point of meeting the other team's umpire, over a glass of ale in the pavilion.

'Now, look 'ee 'ere,' he would say, 'it is for yew to luke after yewre business, and oi'll luke after mine!'

Once on a time a cricket match was about to be played between two village clubs of long and vehement rivalry. An hour before the pitching of stumps a visitor to the district walked on to the ground and inspected the wicket. He was greeted by an old man, a very old man. The visitor asked for information about the impending battle, and the ancient monument told him.

'Is your team strong in bowling?' asked the visitor.

'Ay, sir, not so bad,' was the answer.

'And who gets most of your wickets?' asked the visitor.

'Why, sir, Oi do,' was the reply.

'Heaven,' said the visitor, 'surely you don't bowl at your time of life?'

'No, sir, Oi be the umpire.'

148

But in the highest realms of county and Test cricket the umpire, though frequently the source of humour, is seldom allowed to share in it. A crucial blunder might mean an end to his livelihood. He deserves all the help he can possible be given. Is not his job difficult enough in itself without the addition of embarrassments which are the consequence of our hastiness and temper? I appeal to every lover of the game to think of the umpire always, to bear always in mind that, like the backwoods pianist, he is doing his best—in threatening circumstances.

English cricket today is fortunate to be under the supervision of umpires as fine and courageous and clever as Arthur Morton (a rich character), Frank Chester, Hardstaff—to name but a few. Chester is a joy to watch; he delivers his decisions sometimes with immense irony. I have seen him signal a snicked boundary by means of a gesture of regal disdain, as though to say, 'What a stroke! I am compelled by the law to rule it worth four; but I reserve the right to say what I think about it.'

I have seen Chester give a batsman out with a finger suddenly pointed to heaven, dramatic in its announcement of ruthless finality. And I have seen him turn his back on a bowler's manifestly absurd appeal for leg-before-wicket—turn his back with the air of a man consigning another to some place outside the pale of all sense and decency.

Arthur Morton is not so spectacular; he believes in the conservation of energy. But county cricketers know well, and revel in, his comments at the wicket, many of them delivered out of the corner of the mouth. 'I wish you'd keep quiet,' he once said at the agony of a Lancashire and Yorkshire match, 'it's like umpiring in a parrot-house.'

Parry is the umpire who bends himself into a right angle for every ball when he is standing at the bowler's end; he takes on this terrible burden of physical discomfort so that, as he thinks, he can get a better sight of the ball in a leg-before-wicket mix-up. Merely to look at him for an hour is to go home suffering from lumbago. They all of them are worthy of our applause, the men who serve the game by standing—and waiting for the end of the long, long day.

AUSTRALIAN SUMMER

ON THE WAY

LIFE on the ship during the voyage out was not according to my expectations; I began it with some romantic ideas lingering in my mind since my boyhood about the talks and intimacy which would occur amongst a company of cricketers setting forth to play Australia. The team merged with the rest of the passengers until you scarcely knew where they were or which was which; Allen rightly encouraged his men temporarily to avoid cricket. The fun of the voyage was at times not easily to be marked off from the fun of a fashionable hotel on any evening at Folkestone after a day at the September festival. It became boring and I gladly escaped from it. I even left the captain's table—not disrespectfully I hope. The captain was charming and a marvel of tact. But the time arrived when I was ready either to laugh outright or become sarcastic at the efforts of the social climbers who each evening vied with one another to obtain the captain's recognition. The snobbishness on an ocean-going liner is appalling. I imagine that most captains in the service would like at times to leave the captain's table. But this is another digression.

When we reached the Red Sea, I decided to begin a diary; I did not keep it up of course, for the simple reason that on a ship nothing often happens; Mark Twain achieved the perfect summary:

Oct. 13, Got up, washed, went to bed.
   „   14, „   „   „   „ „ „
   „   15, „   „   „   „ „ „

and so on and so forth. My own entries are a little fuller; here they are:

September 25, 1936—On the Orion
'Passengers may sleep on deck in the vicinity of the forward lounge between midnight and 6.30 a.m.'—so runs, with much confidence, the notice that has today been given prominence in the various premises of the *Orion*. We are in the Red Sea as I write, and there is scarcely a soul on board, not including the ship's cat, who is capable of any form of sleep, either on deck or below the deck, in

cabin or under the starry heavens; the Red Sea is at its hottest, its
stickiest, its cruellist. There is no air in the world, except fetid
breath from the desert; the *Orion* makes not a wisp of a breeze as she
goes her patient course. The sun is merciless, and when we escape
the chastisement of its fiery rods by going under awnings or inside
the lounge or drawing-room or tavern or café, then we are suffocated,
or, rather, put under some evil drug of the Orient. There is one place
only where we can find momentary release from the torment—in
the dining-room (only we don't want to dine), where the atmosphere
is marvellously chilled. Here the temperature is 75 degrees, and as
we enter it we feel as though we have gone into a refrigerator; we
expect, even hope, to see frost and snow appearing over our bodies.
When at last we reluctantly leave the dining-room and pass out
through its swing doors, we go straight, without a second's break,
into an oven.

I have never before dreamed that the world could become so hot,
that people could endure such miseries, that nature could go its ways
so indifferent to mortal needs. For three days the sun has hurled
down on us the light and heat that destroy; for three days the sky has
contained not a cloud, nothing but the pitiless blue of endless and
indifferent space. And hour by hour the sea has grown hotter, so that
at night, after the sun has gone down and a lovely silver horn of a
moon has enchanted the sky, even then we have had no peace, for the
waters hold the day's scorchings and throw them back. 'Passengers
may sleep on deck'—may, indeed! I did not try; I kept to my cabin
and hopefully manipulated the device that blows air upon you, risking sore throat, stiff neck, double pneumonia. Anything would be
better and more merciful than to 'pass out' from Red Sea humidity,
either by oozing away or by going mad and diving overboard with
such despair that one hit the floor of the ocean and perished as much
from concussion of the brain as from drowning.

The other evening, a quarter of an hour before dinner, I met
Captain Howard on the staircase; the manager of the M.C.C. team
had only ten minutes ago changed into his dinner jacket. His collar
was already a rag; Mr. Gladstone, after four hours or so of eloquence,
never more drastically reduced stiff linen to this state of shapeless
wetness. From the foreheads of all of us waterfalls have descended,
splashing and dashing like the cascades of Southey's poem. (Was it
Southey?—it still too hot to think here, though at last we are emerging from the Red Sea and a breeze is stirring, giving us a sense of
resurrection of all the world from the dead.) At the first hint of this

heaven-sent zephyr R. W. V. Robins stripped off his evening jacket and, regardless of dignity and braces, went to the promenade deck and, feeling the faintest suggestion of a wind, said to me, 'We seem to be cooling as we direct our course towards the Antarctic.' Robins has suffered much and has borne it all with humour and an Alfred Lester sort of fortitude.

Everything that science can do towards the defeat of the Red Sea is done on the *Orion*, but nature, as Mr. Squeers said, is a 'rum 'un'. 'She's a lovely ship,' said Hammond, 'but I wish she—well had wings!' I tell of these hardships not out of desire to present ourselves as martyrs and heroes but to console those we have left at home on the brink of an English winter. 'Lucky you!' they said as we departed from Southampton a fortnight ago; 'oh lucky, to be going into the sunshine, while we shiver in the east winds and hug our hot-water bottles!' At the moment of writing, there is scarcely an English man or a woman on the boat who would not cheerfully give pounds and pounds sterling for one hour of Manchester's wettest rain and coldest cold. Happy days are probably waiting for us in Australia— we shall deserve them, for we have suffered in the Red Sea's cauldron. But such is human nature that while we were writhing and dissolving in the Red Sea, we persuaded ourselves that the Red Sea was really behaving with unusual moderation; then the moment we sniffed a wind of the Indian Ocean we agreed unanimously that the Red Sea had broken records in heat and life-destroying humidity, and we went about amongst ourselves distributing medals for patience, endurance and philosophy, so to say. The probability is that we revealed ourselves as so many comfortable creatures of the temperate zone of the earth; it is said by the knowing ones of these parts that the more intelligent inhabitants of the Nubian Desert sometimes visit the Red Sea to enjoy its bracing climate—to them the Red Sea is the Skegness of the Tropics.

Pleasures there have been for us, of course; lazy days in the Mediterranean, when the sunshine has been friendly and the swimmers in the bathing-pool have splashed about, before stretching themselves luxuriously in the lovely slanting light of the late afternoon. Then the evenings. First the sunsets, and the peacefulness that comes over the ship before dinner; people have retired to dress, and the solitary watcher, leaning on the ship's side, has the sense for a moment that he is being divested of personal identity and absorbed into the deepening beauty of the hour of twilight over the ocean as the evening star appears. At night the dancing begins, and here again it is good to escape from the glitter and animation, to withdraw and watch from a point apart. Then it is possible to feel the pathos of contrast—the light and happy intimacy of life brought together for a moment by chance; and the surrounding and lasting immensity of the Indian Ocean. And while all the laughter of young people goes on, and elders sit domestically in lounge and drawing-room enjoying familiar comforts, the ship moves on, a beautiful sensitive creature, with the flexibility of a canoe and the power and grandeur of an ocean-going liner; through the night it moves, throbbing with a poised life of its own, making a wake in the water delicate as a chain. At the moment we are well beyond Aden, a sun-cursed pile of brown rock, oleaginous, with the refuse kites flapping in the air—a place where the White Man's Burden—and the Black Man's Burden too—can be felt as a weariness to flesh and spirit. We are following the track of a monsoon, and the ship is rolling. In the middle of the night it is thrilling for the landsman to listen from his cabin to the surge outside and to feel the whole of the boat's nervous system working; you can hear the heart of it. I have grown to love the ship and the quiet certainty of the men who control its strength, grace and nobility.

GOODBYE TO THE *ORION*

October 17

NOT without mixed feelings did we come to the end of our voyage on October 13th, for glad as we were to set foot in Australia it was sad to say 'Goodbye' to the *Orion*. Life on a ship is concentrated in so small a space that in a month a man exceeds the common length of days. The distractions and responsibilities of the world come for a while to an end; as the hours go by we can almost count each pulsation of existence; consciousness and sense of personal identity become pure and absolute. And a strange sort of pathos falls on the little world we make for ourselves during the voyage; we know it cannot last long, that friendships almost certainly will come to an end soon, that all our efforts to reproduce the world we have left on land must end in irony—yet we do indeed reproduce it, I am afraid, with as many as possible of its foibles and pretensions. We live as though in a bubble which we have ourselves blown up, and as the voyage goes on the more does the bubble swell to bursting-point.

I have loved the evenings sitting in the 'Tavern' before dinner, watching the swimmers in the bathing pool while the sun sank over the Indian Ocean and the sky turned to a sudden purple and stars appeared as though kindled one by one. I loved the careless fun of the games deck, the fun with the children in their own playground. I loved to go at half-past ten every morning into what I called the 'Market Place', because it was there that C. B. Fry held court amongst the deck-chairs and the passing life of the ship; where we discussed all things under the sun. Perhaps our arguments were rather too contrapuntal to be easily followed by the listening throng; we each went our way, talking for art's sake, keeping count of our own bull's-eyes. But one day, just to tease him, I said, 'Well, Charles, good morning. No hemlock yet? Give us your views on the origin of the Iambic.' It was a pure piece of banter; the word 'Iambic' came to my mind by the merest chance. I might as well have asked him to explain the origin of King Cole or green cabbages. But Fry, without a moment's hesitation, launched into a remarkable piece of virtuoso exposition; in half an hour he sketched, with a swift touch and comprehensive illustrative detail, the history of prosody. And he had not finished when I left him and went for my morning walk seven times round the deck, making a mile. Each time I passed the ship's centre (the 'Market Place') he was still at it—'You see what I mean? However . . .' He wore a confusing variety of clothes day by day, clothes of strange dyes, patterns and purposes. Only once did he appear (save at dinner) in tolerably reasonable guise, and that was at a fancy dress ball, when he simulated an ascetic yet genial scoutmaster. The next day he wore what I called his deep-sea fishing attire, and I said, 'Glad to see you back in fancy dress, Charles.'

The team went quietly about their pleasures. Verity read *Seven Pillars of Wisdom* from beginning to end; Hammond won at all games, from chess to deck quoits. Maurice Leyland smoked his pipe, and Duckworth danced each evening with a nice understanding of what, socially, he was doing. Wyatt took many photographs and developed them himself. Fry, armed with a most complicated camera, also took many photographs, and none of them could be developed.

After we left Colombo the heat mercifully cooled down and a fresh wind blew. We came upon the Cocos Islands suddenly on a windy morning. Never shall I forget the romantic beauty of this experience. All the adventure stories of my youth sprang to life; here were Stevenson, Ballantyne, Defoe. On the little beach, silent and empty, there was surely Man Friday's footprint; the colours on the water evoked visions of enchanted lagoons, treasure and coral. In a towering sea two little boats came bravely to take a barrel from the *Orion* containing the quarterly supply of rations for the handful of men who work on the islands, supporting the Empire and the White Man's Burden. The barrel was taken on board, and mighty waves swept past the two boats, sometimes hiding them from our view. On the *Orion* we all leaned over the side and waved farewell. And the last we saw of the little boats was their plungings and swayings as they returned to the island, with the men waving farewell in return; there was not a person on board the *Orion* who did not feel the emotion of the scene. 'It makes a lump come into your throat' said William Voce of Nottinghamshire.

When we reached Fremantle it was seven in the morning. We had to be up and about early. Many times on the voyage I had wakened in the dawn and looked through my porthole. There is magic in things seen from a ship's porthole; it becomes a magic mirror. I saw the sunrise on the Indian Ocean through my porthole and felt ashamed to be prying into an act of beauty so secret and removed from human interference. Through my porthole I saw Australia for the first time.

BRADMAN AND HAMMOND

THE two great batsmen of the day are, of course, Bradman and Hammond. Two citizens held argument in the streets at Melbourne on New Year's Day; it was settled by force because, no doubt, it became more metaphysical than language could stand. If I were to be asked to make a decision on the point—which of the two batsmen is the greater—I should vote for Bradman on a good wicket. I do not say that Bradman cannot cope with a bad wicket, but up to now he has failed to do so in my presence. There is not the slightest doubt that Bradman, given opportunities to practise on bad wickets, would master the technique needed; in fact his flexible style, his quickness of foot, are born, so to say, for the turning ball. He is a much more dynamic player than Hammond, whose methods seem often to me to be static, with genius transforming to greatness a conventional classicism. The innings of Hammond on the impossible pitch at Melbourne could not have been excelled by any other cricketer, for balance, poise, science and constitutionalism in conditions which were revolutionary and disruptive. But though Hammond stayed in an hour and a half that day, he scored only 35; and all the time the wicket was getting more and more impossible.

The difference between Bradman and Hammond can be stated in a few words: Hammond can be kept quiet, Bradman never. Hammond in the Test match at Sydney batted nearly eight hours; and even on the third morning, when he was still not out, he had not made England safe. Bradman in the same time would have put all bowling to rout. At Adelaide, when Australia began their second innings, everybody knew that the match and the rubber depended on Bradman. England enjoyed a slight lead; a failure by Bradman would put the issue beyond question. Bradman played carefully— for him. Allen set a wide protective field, and Bradman declined to do anything silly or rhetorical. I was writing for evening papers in Australia, and I had to send messages away every half-hour. As I saw Bradman putting his bat to the ball, with a short 'lift up', body near the line, I wrote something to this effect; 'It will be a pity if Test matches are going to ruin even the stroke-play of Bradman.' At the end of an hour Bradman was fifty—and not once a single flash or thump or flourish. Without his major hits, without risk or hurry, he can score faster, over a long period, than any other batsman in the game at the present time. I think he is a finer player today than ever he has been; he was, I thought in Australia, just beginning (so to speak) to see the ball. Once he had got over the difficulties which beset him at the beginning of the tour, his confidence in himself was terrifying in its quiet modesty. If I had to choose a batsman to play for my life, on a good wicket, I should of course name Bradman— and after doing so, I should take out an annuity.

At Adelaide, in November, on a night I shall never forget, he told me of his plans to win the rubber. He expected that O'Reilly would tie up Hammond by a leg-stump attack of good length. For the whole evening, he discussed cricket—we were alone in his house. At eleven o'clock he told me he would have to turn me out, as he had a call to make at the hospital. But as the hospital was on the way to my hotel, he drove me into Adelaide, on a night of great beauty. He ran up the steps of the hospital and I waited in the car. After a short while he came back, took the wheel and said: 'I'm afraid the poor little chap

isn't going to get through.' The next morning the death of Bradman's baby was announced.

I hope I am reticent enough about this night's happenings; I hope
nobody will misunderstand me. I want to give an idea of Bradman's
character. I am tired of hearing him referred to as a run-making
machine on the field, and a hard Australian off it. (In any case, are
there no 'hard' Englishmen between Newcastle, Huddersfield and
the 'city'?) To return to our discussion of his cricket: when does a
batsman who commands all the strokes and plays them rapidly and
scores 300 in a day in a Test match, when does he cease to be an
artist and degenerate into a 'machine'? I suppose this unintelligent
objection to Bradman is much the same as the objection to Bach;
it is excusable in fallible humanity to regard the illusion of mastery
as bloodless and remote and automatic. But Bradman, like Bach—if
he will allow the comparison—is full of blood; no other batsman
today is as audacious as Bradman. His hook is the most dramatic hit
seen since Jessop; it is a boxer's blow. And for all the rare organization of his technique, nature is in it always. Bradman has not allowed
enormous skill to ruin the salt touch of his original self. The *gamin*
comes out in a sudden cross-bat solecism.

When I arrived in Adelaide in November, Bradman assured me
that he did not intend to score 'any more two hundreds in Test
matches'. He thought there were other batsmen in the Australian
team ('If ever you see Ray Robinson and myself batting at the same
time, you'll forget me, and remember only *his* shots, when the day's
finished'); he wished to enjoy himself. As events turned out Bradman was compelled again to shoulder responsibility. Before the fifth
Test match began in February, I saw Bradman one evening outside
Usher's Hotel in Sydney; I chaffed him about the promise he had
made in November. 'Well,' he said, 'whose fault is it? You'll have to
admit that I got out at Brisbane in the first innings having a crack;
and that at Sydney in the second innings, and at Adelaide in the first,
I tried to hit the ball over the on boundary. But I'm not a fool. When
the English field was set to save fours—well, I wasn't going to risk a
hook for nothing. I believe I've taken my reasonable chances in
Tests and nobody can say that I've ever turned down a reasonable
challenge to score quickly. I like to hit the ball about. But a run-
saving field, everybody deep, was no good, and I reckon a good
player can score fifty an hour by twos and threes if the field is
scattered.'

There is a thoughtfulness in all that Bradman does, save in

moments when he seems to rebel against his own mastery, as he did in England at the beginning of the season of 1934. His cricket for weeks that year was hectic; he seemed to try to hit every ball past mid-on, off the back foot, a punch not a stroke. But at the crisis he was ready, cool and grim. Australia lost three wickets for 39 at Leeds, and next morning Bradman drove Bowes's first two balls straight for four. 'Hello!' somebody said. 'The little ass is going mad again.' But the two drives had been made with the body so close to the ball that I knew the worst was coming. I fancy I can read Bradman well; I lived much with him through his difficulties of 1934. I can 'sense' a big score from him. And he has never yet failed Australia whenever it has been necessary that he should play an innings, and not merely of a hundred but one of two or three hundred. Concentration is the main reason of his mastery; that of course added to a superb technique. His strokes cover the whole field. At Leeds in 1930, after he had scored 304 in a day—a hundred before lunch, a hundred between lunch and tea, and a hundred between tea and close of play— a writer on cricket stated that Bradman had few strokes on the off side in front of the wicket. A diagram of his strokes that day was like the spokes of a bicycle wheel, or rather, like the old advertisements of electric belts with rays of vitality flashing out everywhere. No innings played by anybody, 'alive or dead' (I am reminded of Horowitz, but this is a joke secret to my friends), has exceeded in brilliant stroke-play, in combined audacity and skill, the hundred which Bradman made one Saturday evening at Lord's, against Middlesex, in 1934. What on earth do people mean when they say that Bradman is mechanical? Of the two batsmen, Bradman and Hammond, I should say that Hammond is the one more likely to dull the mind by monotony, by the suggestion of habitual professional efficiency, stately and not variegated, and never explosive.

It has been said that Bradman does not 'like' fast bowling. Once on a time I shared for a moment the same doubt. In 1930, at Liverpool, Bradman moved a yard—across to the off side—and allowed a terrific break-back from Macdonald to bowl him. At the time I wrote a rather severe criticism of this piece of poor cricket. Again, in 1930, at the Oval, Bradman was seen once or twice to retreat from Larwood. But this time the retreat was away to the leg stump, and Bradman usually tried a cut, or a hit to the off. During the 'body-line' campaign in Australia, some of us tried from this country to reconstruct what was happening whenever we read that Bradman was 'running away'. I risked the opinion that Bradman had declined to be enchained in the leg-trap. Like a great player, he sought to solve the problem by creative batsmanship; he moved aside on quick feet, and *cut* or slashed the fast bowling, which was head high three or four balls an over, sending his strokes to the vacant off-side field. It is silly to say, 'He didn't intend to get hit, or to settle down.' 'Body-line', bowled at Larwood's pace, allowed no batsman to settle down. The truth is admitted now by the majority of cricketers in England that 'body-line' made batsmanship almost impossible, and that nobody but Bradman, of contemporary players, could have driven it to the off side, and scored against it at an average of 56. Against Larwood and the leg-trap, Bradman is still supposed by many folks to have failed; his scores against 'body-line' in the Test matches were 0, 103 not out, 8, 66, 76, 24, 48 and 71. In all Test matches, against England, South Africa and the West Indies, Bradman's scores in Test matches take the breath away; 18, 1, 79, 112, 40, 58, 123, 37 not out, 8, 131, 254, 1, 334, 14, 232, 4, 25, 223, 152, 43, 0, 226, 112, 2, 167, 299 not out, 0, 103 not out, 8, 66, 76, 24, 48, 71, 38, 0, 0, 82, 13, 270, 26, 212 and 169.

The point is that this incredible sequence of scores has not been done by slow covetous cricket, but in every instance by strokes powerful, supple, swift. He cannot be kept quiet. If, as often happens, people say, 'Oh, but he hasn't the charm of McCabe, or the mercury of Macartney, or the dignity of Hammond', the objection is a little unintelligent, as though a lion were criticized for lacking the delicacy of the gazelle, the worrying tenacity of the terrier, and the disdainful elegance of a swan or a camel. Or we might as well sigh, at Bayreuth, not for the sweep and dynamic energy of Wagner, but for the poignant delicacy of Mozart as heard in the Residenztheater of Munich. We must pick and choose—and all sorts are needed to make the world's fairground. 'He's the best I ever saw,' said Wilfred Rhodes to me a year or two ago; then he shrewdly modified the opinion, as he of course would—'He's the best back-foot player I ever saw.' Bradman is seldom, if ever, detected in the act of playing foward 'full-stretch'. That is another of his secrets; he sees the ball so quickly, so soon and so late, that he is only at rare intervals—once or twice in a season—in the wrong position when the ball pitches. It is almost impossible to bowl a difficult length to him; in fact, whatever you bowl is usually wrong. He is a ruthless critic of himself and of others. At Melbourne, after the fifth Test match, we spoke together of Worthington's wretched luck. Worthington had gone through the tour without a decent score in a Test match, but at last he found form, played as though about to get a century and trod on his wicket at 44, while performing a splendid hook. 'Yes,' said Bradman, 'he was playing well and it *was* a shame.' Then, after a pause—'Still, you know, a batsman *shouldn't* tread on his wicket.' A terrible little man, but likeable, and with a wistful something about him, probably that melancholy which Aristotle says is the mark of all great ones of the earth.

Hammond was, in his first years of county cricket, a stroke-player of audacity. He came to Old Trafford one Whitsuntide and hooked Macdonald many times in an innings of nearly two hundred. In those days Lancashire had one or two old soldiers of bowlers who knew how to check strokes. But nobody could stop the course of Hammond that day. He was, as a young man, so rapid and brilliant a player that a member of the Selection Committee of the period assured me that Hammond was too reckless for a Test match cricketer. In the passing of time, Hammond grew older and conformed to the Test match policy which was enforced under D. R. Jardine, a grim policy indeed, which, in Australia especially, distrusted all strokes not controlled cannily. I believe that Hammond is the only contemporary English batsman who could go, without fear of becoming anonymous by contrast, into the company of Mac-Laren, Trumper, Tyldesley, Hutchings, and others. But also I believe that under MacLaren's captaincy, Hammond would have remained to the end a match-winning Test match batsman, an annihilator of all bowling, not only a beautiful stylist, weighted with responsibility, and glad of an escape into the gentler atmosphere of Gloucestershire cricket. For it is to the Hammond of county matches that we have had usually to look for the free and happy Hammond. In Test matches he has often seemed to carry the whole weight of his side's responsibilities, and though the burden has not submerged his genius it has subdued his spirit. The Australians set themselves to 'keep him quiet'. On good wickets they were satisfied not to try particularly to get him out so long as they checked his hits. A sort of a compliment, after all. But though my admiration of Hammond as a batsman is second to none—not to admire him would be myopic and idiotic—I sometimes feel sadly that circumstances have hindered his proper way of development. He belongs, in his methods, to the Golden Age, the pre-war period when we did not consider it criminal for a player to get caught at long-on in a Test match for less than two hundred.

DIGRESSION ON LARWOOD

WHEREVER I travelled in Australia, I heard praise of Larwood; also I heard expressions of regret that he was not with us now. He was not blamed for his contribution to the 'body-line' controversy, which was caused by a form of attack now condemned by nearly all English players actively taking part in first-class cricket. 'Larwood did a job of work under instructions'—that was the Australian comment in all places between Perth and Woolloongabba. Larwood's attack was first admired in Australia when he bowled at Brisbane and shot wickets down one after another. Chapman won the match by nearly 700 runs—and Larwood was hailed as the finest fast bowler from England in living memory. Hence the tribute I have now written and not, I hope, irrelevantly included in this book.

From time to time the glossy moral unction of the game is temporarily rubbed off by some savage who has more energy than is good for him. He rushes into the drawing-room and, before he can be stopped, he is on the royal hearthrug; and the ruling caste of the Dedlocks turns faint with horror. In the 'eighties or early 'nineties the professionals went on strike for more money. 'Good heavens,' spluttered the Dedlocks, 'more money? What do they want it for?' In our own time the traces have been kicked over by Parkin; by that beautiful cricketer Jack Newman, who actually kicked the wicket over in public view under the eyes of Lord Tennyson; and by the great Cid of cricket, A. W. Carr. These men would not, could not, toe the conventional line; how they embarrassed the upholders of taste! They made it hard for the Dedlocks to open their annual cricket-club bazaars with the old talk about 'Playing cricket'— 'It's not cricket'—as though cricketers came before footballers and jockeys in the eyes of the Lord.

Then Larwood threw his bomb. Of course we all applauded the act for a while, so long as the bomb fell in the midst of the enemy. 'Body-line' was the nation's answer to Bradman and his double centuries. But the worst of these storm-petrels is that they will go on following us and screaming and flapping disturbed wings long after the unfriendly and alien seas have been left far behind and we are back in safe home waters. Larwood actually thought that what was good enough for Bradman and Australia would be considered good enough for the peaceful cricket fields of England. And so photographs were taken of the bruised anatomies of men who had fought the good fight along with Larwood in the realms of the barbarian, photographs of ribs tickled by this same Larwood, and of good honest Lancashire thighs and buttocks stamped with the name of the maker of the ball—aimed by Larwood who, demented spirit, could not make the proper English compromise at the right time. Of course, he was stopped; there is a limit. And Nature took a hand in the affair; she destroyed some secret pivoted place in Larwood's toe; she, who does not really love her own earthquakes and tidal-waves, 'larned' Larwood not to be himself in excess.

By the power of his genius Larwood gave us all a good shaking. The firing of that first cannon-ball in the history of warfare did not cause as much consternation as Larwood's first fast ball bowled past the batsman's left ear to a crouching leg-trap. Bradman sat enthroned, a Moloch easefully digesting his year's diet of poor enslaved trundlers. Larwood arrived in the burgeoning land tiny as Gulliver in Brobdingnag. In a moment the god was thrown down, by a pebble from a catapult. Think of it, the blistering Australian heat, the polished turf, the crowd ravenous for another record by Bradman. Larwood begins with the usual chaste field—four slips, cover, extra-cover, and only one man on the leg side, near the boundary and fine, to save the four. Larwood bowls a few conventional overs, formally doing homage to the 'new' ball. Crack! bang! sounds the bat. Australia 20 for none in no time. Jardine makes the sign—the comprehensive wave of the arm that moves the four slips, and nearly everybody else, to the encircling net of the leg-side body-snatchers. 'Closer up,' says Jardine to the Nawab of Pataudi, who takes a few strides nearer to the left pocket of Bradman. 'A bit closer, Pat,' orders Jardine, and Pataudi sits under Bradman's chin, and notices how carefully he has shaved today. The thunderbolts flash through the air; the scene is suddenly changed; a few minutes ago the Australian ship prospered in calm waters; now she is sinking with all hands; holes through her sides, mainmast swept away. The perfect Sydney wicket—to try, for a change, another metaphor—was not long ago a batsman's cushion stuffed with runs; it is now a rack of nightmare. Bradman, like a man of genius, tries to retaliate, and he achieves brilliance. But the old lease at the wicket has lapsed; he is under notice to quit; each of his boundaries is a farewell supper. By strength of his right arm and a new dodge, Larwood solves the problem of years—how to put an end to the tyranny of the perfect pitch, and the great batsman's endless reign on it. Was it not cricket? Is there not a higher order of ethics than the common one? But the great ones of the earth have always been brought down in their empyrean flights, their reckless wingings into the sun, which blind them and make them mad—madness being what occurs to a man who upsets the pleasant equilibrium of things. A race of Larwoods would have wrecked cricket, no doubt. But, by the measure of genius which is employed by the amoral gods, Larwood's deeds in Australia were wonderful. As I say, it was all right so long as he let his sling go flying into the ranks of the foe. Old men in the West End clubs staggered to their feet, seized the tongs and the fire-irons, and demonstrated where Bradman was wrong in technique and temperament. Today the old men are still warlike, with their walking-sticks and pokers, but, as I say, no contemporary county cricketer has a word to say on behalf of the method of attack which won the rubber in Australia a year or two ago.

Fast bowling is dying out. There are one or two believers yet, maybe, in the old faith, who call for four slips and ask the wicket-keeper to stand back. But it is all nothing but a rite performed in a temple from which the spirit has long since fled. Batsmen play to the pretence; they go to the wicket heavily padded, huge leg-guards, and their bodies encased in circular wadding, until they look like advertisements for Michelin tyres. And Gover runs on the flat of his feet, and bowls not much faster off the pitch than the Larwood of today; Larwood who now is compelled to use the canter of compromise instead of his old lovely gallop over the earth, head down, like a young colt chafing his bit. In a few years from now, the modern sceptics will deny there ever was fast bowling. We can hear them; 'Fast bowling?—a Victorian and Edwardian crudity, a form of current and brutal Jingoism. We are subtler and more sensitive, with our in-swingers and googlies. Besides, were your Richardsons and Brearleys really fast? What were your standards of speed, what had you to go by? Today we have seen the aeroplane and the breakneck velocity of the dirt-track. What did the Victorians know of pace? They used to send a man with a red flag in front of a traction engine. People used to get run over in the streets by hansom cabs; how did they manage it? No wonder they thought Arthur Mold was quick!'

Larwood was the last of the classical fast bowlers; he showed his left side to the batsman, as Tom Richardson did. His body swung over the right hip, and his follow-through was thrilling. Even yet you can see these beauties of rhythm in his action, reduced though they are by physical hurt sustained in Australia. If ever a cricketer wore himself out in the service of his country, Larwood is his name. He stood to his guns in the face of a roaring outraged continent. And what guns they were, right or wrong. Australia has been the graveyard of fast bowlers. Take these figures, all of them epitaphs to doomed endeavour on the hard earth of Sydney, Brisbane, Adelaide, Melbourne: Richardson, average a wicket 30; Lockwood, 68; Hirst, 42; Cotter, 30; Howell of Warwickshire, 66; Gregory, 31; Macdonald, 65; Fielder, 27; Ernest Jones, 27; Frank Foster, 21. In 1928–29, Larwood's bowling analysis, for Test matches in Australia, was 18 wickets for 728 runs, average 40·44. On English wickets, in 1930, Larwood against Bradman and the Australians took four wickets for 292, in 101 overs, average 73·00. The cruel pitches frustrated him, and so the leg-trap was invented. But, as Burke pointed out, the march of the human intellect is slow.

THE 'MANCHESTER GUARDIAN'

GENTLEMEN *v.* PLAYERS, 1938

FIRST DAY

GENTLEMEN
First Innings

B. O. Allen, c Price, b Pollard	10
P. A. Gibb, lbw, b Smith	18
R. E. S. Wyatt, lbw, b Smith	4
W. R. Hammond, c Compton, b Pollard	46
N. W. D. Yardley, c Price, b Smailes	88
H. T. Bartlett, not out	175
R. H. Moore, b Nichols	24
F. R. Brown, c and b Smith	23
R. J. O. Meyer, lbw, b Smith	0
J. W. A. Stephenson, c Price, b Nichols	6
K. Farnes, c Price, b Pollard	10
B 2, lb 3, nd 2	7
Total	**411**

PLAYERS
First Innings

Edrich, c Stephenson, b Farnes	0
Hutton, not out	0
Price, c Hammond, b Farnes	0
Paynter, not out	0
Total (for two wickets)	0

Woolley, Hardstaff, Compton (D.), Nichols, Smailes, Smith (P.), and Pollard to bat.

BOWLING ANALYSIS
GENTLEMEN—First Innings

	O.	M.	R.	W.		O.	M.	R.	W.
Nichols	29	2	117	2	Smith	38	6	140	4
Pollard	28.5	4	60	3	Smailes	21	2	87	1

Umpires: Chester and Hardstaff.

LORD'S, WEDNESDAY, JULY 13TH

AN astonishing outbreak of hitting has taken place at Lord's this evening. The Gentlemen were 329 for nine when Farnes came in. Bartlett, who scored a hundred quickly enough in all conscience, proceeded to give one of the most skilful and jubilant

165

displays of driving witnessed on the ground for years. The Gentlemen's last wicket scored 82 in half an hour or thereabouts; Farnes's share was 10. Bartlett, a left-hander, has been coached by Woolley, and so the match already has honoured the captain of the Players in his season of farewell.

The sun shone plenteously, and those of us who had come from Manchester blinked our eyes like bats; the transformation was like an escape from a dripping tunnel, or like the rebirth of the earth after winter, or like the change from Davy Jones's locker in a pantomime to the second scene, which always takes place in the brilliant light of the village green, where the boys and girls sing merrily and the dame comes on and tells us of her matrimonial vicissitudes, with several far-reaching allusions to her 'first'. I felt ready to burst into poetry and chant the verses which begin Act 2 of Goethe's *Faust*, only I could not quite remember them. The cricketers seemed glad to be alive once more.

It has been a good day, and a summer's day, and we have seen a cricket match, and more than a hundred made by a player who yesterday was only a name to a few of the knowing ones and tomorrow will be famous as perhaps our most magnificent driving batsman. One of his hits this evening threatened to demolish the grand stand.

At half-past eleven Woolley led his team into the field, walking as of old his quiet, high-shouldered walk, only his legs moving and no other part of him. He looked almost the same Woolley who won our hearts more than thirty years ago; time has passed him by after giving him the gentlest and friendliest touch on the shoulder. When Gibb and B. O. Allen began the Gentlemen's innings Lord's made the perfect picture of summer in England; the grass held the glow from the sky gratefully, the white clouds poised themselves over us and the air hummed with the pastoral music of aeroplanes.

On a comfortable wicket Pollard and Nichols attacked, Nichols rolling along with a list to the port side; he has a nautical air. But he scarcely suggested an England fast bowler, for though he beat Gibb by means of a gorgeous out-swinger his bowling for the most part fell short of real velocity, and often his direction wasted the new ball. Pollard maintained a steady length and once or twice compelled a hurried stroke. Gibb, with a late stab, forced Pollard for four to the off; this was the only visible hit for half an hour. B. O. Allen was a model of left-handed congestion—also he was anonymous. Peter Smith came on instead of Nichols, who veered to cover-point. Allen secreted six runs in forty minutes, then sent a sharp chance to Nichols at second slip, off Pollard, and Nichols missed the catch and proceeded to expostulate in dumb show—to quote John Nyren. Gibb, who showed form and a quick judgment, was suddenly out to Peter Smith, beaten entirely before the ball pitched. He made the full use of his pads, like a true Yorkshireman, and was triumphantly lbw.

I liked watching Compton in the field; he was so eager and boyish. He does not throw in—he aims, like a lad playing with a stone on the way to school. I suspect that he carries a catapult in his pocket. In 50 minutes the Gentlemen made 31, and now Allen was beaten by pace off the pitch from a ball of Pollard's; Price held a catch at the wicket by pure instinct. The batting lacked decision and footwork, especially against the slow leg-spin of Peter Smith, who is at first glance a lethargic bowler, but really can turn the ball. His googly is excellent. I doubt, though, whether Australian batsmen would wait for his often overflighted length as politely as some of the Gentlemen waited for him this morning. Even Hammond played back to Smith and received him almost ceremoniously. Wyatt was leg before to Smith at 35, the third out, and he, too, declined to employ aggressive feet.

Yardley at once lent style to a morning of amiable utility, in spite of a preliminary snick behind his back off Smailes, who bowled when Pollard rested after an hour of honest length and direction. He forced Smailes to the on boundary with a simple flexion of the right forearm; nobody excepting a born batsman could make such a stroke. A cricketer is under no obligation to bat all day to convince us of distinguished ability; one revelation of his best is enough, if it is of the best, for man cannot by thinking add an inch to his stature. A good maiden over by Smith to Hammond provoked applause from the crowd, which was browning in the sun like meat at roast on a spit. But Hammond, as I say, was not in his throne-room mood; he was performing an official job, opening a provincial art gallery or something. He seemed satisfied to leave the speech-making to Yardley, his equerry. Yardley played admirably and pulled Smith for four from two consecutive balls. Nichols, on the starboard bow, or rather cover, picked up one or two hits with an obvious 'Aye, aye, sir!' At lunch the Gentlemen were 100 for three, and everybody was happy that the cricket season was returning. I felt encouraged to leap on the grass like a spring lamb, but after all Lord's is Lord's.

After lunch Yardley reached a capital fifty with a pretty late cut

off Nichols, who went on with the pavilion behind him, not to say
the mainmast and the captain's bridge. He worked hard and, whatever he lacked of style, showed character. Hammond at last became
interested; his bat began to send out the proper regal sound. How
beautifully he runs between the wickets, and how he relaxes when
he sees that only a single can be obtained! They used to say that
merely to see Forbes-Robinson walk accross the stage was a classical
education in the actor's art. To see Hammond running a single is a
classical education in the poise and dignity of our national field
sports. A cut for four by Yardley off Nichols was swift and handsome; even in a slow-motion photograph the stroke would have held
its own luminous velocity. And Yardley cut the next ball square, also
for four.

At half-past two the Gentlemen had pulled through from the
awful beginning of 35 for three. The score now was 137 for three,
Yardley not out 63, Hammond 37, but Hammond faltered once more
when he sliced Pollard for three, intending a forward drive. Yardley
continued to cut short balls against all Yorkshire precedents—no,
not all, for there was once a Yorkshireman named J. T. Brown and
another named Denton. Still, on a lovely lazy day of high summer a
little licence is permissible in a cricket report. It is a pleasure to be
writing at all on cricket. Only Nichols remains to remind us of the
heavy seas experienced at Old Trafford.

Hammond watched the fine, dashing play of Yardley obviously
with as much pleasure as anybody in the crowd. He played the part
of the Regent. He handed over the prerogative to the young man
who some day will succeed him as England's captain. The Players'
captain fielded at first slip, tall as—in fact, tall as Woolley. He
seldom received a ball, but his every movement was evocative of
history.

The ease of the pitch defeated the fast-medium bowlers, and
Pollard toiled in vain. Peter Smith alone caused the batsmen to
watch the ball to the last second of time. Price, though eager to prove
his ability behind the stumps, found little opportunity. Now that
Hammond and Yardley were set he might have been provided with
a shooting stick or a deck-chair. When two batsmen settle down to
thorough mastery an 'accident' is needed to dig them out. At 155
Hammond made a hard, forcing hit, correctly executed, from
Pollard's in-swinger, and Compton, at short forward leg, gripped a
grand catch. Hammond's 46 occupied rather less than two hours—
a studied piece for an Occasion, like a Poet Laureate's ode indited on

a given day or date. Hammond and Yardley added 120 in 104 minutes.

Bartlett flashed his bat contumaciously and unscientifically at Pollard, and fortune was with him. Yardley failed to make the century he deserved, for Price caught him like a good wicket-keeper, and then Bartlett delighted the crowd with an innings which was a remarkable mixture of powerful and brilliant hits and hazardous misses. When he did play a stroke he might have been a not far distant relative of Woolley. Finer straight-drives and finer cover-drives could scarcely be imagined than Bartlett's. Yet every over seemed his last. His one defensive stroke, a half-cock thrust at the pitch of the ball, kept his wicket safe, though it was shaved to an inch more than once. This was an innings of a proper gentleman of England—no trained labour, nothing but natural hitting, not by any means crude. Often he looked a born batsman, just a little short of experience and discretion. The Players' bowlers should have got him out for a reasonable score all the same. Woolley worked Pollard and Smailes too hard at one period; perhaps in his modesty he forgot he was captain and was wondering 'What is the matter with Wally Hammond—why doesn't he make a change?'

Moore shared an invigorating stand with Bartlett, and, to the joy of thousands, Bartlett reached a century of dashing and crashing boundaries. So, at the end, the Gentlemen achieved a substantial total and also emphasized in no uncertain voice that the bowlers chosen to play for England at Manchester were in one or two instances not the best available by far. Nichols is not in the class of Farnes, and on a good wicket Smailes is merely useful. Pollard confirmed the view that he can be relied on for steadiness even on a day which finds his attack not at all deadly. Peter Smith, I fancy, is too slow through the air to trouble Australian batsmen.

At the end of the day Farnes struck two more resounding blows for the Gentlemen. A rising ball caught Edrich on the glove, thwacked him on the head, and bounced merrily on into Stephenson's hands in the gully. Price came in after Edrich had been revived sufficiently to retire from the wicket, and at once gave Hammond a simple slip catch. No doubt the Players were now feeling like Sir Richard Grenville's seamen, 'We have children, we have wives, And the Lord hath spared our lives. We will make the Spaniard promise, If we yield, to let us go . . .'; but out Paynter had to go to face the music. To his credit he survived the rest of the over and lives to fight again.

GENTLEMEN *v.* PLAYERS, 1938

SECOND DAY

GENTLEMEN

First Innings		Second Innings	
B. O. Allen, c Price, b Pollard	10	b Pollard	5
P. A. Gibb, lbw, b Smith	18	c and b Smith	24
R. E. S. Wyatt, lbw, b Smith	4	c Smith, b Smailes	30
W. R. Hammond, c Compton, b Pollard	46	c Price, b Smith	37
N. W. D. Yardley, c Price, b Smailes	88	not out	16
H. T. Bartlett, not out	175	c Compton, b Smith	1
R. H. Moore, b Nichols	24		
F. R. Brown, c and b Smith	23	b Smailes	6
R. J. O. Meyer, lbw, b Smith	0		
J. W. A. Stephenson, c Price, b Nichols	6		
K. Farnes, c Price, b Pollard	10	not out	0
B 2, lb 3, nb 2	7	Lb 1	1
Total	411	Total (for six wickets)	120

PLAYERS

First Innings

Edrich, c Stephenson, b Farnes	0
Hutton, lbw, b Farnes	52
Price, c Hammond, b Farnes	0
Paynter, c Gibb, b Stephenson	36
Hardstaff, b Farnes	25
Woolley, c Gibb, b Meyer	41
Compton (D.), b Farnes	6
Nichols, b Farnes	23
Smailes, b Farnes	19
Smith (P.), not out	9
Pollard, b Farnes	5
Lb 2	2
Total	218

BOWLING ANALYSIS

GENTLEMEN—First Innings

	O.	M.	R.	W.		O.	M.	R.	W.
Nichols	29	2	117	2	Smith	38	6	140	4
Pollard	28.5	4	60	3	Smailes	21	2	87	1

PLAYERS—First Innings

	O.	M.	R.	W.		O.	M.	R.	W.
Farnes	21.3	6	43	8	Meyer	9	0	34	1
Stephenson	21	4	46	1	Wyatt	5	1	11	0
Brown	24	3	82	0					

170

The clouds returned today, with a wind, and, as usual, the weather entered the cricket's bones and mine also, as well as into the intellect, so that Wednesday's freedom of thinking became impeded. Sunshine is wanted for the roaming of fancy, from Nichols to Goethe and Tennyson. This morning I watched Hutton's carefully studied science and felt like writing a treatise on rational footwork. The Players had to struggle hard for runs, and at the interval five wickets were down for 119, four of them taken by Farnes, who this time bowled a length and put behind him the temptation, which overwhelmed him on Wednesday evening, to knock the batsmen over as though playing a turbulent young god's part in a human skittle-alley. He defeated Hutton on the point of lunch with a glorious late swinger; only by use of his extraordinarily quick feet did Hutton save his wicket from splintering downfall—he was resourcefully leg-before-wicket.

The only piece of triumphant batting on view during the first two hours was Paynter's; he was at his nimblest and most lusty. He stood up to a few preliminary 'kickers' sent by Farnes as a sort of alarm-clock announcing the morning's awakening; he drove Farnes to the off for three and scampered up and down the pitch on feet that twinkled so brightly that you could not tell which was which. Then when Brown came on, he struck four fours in an over, three from consecutive balls—a swinging square-leg hit, a pretty cut, a square cut out of the game's smithy, and a strong push to the on. To everybody's sorrow, Paynter succumbed a moment afterwards, caught at the wicket from a nasty running-away ball of Stephenson's. Gibb was a good wicket-keeper now, quiet and clean. His form against Oxford the other week must be regarded as a mysterious deviation from the normal. Still, a wicket-keeper's technique should guarantee that he can never fall below a certain level in any circumstances.

Paynter was third out at 58. Here ensued a stretch of dull activity while Hutton and Hardstaff added 46. Hutton always satisfied the lover of thoughtful batsmanship; now and again he revealed strokes of distinction. He is certain to go far, his method is so good. Always is he over the ball, head down. And he gets into position swiftly, and usually without a hint of awkwardness. Hardstaff is excellent against fast bowling, but once or twice he reached out speculatively to Brown and caused some of us to feel again the anguish of mind that we suffered in Australia when we saw Hardstaff groping at slow leg-spin and falling over himself trying to find it. He drove the quick stuff stylishly until he played on to Farnes; he tends to flick late in his defensive stroke. He is a splendid natural batsman who somehow seems to lack governing ideas.

Ten minutes before lunch Woolley went out to bat, cheered all the way. He looked slim and youthful, with a bronzed face. He might have been making his first appearance at Lord's. When he reached the wicket the applause broke out once more, and Hammond, who always does the courteous and right thing, came forward and welcomed him. It was a scene of charm and some emotion. Woolley's career rolled out in memory, a lovely frieze. No cricketer has given a choicer pleasure than he; he has never played a dull innings, a mean one, a covetous one. No wonder time is afraid of touching him. After lunch Woolley again walked to the wicket, this time with Compton at his side; I expected to see Compton asking for Woolley's autograph at any moment.

Woolley was beaten once or twice by Farnes, but played him to leg elegant as ever, then caressed Brown to the square-leg boundary, and hit him with a leisurely swing of the bat to the far-distant off boundary, under the clock tower, with no more effort than an indolent man stretching his arms. Compton watched these strokes with eyes glowing with hero worship, and at the first opportunity told of his inspiration by driving Farnes magnificently for a straight four. In the same over he played forward correctly and missed a superb ball which came from the earth at a devastating speed and shattered the off stump. Farnes had so far taken five out of the six wickets, and the total was a paltry 139. Thus did Farnes tell the Selection Committee who is the best fast bowler in England. A stroke by Woolley off Brown sent out a terrific crack, and the ball rebounded yards back into the field after hitting the railings (I decline patriotically to say fence), but there was not even a hint of effort in Woolley's action; he was all curves and nonchalance. Nichols, his next partner, is also a left-handed batsman, but compared to Woolley his was a left-handedness which reversed the order of nature. Woolley causes even right-handers to appear contrary and odd.

Hammond, who controlled his bowling well, was obliged to bring on Wyatt to cope with Woolley, and Wyatt's first ball was rather luckily tapped through the slips. Nichols played forward like a picture of cricket by G. F. Watts; sometimes he hit the ball, sometimes he missed it and at the end of the over he leaned on his bat with legs crossed negligently. His strokes were often hard, but did not always bring him runs; they got stopped by the port-side scuppers, I suppose. Wyatt bowled intelligently, and even compelled Woolley to stab late at the off side, and twice did Woolley fail to time the ball. The weather brightened now, or was it an illusion caused by the presence of Woolley? He can make the dullest day luminous; the sun never sets while he is batting; he is a giver of light.

Farnes was rested by Hammond, who is far-seeing in the treatment of his bowlers, and Meyer tried his arm from the pavilion end, and at once got Woolley caught by Gibb, another piece of rapid-eyed wicket-keeping. Woolley batted an hour, every minute a delightful pulsation. When he left the scene, and by doing so impoverished it, the Players were 168 for seven wickets. Seldom in recent years have the Gentlemen shown as much mastery in this match; their attack was far better than that of the Players, steadier in technique and more threatening.

Smailes, yet another left-hander, joined Nichols, and 93 runs were needed now to save the Players from the indignity of a follow-on. Thirty-five were gathered in devious ways for the eighth wicket, and Nichols performed one late cut with a lightness of touch that diverted us; his strokes, indeed, are in humorous contrast to his rolling, lumbersome physical movements. As soon as Farnes returned with the new ball Nichols was bowled, and he returned to the pavilion almost imperceptibly. Stephenson stopped a violent return drive from Smailes by the simple expedient of sitting on the ball, amid cheers and merriment; Stephenson bowled ably, but the menace to the Players was always Farnes, who shot Smailes's off stump yards out of the earth at such a catherine-wheel velocity that a girl sitting in the seats near the pavilion bounced into the air, startled out of her senses.

One of the day's best hits was a drive past cover by Pollard for four, off Stephenson; he, too, was bowled straightway by Farnes, who has seldom, if ever, exhibited a finer attack—this was fast bowling of the proper kind, overwhelming to the soundest defence, and, as they say, leaving the batsman standing. He hit the stumps five times and took eight for 43 in 21 overs and three balls. I have a prejudice for the bowler who sends a wicket reeling along the ground —the finest sight in cricket.

Hammond decided not to ask the Players to follow on; presumably he wished to give Farnes a rest. The Gentlemen went in again as though they, and not the other side, were saving the match. Pollard bowled admirably—few batsmen could have treated him

173

light-heartedly. But no attempt to get on with the match was palpable in the batting of Allen, who fell to a grand ball by Pollard, or Gibb or Wyatt, who received a gentle amount of ironical comment from the crowd, and a cheer when at last he was caught endeavouring to make a concession to the vulgar.

Hammond himself was stately rather than anything else, and Brown, apparently sent in to hit, quickly became bowled and to the joy of everybody Bartlett batted next, only to provoke disappointment and a general move towards the exit gates, for he drove at Peter Smith, and was caught at deep long-on, beautifully caught, too, by Compton, who came forward to the wicket to talk over the matter with the grown-ups. The Players will have to play hard to save themselves now and deprive the Gentlemen of their second victory in the fixture since the war. It is a healthy sign to see the Players struggling against the Gentlemen again, as they often were seen in the Golden Age. At twenty minutes past six Hammond's indifferent innings ended; still, in spite of their poor show this evening the Gentlemen should win. The Lord's wicket on a third day is likely to stimulate Farnes to further destructiveness—not that at the moment he needs any keener provocation than the Selection Committee.

THIRD DAY

GENTLEMEN

First Innings		Second Innings	
B. O. Allen, c Price, b Pollard	10	b Pollard	5
P. A. Gibb, lbw, b Smith	18	c and b Smith	24
R. E. S. Wyatt, lbw, b Smith	4	c Smith, b Smailes	30
W. R. Hammond, c Compton, b Pollard	46	c Price, b Smith	37
N. W. D. Yardley, c Price, b Smailes	88	b Smith	34
H. T. Bartlett, not out	175	c Compton, b Smith	1
R. H. Moore, b Nichols	24	b Smith	4
F. R. Brown, c and b Smith	23	b Smailes	6
R. J. O. Meyer, lbw, b Smith	0	not out	14
J. W. A. Stephenson, c Price, b Nichols	6		
K. Farnes, c Price, b Pollard	10	not out	16
B 2, lb 3, nb 2	7	Lb 1	1
Total	411	Total (for eight declared)	172

PLAYERS

First Innings		Second Innings	
Edrich, c Stephenson, b Farnes	0	c Gibb, b Meyer	78
Hutton, lbw, b Farnes	52	lbw, b Brown	6
Price, c Hammond, b Farnes	0	c Gibb, b Farnes	5
Paynter, c Gibb, b Stephenson	36	lbw, b Stephenson	12
Hardstaff, b Farnes	25	b Brown	0
Woolley, c Gibb, b Meyer	41	c Moore, b Brown	8
Compton (D.), b Farnes	6	lbw, b Farnes	45
Nichols, b Farnes	23	not out	31
Smailes, b Farnes	19	b Stephenson	20
Smith (P.), not out	9	c and b Farnes	9
Pollard, b Farnes	5	c Farnes, b Stephenson	13
Lb 2	2	B 4, w 1	5
Total	218	Total	232

BOWLING ANALYSIS

GENTLEMEN—First Innings

	O.	M.	R.	W.		O.	M.	R.	W.
Nichols	29	2	117	2	Smith	38	6	140	4
Pollard	28.5	4	60	3	Smailes	21	2	87	1

Second Innings

	O.	M.	R.	W.		O.	M.	R.	W.
Nichols	7	1	17	0	Smith	27	6	68	5
Pollard	22	4	53	1	Smailes	11	0	33	2

PLAYERS—First Innings

	O.	M.	R.	W.		O.	M.	R.	W.
Farnes	21.3	6	43	8	Meyer	9	0	34	1
Stephenson	21	4	46	1	Wyatt	5	1	11	0
Brown	24	3	82	0					

Second Innings

	O.	M.	R.	W.		O.	M.	R.	W.
Farnes	24	6	60	3	Brown	18	3	75	3
Stephenson	21.4	6	60	3	Meyer	16	4	29	1

Farnes bowled one wide.

LORD'S, FRIDAY, JULY 15TH

On a warm, dull afternoon the Gentlemen defeated the Players comfortably, in spite of a wicket made easy by a drizzle of rain which fell just before lunch. Farnes this time tempered the wind to the shorn lamb—that is to say, he conformed more or less to the modern idea that a fast bowler should seldom challenge by a short rising ball a batsman's ability to hook. The only important occurrence during the Players' innings was Edrich's return to form. He batted well, after an anxious prelude, and by his clever play to the on gave signs that he is once more about to belabour his enemies. He will have his chance at Lord's this weekend against Yorkshire.

175

Hammond declared the Gentlemen's innings closed this morning after three-quarters of an hour's desultory play, which was distinguished by an immaculate, not to say immobile, innings by Farnes. Contemporary tail-enders often display a straight and entirely unproductive bat, scorning the good honest clouts of the fast bowlers of old. Peter Smith bowled his googly skilfully again, but his attack is perhaps too slow and easy to reach by quick-footed Australians. Hammond left the Players with 366 to score for victory in a little under five hours.

Farnes beat Edrich three times in his first over, and Gibb missed an opportunity to stump Hutton, though Gibb on the whole, like Price, has kept wicket well enough throughout the match. Hutton was out in the over following the one which gave him another innings; he was beaten by a beautiful spinner from Brown, who has shown a little of his old ability today. Hutton then changed into his ordinary clothes and sat alone under the covered seats watching the match. I have seldom seen a county cricketer watching a cricket match in a solitude as charmingly thoughtful as that of Hutton's this afternoon.

Paynter promised a fine innings by a thumping four to the on, but he lost his wicket suddenly to a ball of Stephenson's especially quick off the ground. And Hardstaff once more revealed his weakness against slow spin and failed rather ingloriously. Woolley, too, disappointed us in his last innings of the great match he adorned for so many years in a period of bigger men than these of the moment. He was caught trying a drive, caught with ruthless judgment and patience by Moore. The Players had now lost four wickets for 64.

Edrich pulled aggressively, but abjured his hook stroke. He watched the ball and played back strongly. He reached 50 out of 76, and Compton helped him to save the Players' innings from the invertebrate. These two Middlesex young men are in their own way excellently contrasted as Hendren and Hearne were in the old years. Edrich is pugnacious and of the people; Compton is elegant, but with an eagerness never known by Hearne, even when Hearne (if ever) was a boy. Edrich makes his best strokes to the on; Compton can ripple the off side as well as the leg side. He has inspired moments when he reminds me, with a terrible sort of joy, of Victor Trumper. Edrich swept Brown twice for fours, and Gibb took a ball on the leg side from Meyer with the instinctive action of a good wicket-keeper; one or two experts in the crowd observed this dexterity and applauded. Edrich was caught by Gibb at 143, and then after Farnes had hurled down a passionate and colossally wide wide he completely overwhelmed Compton lbw after the boy had, to his open unashamed delight, survived an appeal in the same over for lbw.

A few vigorous and nicely balanced hits by Smailes introduced some show of fisticuffs to the Players' dying end, and Nichols attended the funeral with the formal starched sobriety of a mute. At this part of the proceedings four Essex men were in charge—Farnes and Stephenson were bowling at or to Peter Smith and Nichols. A brilliant square cut by Nichols suggested that had he not wasted much of his powers on fast bowling he might easily have become a really good batsman. The game finished with some clean and determined blows by Pollard, and at twenty minutes to six the Gentlemen, captained by Hammond, had beaten the Players for the second time since the war.

THE TEST MATCHES OF 1938

ENGLAND

First Innings

Hutton, lbw, b Fleetwood-Smith	100
Barnett, b McCormick	126
Edrich, b O'Reilly	5
W. R. Hammond, b O'Reilly	26
Paynter, not out	75
Compton (D.), not out	69
B 1, lb 17, nb 3	21

Total (for four wickets) 422

To bat: Ames, Sinfield, Verity, K. Farnes and Wright.

AUSTRALIA.—D. G. Bradman, S. J. McCabe, J. H. Fingleton, W. J. O'Reilly, C. L. Badcock, B. A. Barnett, L. O'B. Fleetwood-Smith, A. L. Hassett, E. L. McCormick, W. A. Brown and F. Ward.

Umpires: Chester and Robinson.

FALL OF THE WICKETS

ENGLAND—First Innings

1	2	3	4
219	240	244	281

The following is the Australian bowling analysis to the end of the first day's play:

	O.	M.	R.	W.		O.	M.	R.	W.
McCormick	23	4	73	1	F.-Smith	30	8	90	1
O'Reilly	38	8	106	2	Ward	24	2	108	0
McCabe	10	4	24	0					

NOTTINGHAM, FRIDAY, JUNE 10TH

ON one of the easiest pitches ever known, England batted first and did not lose a wicket until the time of day was twenty minutes past three and the score 219. Barnett, after a fortunate period, played like a soldier of fortune; in a glorious innings he hit the Australian attack right and left, scattered the field, cut and drove with power and ease and poise. At one point fours ran across the grass nearly every over. He failed by two runs to reach a hundred before lunch and join the company of Trumper, Macartney and Bradman, the only three cricketers who in a Test match between England and Australia have scored hundreds before lunch. He

178

announced to the world that O'Reilly can be forced in front of the wicket; his innings may be said to have lighted a torch that— etcetera and so forth.

Hutton lent a valuable aid to Barnett: his honour was to score a hundred in his first Test match against Australia. He will score many. He was calm and competent today, a craftsman who knew what he was about and what was expected of him. But after Barnett fell the English innings dwindled for too long; the Australian attack was free momentarily to think again that it was tolerably good and would be deadly on a wicket that fell short of an almost unlawful perfection. The bowling did not seem distinguished while Barnett raided it; afterwards it recovered composure and Hammond failed again in a Test match in England.

Bradman risked playing all his spin bowlers, and Waite was badly needed to keep a length at one end. McCormick on the lifeless earth achieved a pace and accuracy which at Lord's might have caused much confusion of mind and much hopping and jumping about. The turf certainly was no use to Fleetwood-Smith, and Ward's length was frequently so short that the ball appeared to reach the batsman under protest. And O'Reilly, but for a few spells, was only diligent and accurate. Rather than bowl on this Trent Bridge wicket I would break stone: if the Australians are granted reasonable luck—as much as came England's way today—they should score at will until replete.

Australia's Barnett kept wicket with exquisite touch and with as much charm of manner as Oldfield himself. And Emmott Robinson called no-balls daintily, not in his Yorkshire appealing voice, which, of course, was right and proper. I wonder if he will one day be the first to appeal for leg-before-wicket. At the day's pleasant fall Compton batted delightfully, and Paynter guarded and waited and matched the warm South with the grand hardihood of the North, not to say the common sense of Clayton-le-Moors, which is in Lancashire, though you might not think so.

As usual on these occasions panic sat up at once and made a noise, for from the last ball of McCormick's first over Barnett was missed in the slips by Brown, a difficult left-handed chance off the bat's edge. Barnett's stroke possessed perspective, so to say: he was a long way from the ball when he sliced it. In O'Reilly's first over Barnett was in difficulties, and then in McCormick's second over Hutton, knocked back by pace, played the ball into his stumps without causing the bails to move. The umpire studied the marvel with meticulous eyes; the double magnifying glasses of 'hextry power' of

179

Sam Weller were needed. Hutton was fortunate to prosper by this temporary suspension of the working of natural law, and the crowd emitted bladders of relief.

For a while Barnett's wicket was charmed; McCormick bowled fast and well, and more than once or twice Barnett's innings seemed about to topple and fall. I was reminded of the Aunt Sallys in the old fair; you kept hitting them smack on the centre of gravity and they staggered half over but came back. England suggested the fall of wickets every moment in the first half-hour; clearly the Australians expected quick wickets almost as a matter of course and by right of possession. Fingleton and Brown crouched low and acquisitively at silly mid-on and silly short-leg, each with as many arms as an Indian god. The atmosphere was tense with incipient disaster for England. And Bradman did his best to get on the nerves of one and all; he changed O'Reilly and McCormick over and in general the fieldsman conducted an enveloping movement.

Barnett obviously decided that his best plan was to trust his stars and drive. A sudden change occurred, fresh as the wind that greets the suffocated liner emerging from the Red Sea. While Hutton defended skilfully, if anonymously, Barnett sailed into the Australian bowlers as though the scene were merely Cheltenham at an August Festival there, where retired colonels who live in houses called 'Curry-Curry' go black in the face at the mention of the name of Lancashire.

Barnett drove McCabe to the off light as Woolley and cut the next ball for another four with a flourish that probably scandalized Emmott Robinson. Then when Fleetwood-Smith came on Barnett sliced him recklessly over the gully, smote the next ball, a full-toss, for four, and drove a three in the same over. Next minute he crashed a no-ball from McCormick past point, thumped Fleetwood-Smith to the off with ease, sent him a high hard return chance which soared away like a homing pigeon for four. Barnett proceeded to hit O'Reilly straight with a grand follow-through: he reached fifty out of 69 in sixty minutes. Then, bless our spectacles, if Bradman did not miss him from a drive at mid-off!

Barnett's innings was played on the rim of mortality: at first it suggested the desperate sword-play of a wounded gallant, one knee on the earth with bloodthirsty foes all around. He carried an amulet; he died and was born again. He found mastery and sent his enemies running.

And Hutton, cool and apparently disinterested, put a Yorkshire bat to the ball; once or twice he felt for it vaguely in front of his left leg. But he was good and trustworthy. England passed the hundred for no wicket at five minutes to one. The innings achieved a rare rally, nay, a resurrection. Hutton drove Ward straight; I have seldom seen so much driving as this in a Test match, and before lunch too. At ten minutes past one Hutton lay back to Ward's leg spin and cracked a magnificent four square to the off and reached his fifty, to the approval of thousands.

The moral of Barnett's cricket needs no italics; he demonstrated that Australians, like Socrates, are mortal, being, as they are, human. The cricket of Barnett became dazzling; the noise of his bat awoke the echoes. And now he was entirely masterful, sure, organized, stylish. A stroke off McCormick past cover was of blood royal; a drive to the on in the grand manner of MacLaren, a stroke which said, 'L'état, c'est moi!'

Barnett swept the first ball after lunch from his presence and attained his hundred. The scene was a fitting place for the innings: a splendid crowd, sunshine and shadow, blue sky and mountains of cloud, and Trent Bridge spacious with history. Barnett and Hutton beat the first-wicket record for England and Australia matches in this country, and at a quarter to three the score stood incredibly at 200 for none. A sudden rainstorm drove the players from sight for a few minutes, a lovely veil of rain shot with sunshine.

O'Reilly attacked desperately after lunch, whirling his arms and looking like one of the windmills in *Don Quixote*. He beat both Barnett and Hutton, but Barnett hit him to the on boundary as soon as he pitched beyond a length. At last somebody was seeing O'Reilly plain, seeing him in the light of objective reality. O'Reilly's good were respected: his bad ones were detected, shown up, demolished.

At 219 a quick ball of perfect length bowled Barnett. At once the Australian attack tightened. Hutton made his century and was leg-before-wicket trying a stroke to leg; his innings was intelligent, as old as the hills in the head, and technically correct. He batted three hours and twenty minutes. Edrich, confident to the point of casualness, played on to O'Reilly: England now were 244 for three, not at all a prolific score on the preposterously easy pitch.

Between a quarter-past two and half-past four England scored in spite of the great prelude, only 105 for three wickets. Towards tea McCormick was a tired if heroic bowler; he should have been hit now. But Hammond and Paynter made heavy labour of their jobs: apparently the English innings had to be begun again. Why do

English batsmen get out as soon as they have obtained their centuries? Australians take the wicket on a 200-run lease at least. After tea O'Reilly bowled Hammond by art skilful and beautiful and deceitful. Hammond had been playing back serenely according to his custom. O'Reilly lured him out further than he wished to go ball by ball, then overwhelmed him with a flighted in-swinger.

Paynter was dour; Australia got the game for a while in some control after all. The batting after Barnett departed became heavily laden, careworn, and not profitable. Thanks to Compton, the English innings smiled again: he was the picture of confident and graceful youth. Here is a cricketer who will for years bring into Test cricket a flavour, a bloom. It was all in all a renaissance day for English cricket, well worth watching and well worth cheers and congratulations.

FIRST TEST (SECOND DAY)

ENGLAND

First Innings

Hutton, lbw, b Fleetwood-Smith	100
Barnett, b McCormick	126
Edrich, b O'Reilly	5
W. R. Hammond, b O'Reilly	26
Paynter, not out	216
Compton, c Badcock, b Fleetwood-Smith	102
Ames, b Fleetwood-Smith	46
Verity, b Fleetwood-Smith	3
Sinfield, lbw, b O'Reilly	6
Wright, not out	1
B 1, lb 22, nb 4	27
	—
Total (for eight declared)	658

AUSTRALIA

First Innings

J. H. Fingleton, b Wright	9
W. A. Brown, c Ames, b Farnes	48
D. G. Bradman, c Ames, b Sinfield	51
S. J. McCabe, not out	19
F. Ward, not out	0
B 8, lb 3	11
	—
Total (for three wickets)	138

To bat: C. L. Badcock, A. L. Hassett, B. A. Barnett, W. J. O'Reilly, E. L. McCormick and L. O'B. Fleetwood-Smith.

FALL OF THE WICKETS

ENGLAND—First Innings

1	2	3	4	5	6	7	8
219	240	244	281	487	577	597	626

AUSTRALIA—First Innings

1	2	3
34	111	134

BOWLING ANALYSIS

ENGLAND—First Innings

	O.	M.	R.	W.		O.	M.	R.	W.
McCormick	32	4	108	1	F.-Smith	49	9	153	4
O'Reilly	56	11	164	3	Ward	30	2	142	0
McCabe	21	5	64	0					

McCormick bowled three no-balls and O'Reilly one no-ball.

The following is the bowling analysis of the Australian first innings to the end of the second day's play:

	O.	M.	R.	W.		O.	M.	R.	W.
Farnes	18	7	31	1	Wright	19	4	47	1
Hammond	5	3	6	0	Verity	4	0	20	0
Sinfield	15	6	23	1					

NOTTINGHAM, SATURDAY, JUNE 11TH

This has been a great day for English cricket, also a busy day. Records have gone tumbling right and left, disturbing distant seismographs. Paynter wallowed in the biggest score ever made against Australia by an Englishman in England, and Paynter is English sure enough, Lancashire by birth and appetite. Compton followed the fashion nowadays of unrazored youth to amass Test-match hundreds at the first sweet opportunity. The Australian attack was routed, scattered, plundered, or, as the man in Dickens would say, smifflicated. The vast crowd roared joy continuously; at three o'clock the premises were closed, and a sign was hung on the wall 'Ground Full', and somebody else added in chalk, to clinch the issue, 'House Full'. The smashing of the records and the setting up of others made the press box behave like Wall Street; I expected defaulting, even suicides.

At lunch some of us actually felt sorry for the Australians (it was easy to be sorry for them while at lunch, and such a good lunch, with the score 589 for six). We cursed the perfect wicket as we drank our coffee, smoked our cigars, and wiped our crocodile tears; we said it was a scandal that the arts of two beautiful spin bowlers should

183

have counted for nothing—or, in other words, for 589—all because of a wicket impossibly perfect and probably with cocaine in it. (We had to have our little joke.) But, then, after Hammond had boldly declared the English innings closed, what did we see? We saw Australian batsmen depressed and insecure; we saw hostile bowling; we saw young Wright spinning nastily where Fleetwood-Smith and O'Reilly had failed; we saw Farnes attacking with velocity where McCormick had toiled. And at last we saw Bradman uneasy of mind, uncertain of touch, out of patience with himself as he faltered. No wonder the crowd rejoiced. 'This,' we said at tea, 'is a Mingling that repays one for much disappointment and vexation.'

Whatever the result of the match, a notable fact is already established; the rubber will be decided strictly in terms of skill, ball for ball: that is to say, the Australians cannot hope now to bluff England out or have us out before we are in. Apparently some of our young men have never heard of O'Reilly; the old complex has been replaced by the new Compton; a cable should be sent at once by Bradman to Grimmett, 'Come home at once, all is forgiven.'

The stand by Paynter and Compton went on at half-past eleven from the point at which it had left off the evening before. The Australian bowlers were not given a minute's notice; a lovely square-drive by Compton opened the firing. Paynter insultingly pushed a ball a yard or two from him and ran; he and Compton proceeded to run many short ones, and the Australian field became flurried and all finger-and-thumbish. Two fours by Paynter, violent and impertinent, swept his score to 88. Paynter ran yards out of his ground to flay McCabe alive; he missed the ball and Barnett missed the chance —poor Barnett, who now fumbled after hours of swift precision. The Australian attack did not recover from this bitter blow. O'Reilly drooped and revived, took off his hat and wiped his brow; and Fleetwood-Smith twisted fingers in vain, and McCormick ran his long run up an almost visible hill. Vanity and uselessness. The harder they bowled the more Paynter liked them. Compton was even more insolent than Paynter, for Paynter did at least compliment the Australians by making a show of effort. Compton played his strokes with leisurely elegance, and reached a century like a young man about town taking a walk for once in a way. He got out in the attempt to pull square over the boundary. Compton is not quite ready yet, but soon he will be. It is strange and significant that nowadays young batsmen, immature if gifted, may compile Test-match hundreds at the first attempt; years ago a severe apprenticeship had to be served by such as Trumper, Hill, Tyldesley, Hayward, before they were able to achieve the great things. Paynter and Compton scored 206 for the fifth wicket, another record (I am told) for these engagements. The flavour and blossoming skill of Compton's innings were delightful; he flicked and forced to leg with supple and balanced power. But I did not always care for his way of reaching forward in front of the left leg.

After Compton had somehow lost his wicket Paynter thumped and blazed away, and occasionally edged and sliced. And Ames drove in style. The Australians wavered; this was a strange and blessed sight. We felt that Hammond performed almost an act of mercy when at a quarter-past three he called the halt. Paynter probably said, 'Hey, but Ah'm only just beginning—live and let live.' He batted five hours and a quarter.

Bradman badly missed a stock length bowler; Fleetwood-Smith, for the first time in his life, found a wicket on which he could not turn the ball. Of course, the Australians contributed to their own hardships; three decisive mistakes were made in the field by men who seldom make mistakes. Everything 'came off' for England and nothing at all for Australia—that much we must all of us compassionately admit, though the warning of Dr. Johnson lingers in the memory: if a man invades your house knock him down first and show compassion at his ill-fortune afterwards. The highest score ever made by England against Australia was duly celebrated by the swarming multitude; ten thousand sandwiches were consumed on the spot and fifteen thousand cakes, and unmentionable quantities of ale. Trent Bridge was a happy sight when at half-past three Brown and Fingleton began Australia's long journey, but few of us did not resign ourselves to the prospect of English bowlers soon as hopeless as Australia's had been.

Brown and Fingleton were each calm and unhurried; 29 were compiled scrupulously in half an hour. Yet for all the air displayed by both of studied calm I felt a change from that assured manner which marks the outset of an Australian innings on a beautiful wicket. There was little sense of attack in the strokes even when a short ball occurred; the burden of 658 runs palpably hung round Australia's neck. Still, the defences of Fingleton and Brown seemed reliable enough at ten minutes past four, when Wright bowled his first ball for England which Brown hit for a straight boundary.

Now came the turning-point of the afternoon; Wright struck the spark of battle in an atmosphere which was breeding stalemate. I do

185

not refer merely to his dismissal of Fingleton: that was another inexplicable accident for Australia. Wright bowled an atrocious long-hop, ready to bounce twice, and Fingleton, trying a forcing back-stroke, played on. It was when Bradman took his responsible stand that Wright won his spurs. He spun the ball from leg sharply if not a lot. And his length was not bad, not worse at any rate than a leg-break bowler's length should be. Bless us, if he did not at once attack Bradman and worry him! There seems no respect amongst the modern young bloods for reputation. Bradman was compelled to reach out at Wright, to grope forward, a weakness never or seldom to be known in his technique. Thirty thousand voices appealed when a ball struck the great man's pads; thirty thousand howls of exultation were emitted when Bradman stabbed late at Wright, terribly late and hurriedly, and sent a ball to Farnes at forward leg; but it was not a catch. Bradman again reached forward at Wright's spin; he looked like a curving mark of interrogation. I have never before seen Bradman as uneasy as this on a batsman's turf. He prodded Farnes with the wrong side of his bat apparently, and tossed back his head in self-chastisement. Then amidst gasps and groans Wright just failed to catch and bowl him; Bradman once again played forward sooner than he ever wishes to play or ever does play; Wright too eagerly thrust his right hand at the chance of a lifetime. But he had won ample enough honour: he had joined the few, the very few, who have lured Bradman out of his own territory, lured him from the great pivot of the back foot.

Bradman was only seven when Wright morally got him; he drew him out again with a leg-spinner going away past the off stump; Ames swept the bails off as Bradman suspended himself in a pyschological mid-air. Then to the jubilation of many Bradman walked away; but he was walking away to tea—this mishap to him had taken place at the last ball before tea. After the interval, Bradman essayed a square-drive past point off Farnes, and the ball flew through the slips, and yet again Wright sicklied over Bradman's face with introspection. Bradman even distrusted Sinfield, who bowls an off-break as venerable as my grandfather. Care sat on Bradman; the uneasy crown. Much as I patriotically wanted him to get out, the sight of his suspiciousness saddened me. It was as though D'Artagnan had been detected in the act of taking out a life insurance policy. We could see, of course, that he was a great batsman, but this time we looked upon a Bradman compelled to struggle. Yet when Verity came on he threatened to break the cordon; in one over he drove to the off brilliantly and glanced to leg. Next over two more masterpiece fours. He was going to escape, going to emerge, and get his usual two hundred! Even when he is out of mood, we said, he contrives to pull Australia from all holes. The light darkened; I am certain the gloom of the late afternoon had its effect on the Australians, as much on their spirits as on their eyesight. Farnes bowled with a power of penetration not once seen in the Australian fast bowling. Brown batted bravely and coolly, satisfied to stay there.

Bradman reached 47 and then sliced without control a ball from Farnes past the right hand of backward point; Edrich should have caught it; he had promised much by his alert fieldsmanship. The stroke told more and more of Bradman's unsettled state. He reached 50 in eighty minutes, though then fell to Sinfield, of all good honest bowlers on a pampered wicket. Sinfield flighted the ball with the craft and pretty curve of long tradition; Bradman, trapped in two mutually exclusive minds, succumbed to a catch at the wicket. Bradman fell just before six o'clock, and in the most trying of all periods known to batsmen, the day's last thirty minutes, McCabe and Brown had to watch out keenly in the encircling gloom.

Even on the doorstep of escape from a dire day Australia were mocked. Brown, who appeared sound and well rooted, snicked Farnes, and Ames devoured the catch. At the finish six or seven or eight English fieldsmen crouched round Ward's bat; time was bringing its revenges with a delectable irony. To save the match the Australians will need all their own capacity to fight back; much depends on McCabe now.

FIRST TEST (THIRD DAY)

ENGLAND

First Innings

Hutton, lbw, b Fleetwood-Smith	100
Barnett, b McCormick	126
Edrich, b O'Reilly	5
W. R. Hammond, b O'Reilly	26
Paynter, not out	216
Compton, c Badcock, b Fleetwood-Smith	102
Ames, b Fleetwood-Smith	46
Verity, b Fleetwood-Smith	3
Sinfield, lbw, b O'Reilly	6
Wright, not out	1
B 1, lb 22, nb 4	27
Total (for eight declared)	658

AUSTRALIA

First Innings		Second Innings	
J. H. Fingleton, b Wright	9	c Hammond, b Edrich	40
W. A. Brown, c Ames, b Farnes	48	not out	51
D. G. Bradman, c Ames, b Sinfield	51	not out	3
S. J. McCabe, c Compton, b Verity	232		
F. Ward, b Farnes	2		
A. L. Hassett, c Hammond, b Wright	1		
C. L. Badcock, b Wright	9		
B. A. Barnett, c Wright, b Farnes	22		
W. J. O'Reilly, c Paynter, b Farnes	9		
E. L. McCormick, b Wright	2		
L. O'B. Fleetwood-Smith, not out	5		
B 10, lb 10, w 1	21	B 2, lb 4, nb 2	8
Total	411	Total (for one wicket)	102

FALL OF THE WICKETS

ENGLAND—First Innings

1	2	3	4	5	6	7	8
219	240	244	281	487	577	597	626

AUSTRALIA—First Innings

1	2	3	4	5	6	7	8	9	10
34	111	134	144	151	194	263	319	334	411

AUSTRALIA—Second Innings $\dfrac{1}{89}$

BOWLING ANALYSIS

ENGLAND—First Innings

	O.	M.	R.	W.		O.	M.	R.	W.
McCormick	32	4	108	1	F.-Smith	49	9	153	4
O'Reilly	56	11	164	3	Ward	30	2	142	0
McCabe	21	5	64	0					

McCormick bowled three no-balls and O'Reilly one no-ball.

AUSTRALIA—First Innings

	O.	M.	R.	W.		O.	M.	R.	W.
Farnes	37	11	106	4	Wright	39	6	153	4
Hammond	19	7	44	0	Verity	7.3	0	36	1
Sinfield	28	8	51	1					

Wright bowled one wide.

The following is the bowling analysis of Australia's second innings to the end of today's play:

	O.	M.	R.	W.		O.	M.	R.	W.
Farnes	8	0	26	0	Sinfield	10	4	9	0
Hammond	4	3	1	0	Verity	19	11	20	0
Wright	12	2	24	0	Edrich	7	1	14	1

NOTTINGHAM, MONDAY, JUNE 13TH

Today McCabe honoured the first Test with a great and noble innings. At one time Australia was only 263 for seven, with no survivors to help McCabe except McCormick, O'Reilly and Fleetwood-Smith. McCabe changed the gravest situation with the ease of a man using a master key; in an hour he smashed the bowling and decimated a field which for long had been a close, keen net. He pulled his side out of a terrible hole and gave Australia a chance to save herself. Today he scored 213 out of 273 in three and a quarter hours while seven wickets fell. The dear valiance of his play won our hearts. And, believe it or not, when Brown and Fingleton began an uphill job of work a large portion of the crowd actually barracked because Brown and Fingleton played safely and declined to betray McCabe's skill and courage, which they would have done had they attempted indiscreet strokes. Never before have I heard barracking of more stupidity than this. McCabe gave the crowd their money's worth and snatched the match temporarily at least out of England's almost certain grasp. Fingleton and Brown would have been traitors to McCabe had they batted in any but a sound defensive manner; runs now were a secondary condition. Brown and Fingleton possibly carried caution to excess, but the ironical part is that during the period in which they were jeered at they scored only some fifteen runs fewer in two and a quarter hours than England scored in two and a quarter hours after lunch on the first day of the match when Barnett had landed the lunch score at the vantage point of 169 for no wicket. Fingleton no doubt incensed the crowd by sitting down on the grass, perhaps an unwise gesture. But an appeal against the light was not probably justifiable. But let me get away from paltriness and tell the tale of McCabe's masterpiece. And I will try to describe it in the rhythm of its occurrence, and I hope that my narrative will give the faintest idea of the grand crescendo which crowned all.

Warm sunshine blessed the scene at last this morning, and we now had reason to thank Heaven that Bradman got out in Saturday's darkness; this was his own weather and the wicket still contained runs for the picking, even though marks made by Australia's heavy artillery had slightly roughened the surface. McCabe at once drove Farnes effortlessly through the covers for four; then Farnes bowled Ward. The day began now with Hassett in, small and immaculate as Quaife; he almost played on to Farnes forthwith; the ball gyrated from his bat like a kitten seeking its own tail. Trent Bridge looked

189

handsome; bunting and coloured flags suggest royalty or a fairground with cocoanut shies at Australia's batsmen two a penny. Wright bowled with Farnes straightway, and Hassett tried to drive a quick leg-break on the half-volley; spin caused him to slice the stroke, and Hammond held the inevitable catch at slip. Wright dropped the ball in the rough stuff high enough up the wicket; it would have been impossible to cause as much spin as this on Friday on any part of the pitch. Australia 151 for five, and, I imagine, much distress in the Anthenaeum Club, Melbourne, in the lordly mansions of Toorak, in Castlereagh Street, Sydney, in Wagga Wagga, Bondi, Southport, which is near Brisbane, Adelaide, Perth and Kalgoorlie; in all these places the time would be evening at nine o'clock and the people would be listening, incredulously to the wireless, men and women and boys and girls, even the babies allowed to stay up late for the occasion. And patient ships moving without seeming to move through the blue water of the Pacific on the long way from Colombo to Fremantle would be listening too; cricket girdles the earth nowadays; but I must cease or I shall sound like a cricket dinner at Lord's with Sir Pelham in full song.

McCabe was a great player all the time; he has been out of form, but now, in a severe hour, he held himself calmly, masterfully. But he inspected the pitch once or twice and stabbed late at a ball from Farnes which kept low. The situation became one in which a logical policy of batsmanship was difficult to shape; noon on the third day is too early for defence without runs, yet Australia's position chastened a free swinging stroke. Badcock endured for a while an unnatural life; he reached forward to play back. The English bowling seemed merely steady; I thought to myself now, 'Heaven protect this attack the day Bradman and the others get off with a flying start.' Things continued to go awry with Australia; Badcock tried to cut a potential half-volley, and like Fingleton he played on.

The innings was rent in twain now; McCabe was left standing on a solitary rock of sound technique; between him and the rearguard yawned a chasm. He proceeded to play the cricket of heroic loneliness; he hit Farnes for six to square leg with the serenest sweeping movement. He cut late with the touch of intimate art. Impending disaster did not ruffle him; even a snick through the slips off Farnes was tranquil and graceful. Farnes bowled keenly, accurately, ominously, and fast; Wright at the other end turned his leg-break now and again and avoided too much short stuff. Sinfield's offbreaks had an amiable aspect, but he more than once troubled even

McCabe; clearly the turf was now not entirely insensitive to spin. In one other point, too, the English attack at the moment excelled Australia's, a point which had nothing to do with winning the toss; the length was never, or seldom, loose. Barnett defended while McCabe took charge; it is the sure sign of a great batsman that he can at a challenge take charge; what does the term master mean if it does not mean mastery? With his team cornered McCabe played the innings of the match and to make him this compliment is not to forget our Barnett's courage and skill on Friday. But McCabe was so sure an artist, so ripe and, with all his aggression, so stylish and courteous. Australia's Barnett ably put the straight obstructive bat to the ball until after lunch he decided to drive Farnes, in spite of the new ball; ambition was his undoing, but he served Australia well in a last-minute stand of 67.

Now came the death and glory, brilliance wearing the dress of culture. McCabe demolished the English attack with aristocratic politeness, good taste, and reserve. Claude Duval never took possession of a stage coach with more charm of manner than this; his boundaries were jewels and trinkets which he accepted as though dangling them in his hands. In half an hour after lunch he scored nearly fifty, unhurried but trenchant. He cut and glanced and drove, upright and lissom; his perfection of touch moved the aesthetic sense; this was the cricket of felicity, power and no covetousness, strength and no brutality, opportunism and no meanness, assault and no battery, dazzling strokes and no rhetoric; lovely, brave batsmanship giving joy to the connoisseur, and all done in a losing hour. One of the greatest innings ever seen anywhere in any period of the game's history. Moving cricket which swelled the heart. Not once but many times McCabe has come to Australia's aid in a crucial moment and has played gloriously when others have lost heart; he is in the line of Trumper, and no other batsman today but McCabe has inherited Trumper's sword and cloak.

When McCormick was bowled McCabe was 160; he now scored fifty in a little more than a quarter of an hour. He blinded us with four fours in an over from Wright; his innings became incandescent; he reached his two hundred and received worthy acclamation. He passed Paynter's score with a gesture of magnanimity. The English bowling suffered demoralization; length and accuracy vanished. A majestic on-drive sent Australia's total beyond four hundred. With consummate judgment he kept the bowling; Fleetwood-Smith was almost as much a spectator as I was. This gorgeous sirocco had a

191

calm pivotal spot; McCabe's mind controlled the whirlwind; his shooting stars flashed safely according to an ordered law of gravitation. He scored 72 out of 77 for the last wicket in half an hour; after lunch he scored 127 in eighty minutes. In all, he scored 232 out of 300 runs in 230 minutes, and hit a six and thirty-four fours.

Brown and Fingleton made, or declined to make, more than 89 in two and a quarter hours; a wonderful left-handed catch by Hammond then accounted for Fingleton amid universal rejoicing. At the evening's misty fall Bradman was as dour as Brown himself; tomorrow he will move heaven and earth to express his gratitude for McCabe's lifeline; and England will move heaven and earth to overwhelm him and all. Another famous day.

FIRST TEST (FOURTH DAY)

ENGLAND
First Innings

Hutton, lbw, b Fleetwood-Smith	100
Barnett, b McCormick	126
Edrich, b O'Reilly	5
W. R. Hammond, b O'Reilly	26
Paynter, not out	216
Compton, c Badcock, b Fleetwood-Smith	102
Ames, b Fleetwood-Smith	46
Verity, b Fleetwood-Smith	3
Sinfield, lbw, b O'Reilly	6
Wright, not out	1
B 1, lb 22, nb 4	27
Total (for eight declared)	658

AUSTRALIA

First Innings		Second Innings	
J. H. Fingleton, b Wright	9	c Hammond, b Edrich	40
W. A. Brown, c Ames, b Farnes	48	c Paynter, b Verity	133
D. G. Bradman, c Ames, b Sinfield	51	not out	144
S. J. McCabe, c Compton, b Verity	232	c Hammond, b Verity	39
F. Ward, b Farnes	2	not out	7
A. L. Hassett, c Hammond, b Wright	1	c Compton, b Verity	2
C. L. Badcock, b Wright	9	b Wright	5
B. A. Barnett, c Wright, b Farnes	22	lbw, b Sinfield	31
W. J. O'Reilly, c Paynter, b Farnes	9		
E. L. McCormick, b Wright	2		
L. O'B. Fleetwood-Smith, not out	5		
B 10, lb 10, w 1	21	B 5, lb 16, nb 5	26
Total	411	Total (for six wickets)	427

FALL OF THE WICKETS

ENGLAND—First Innings

1	2	3	4	5	6	7	8
219	240	244	281	487	577	597	626

AUSTRALIA—First Innings

1	2	3	4	5	6	7	8	9	10
34	111	134	144	151	194	263	319	334	411

AUSTRALIA—Second Innings

1	2	3	4	5	6
89	259	331	337	369	417

BOWLING ANALYSIS

ENGLAND—Fist Innings

	O.	M.	R.	W.		O.	M.	R.	W.
McCormick	32	4	108	1	F.-Smith	49	9	153	4
O'Reilly	56	11	164	3	Ward	30	2	142	0
McCabe	21	5	64	0					

McCormick bowled three no-balls and O'Reilly one no-ball.

AUSTRALIA—First Innings

	O.	M.	R.	W.		O.	M.	R.	W.
Farnes	37	11	106	4	Wright	39	6	153	4
Hammond	19	7	44	0	Verity	7.3	0	36	1
Sinfield	28	8	51	1					

Wright bowled one wide.

Second Innings

	O.	M.	R.	W.		O.	M.	R.	W.
Farnes	24	2	78	0	Verity	62	27	102	3
Hammond	12	6	15	0	Edrich	13	2	39	1
Wright	37	8	85	1	Barnett	1	0	10	0
Sinfield	35	8	72	1					

Wright bowled four no-balls and Edrich one no-ball.

NOTTINGHAM, TUESDAY, JUNE 14TH

The Australians saved the game in the first Test match here by superb defensive cricket. Even this elaborately pampered turf began to help spin. England's bowlers were late in the day finding the worn places; there was a want of hostility in the attack before lunch; the field for too long was spaciously and protectively set. From the outset there should have been an intimidating show of clutching hands. All day Bradman played a skilful and politic game; he covered the dusty spot at the pavilion end; he carried his team on his shoulders, for though Brown ably helped him it was Bradman who governed the tactical plan. He forswore vain deeds; he curbed his bat and played for Australia, played consummately. He occasionally deceived us into thinking the pitch was as inert as it was on Saturday, but now and again we could see him in difficulties. He conquered by his remarkable technique and by his cool concentration. Many, but not all, English experts agreed that on the same wicket Fleetwood-Smith and O'Reilly might have won the match in an hour or two. This can be written without invalidating the case against the building up of a turf on which in four days only twenty-four wickets fall while some 1500 runs are amassed.

The match died after a few spasms, no doubt of fatty degeneracy of the heart. The wicket for too long was the enemy of evenly contested sport between bat and ball; a preposterous wicket to prepare for a match confined to four days. The absurdity of Test matches in England is that we give them a time-limit and then let them be played on turf which is actually more an enemy of bowlers than is the turf of Australia.

With grim watchfulness Bradman and Brown kept up their wickets; we had expected a severe struggle, but scarcely got it at once; the first overs of the morning bred the deadening air of stalemate. The crowd was small and quiet; disappointment and disillusionment could be felt everywhere. Neither Bradman nor Brown attempted a forcible stroke; apparently they were intent not only on saving Australia but also on exposing the futility of the four-day Test match on a pitch nursed and rolled overmuch. With no time-limit this morning's negative batting of Brown and Bradman would have been not only meaningless but dangerous to their side's position. The best wicket in the world does not get better as time rolls on; even this wicket deteriorated. If this match had been a fight to a finish Bradman and Brown would have played with a reasonable eye for runs. Killing time for the sake of killing time never occurs when there is no time-limit to look forward to as to a rescue party. It is in England, not in Australia, where the risk of dull, futile, and barren Test matches is constantly run. Not that this match has been empty; but it deserved a decisive end.

People today groaned and said it was all boring; this morning's cricket certainly was boring to the patriots. But how churlish the patriots were to forget so soon the brilliance of England's innings, the drama of Australia's struggle, and Bradman's downfall on Saturday evening, the last-minute heroism of McCabe, and Bradman's supremacy today. Suppose in the same circumstances Hammond had snatched his side out of the jaws of the enemy, changed fate in an hour by glorious strokes, and then suppose, say, Paynter and Hutton had supported Hammond's work of salvage by getting down to the job of hauling the ship safely ashore. Would we not have cheered and smote our breasts and said 'Great cricket'? The criticism which was open to be made was not against the strokeless methods of Bradman and Brown before lunch but against the laying down of a sinfully perfect pitch for the needs of a four-day match. The English attack could apparently find little or no aid until too late in the few sullied spots at the pavilion end, though the spots were certainly there; in less than an hour in the morning effort seemed to relax.

Bradman at the end of two hours was only thirty; dourness did not please him; he frequently felt for the ball and looked unhappy, sometimes unsafe. For the cause he scorned delights and lived laboriously. Brown reached his hundred in three hours and a quarter, and for all the want of animation this speed was not far behind the speed in which many of our county batsmen go about the daily routine of compiling their hundreds. At lunch Australia was 199 for one; in two hours 97 runs had been somehow scored on a morning of luscious sunshine under a blue, cloudless sky.

After lunch, as the situation became temporarily easier, the batsmen deployed their hits; 60 were added in forty-five minutes. Then Brown swept to leg gaily and was caught. His innings, if occasionally fortunate, was a tribute to temperament and a sound upright technique. Bradman continued to watch the ball, and the wicket, when McCabe came in at three o'clock. The arrears had just been wiped off. And McCabe's first scoring stroke was edged through the slips from a turning ball by Verity. The fact that spin was not impossible at the pavilion end caused the batsmen to check their strokes; Bradman at times bent himself nearly in two.

Verity bowled well after lunch; as far as style goes he was easily the best of England's lot. McCabe lofted a ball from Wright perilously over mid-on's head and the next ball compelled another and similar uncertain hit. The bowling was now more aggressive than it had been in the day's crucial beginning. I was at a loss more than ever to account for the amiability of England's attack between half-past eleven and half-past twelve. McCabe played tranquilly until four o'clock; he then was caught at slip off Verity, who once more found the rough sensitive spot.

195

Bradman, obviously disturbed by McCabe's dismissal, spoke to Hassett, who came in next; Australia was only 84 ahead and two and a half hours remained for action. Bradman reached his century, the hardest of his career; it occupied him for four hours and a quarter. Hassett died instantly; a ball from Verity astonishingly kicked as though on a gluepot; Compton flung himself flat and held a catch at silly point. The match came again to vivid life, another resurrection, Bradman was in a responsible position in this unexpected onrush of crisis, the crowd woke up and gasped as he played a bad stroke off Farnes. Badcock immediately popped a ball up from Verity not far in front of silly mid-off; the spot at last was growing seemingly in extent and spitefulness; I was glad that England had won the toss. Bradman put on his greatness; he showed Badcock between overs how to smother Verity's spin.

After tea Wright beat Bradman once and Badcock twice and then clean bowled Badcock; each time the spin was quick; clearly we knew now the match had been saved by no common craftsmanship and power of will. I doubt, indeed, if ever a match has been so finely saved as this one; at lunch yesterday Australia was not only under sentence of death; she was pinioned and ready for the quick drop and the instantaneous death, after a more or less hearty breakfast, or, I should say, lunch.

SECOND TEST (FIRST DAY)

ENGLAND
First Innings

Hutton, c Brown, b McCormick	4
Barnett, c Brown, b McCormick	18
Edrich, b McCormick	0
W. R. Hammond, not out	210
Paynter, lbw, b O'Reilly	99
Compton, lbw, b O'Reilly	6
Ames, not out	50
Lb 12, w 1, nb 9	22
	—
Total (for five wickets)	409

To bat: Verity, Wellard, Wright, and K. Farnes.

AUSTRALIA: D. G. Bradman, J. H. Fingleton, W. A. Brown, S. J. McCabe, C. L. Badcock, A. L. Hassett, A. G. Chipperfield, B. A. Barnett, W. J. O'Reilly, E. L. McCormick and L. O'B. Fleetwood-Smith.

Umpires: Smith and Walden.

FALL OF THE WICKETS
ENGLAND—First Innings

1	2	3	4	5
12	20	31	253	271

LORD'S, FRIDAY, JUNE 24TH

England's batsmen got themselves into a palpitating state during the first half-hour of today's argument—and achieved a remarkable recovery. The wicket seemed a little damp for a while, almost a green wicket, as they say in Yorkshire, and because McCormick bounced a few balls, not against any known ethic of the game, three wickets fell, or conspired to be taken, for 31 runs. The panic was nipped in the bud immediately, much as a mild outbreak of fire is dowsed by an honest bucket of water. Hammond at last found his proper style and ability against the Australians in this country, and Paynter again expressed a northern indifference to all crises, actual or potential. He batted as though playing Northamptonshire bowling. Perhaps at times he really thought he was. The stand of Hammond and Paynter for the fourth wicket added 222 in some three hours. It was a great stand, though everything was done perhaps too easily—greatness should be made of sterner stuff, and, to say the truth, the Australian attack quickly dwindled to laborious ineffectuality. O'Reilly and Fleetwood-Smith were almost as harmless as they were on the immaculate sward of Trent Bridge. Neither of them could force home the offensive taken by McCormick—I cannot remember ever before seeing tables turned on Australia as rapidly and as easefully as they have been turned today—at least for the moment. Let us be content with that and unfold the story.

From the early hours the scene at Lord's was tumultuous; as soon as the gates opened the populace swarmed prodigiously. It was as though a great stone had been suddenly turned over on the untilled field of the universe. People ran about looking for places; their faces wore strained unhappy looks. Those who had got good seats were the objects of hatred. Men and women near the pavilion walked about wearing round badges like prize cattle. Gaunt contraptions reared to the heavens, devices of television, broadcasting. I thought I had wandered into a drawing by Heath Robinson. And all this for the simple and rather foolishly decorative game of cricket. In the seats of the mighty sat the members in almost indecent comfort—staunch survivors of the line of the Forsytes, with here and there a

Colonel Blimp ready to go red and denounce all cads. The sun shone upon the imposing scene; we were reminded of the match against the Borealians described in the book by A. G. Macdonell. We only needed some music by Elgar, and a display of Union Jacks. Bradman and his men took the field promptly, and as he led his men out a solitary 'coo-ee' came screeching from the Australian enclosure, recalling the loneliness of the bush, the empty spaces of the Mallabar Desert, and the congested assembly in the long bar of the Australian Hotel at Sydney on any evening at five o'clock.

To begin with, the wicket certainly held a little of the moisture used in the process of preparation. McCormick caused the ball to rise hip high at once, and though he committeed a no-ball and bowled all over the pitch, I did not like the way he was tackled. There were only three men on the leg-side—Brown and Fingleton close to the wicket, at silly short-leg and silly mid-on, and Badcock, far off near the boundary. Barnett struck the no-ball for two, and next ball he forced for three to the on. Then he obtained a two through the slips, but his nose was elevated and his vision tended to embrace the clouds above. Another no-ball from McCormick, wild as the wind, was snicked for four to leg, and the next ball jumped up to Hutton's breast-bone, and he put out a hopeless bat and spooned it wanly to Brown on his very doorstep. It was a startled stroke.

McCabe delivered the new ball conscientiously, and the batsmen competed to get to his end. Barnett square-drove McCabe with a breeze of relief, but still suggested discreet withdrawal against McCormick. Edrich then scandalized us by a terrible heave across a length ball, one of the few length balls sent by McCormick in his first deadly spell, deadly because for all his inaccuracy he can work up a pace not common in these days of enfeebled fast bowling. Edrich was out, to the noise of a frightful rattle of his stumps. His stroke caused general horror. It was ugly and not of his own choosing—it told of a hectic state of mind. The English innings began that way, flushed like the face of a consumptive. Edrich deserved his end even though he did pull the fatal ball into his wicket, for just before he succumbed he hurled his bat at a rising ball in a desperate effort at a blind hook.

At twenty minutes to twelve Barnett fell, much as Hutton fell— another reflex prod at a ball from McCormick, which came up abruptly to his stomach. And so England lost three wickets for 31, lost them because of open and unashamed dislike of the occasional fast ball which drops a little short. Nobody's head was threatened during these disasters. Barnett remained at, or contiguous to, the wicket for half an hour.

In a terrible silence Hammond set himself to retrieve the heavy hour, with Paynter his honest henchman. McCormick paled his fires, and Fleetwood-Smith and O'Reilly came on. From Fleetwood-Smith's first ball Hammond hit a great four to the on, a late, forcing blow from a good length. Apparently he had no room for the execution of such a stroke, but he wonderfully made room. A full-toss in the same over was consigned to the boundary, straight and disdainfully. When McCormick rested his analysis was six overs, no maidens, eighteen runs, three wickets—a case of almost fast, erratic bowling and unhappy, unnerving batting. Fleetwood-Smith and O'Reilly could not spin or even keep a length.

Hammond played serene cricket, masterful without the least show of aggression, powerful yet reserved. He was a grand sight, the captain of English cricket wearing his robes modestly, remembering only that he was our best batsman and our hope and stay. He drove Fleetwood-Smith and O'Reilly in front of the wicket for fours which were perfect in poise, resonant fours, strong in the arm. Magnificent fielding by Fingleton frustrated one of his major hits, but in the same over he dismissed another half-volley by Fleetwood-Smith from his presence. Paynter put his Lancashire bat to the ball, watchful and entirely untroubled. At the crisis he was as imperturbable as Oswaldtwistle in a bowler hat. The Australian attack lost grip with surprising swiftness. The visitor to the ground arriving now would have questioned the evidence of the score-board; surely these two batsmen were on a winning side, surely the Australians were uneasy of mind and hot and perspiring of body. The fielding was not in the ruthless Australian tradition. Fingleton and Brown and Bradman flashed now and again, but we did not get the old sense of barbed-wire entanglements round the wicket. There were, on the other hand, a few solid sandbags. Hammond reached fifty in an hour, and seldom have I seen him more at ease than this in a Test match in England. It was a throne-room innings. Paynter smote Fleetwood-Smith to leg for six, a terrific crack as much as to say: 'Aye, and we can have our bit of fun in t'scullery too, and Ah'm always telling thi mother so.'

When McCormick returned to the attack just after one o'clock he was a spent force, a pop-gun with the mainspring gone, a man hurling remnants of physical effort against a door that was not there. In some ninety minutes the stand by Hammond and Paynter became worth a hundred runs, and at lunch England had emerged from the ruins of 31 for three to the eminence of 134 for three. I have not often known a match change atmosphere as abruptly as this one this morning. Crisis passed from England's innings like the bad dream which all of us wake up from, breathing relief that we are comfortably and respectably in bed and not walking in shame about the city streets with no trousers on. Hammond, not out 70 at the interval, played greatly and deserved better bowling. Paynter enjoyed some luck; when he was six he sliced over the slips against the spin. But, like Hammond, he got over the ball for the most part. The pitch eased as the moisture dried, but the dire situation of England was salvaged mainly because the batsmen kept close to their bats and did not use them telescopically.

Before the game was resumed at a quarter-past two the King shook hands with the players, and Earl Baldwin accompanied him. I liked Hammond's bow; it was as handsome as his innings. The ground put forward a magnificent sight. The sunshine blessed all, King and people. A gentle breeze rippled the green leaves beyond the Nursery; this was Lord's in June, with London spread round us. If Hitler could have looked upon the scene probably he would have said, 'Still kicking the cricket ball about.'

A glorious flick to leg by Hammond off Fleetwood-Smith enchanted us; and a mighty straight drive by Hammond off a no-ball by O'Reilly thrilled us. It was a joy to see Hammond at the crown in a Test match again. And Paynter in his own way was as capital; he played a ball from McCormick down for a four through the slips with time to spare, and the applause rattled like a machine-gun's enfilading. O'Reilly tried his arm at the Nursery end, from which the slope of the ground would help a leg-break. But he could not spin a leg-break with his venom of four years ago. From time to time McCormick was able to lift the ball hip high, even after lunch; but his length and direction still wandered vagrantly; a great fast bowler would have loved the wicket. A delicate glance to leg for four by Paynter said to us in plain Lancashire, 'Aye, and we can behave well-off in t'scullery an' all, Ah'm tellin' thi.' An over by McCormick hereabouts comprised two full-tosses, a no-ball, two long-hops, and one ball whose length I could not define.

Paynter attained his fifty with a mighty pull off another no-ball, this time by O'Reilly, who toiled hard and scarcely ever compelled the batsmen to reconsider first thoughts. At 174 for three McCabe was resorted to for a change, old ball at that. I thought now that only by some absence of mind on the part of Hammond or Paynter would another wicket fall. The attack seemed to live entirely on hope and perseverance. Not a ball beat the bat for hours. When Chipperfield bowled again Paynter hit him straight; the bowler half-stopped the blow, but it thundered for four. The next ball sped to the off boundary; Paynter was helping himself before the new ball arrived. Then Hammond came to his century, after two hours and twenty-five minutes of unflawed play, ripe as the harvest. A brilliant square-cut by Paynter off Fleetwood-Smith celebrated England's 200, still for three wickets. And in the following over, wheeled up by Chipperfield, Paynter cut again for four, sweet and late, and flicked a leg ball saucy as a kitten for four. Paynter was at this period brilliant, a gorgeous mixture of brawn and celerity, humorous, yet in the eyes of the bowlers no laughing matter. Every over the crowd roared home the fours. Fingleton ran and fielded gloriously, but not once did we see a good ball. Either the attack was unequal to one or the batsmen declined to allow one. Both Hammond and Paynter were leaving their ground with impunity. Not until the score was 223 was the new ball claimed. McCormick endeavoured to begin again. His third ball, a no-ball, went for four to the on. Hammond threatened to smash his bat in two in the lust for power.

Paynter paused in the nineties, but was safe enough. He arrived at 99, and the packed thousands took in large amounts of breath, ready to roar. He was leg-before-wicket, and approbation expired in a sad, pricked bladder. O'Reilly sent a quick ball, knowing Paynter would try a glance for a single. Paynter missed aim, and walked to the pavilion with noble sounds of acclamation and sympathy following him. For a little more than three hours he had held the fort in one of the finest innings of his life, an innings chock full of grit, skill, and character. 'A grand little chap,' said the crowd, which he is. After lunch Paynter scored faster than Hammond—proof enough of the form he was in.

Compton, like Edrich, failed through the impetuosity of the young; he hit recklessly across a length ball from O'Reilly and was leg-before. And so, after all, England were not happily placed at a quarter-past four, for 271 for five is not a good score against Bradman, McCabe and the others. The Australians sought to thrive on their fresh situation; the bowling looked up and McCabe surprisingly got life out of the wicket— which will misbehave itself on the fourth day if no rain gently falls. McCabe even spun a leg-break at Ames, and a very good leg-break it was. Hammond scrutinized the spot on which McCabe achieved his vitality, then hit McCabe for a sumptuous four to square-leg. But Hammond had to move responsibly after Paynter's mishap; at tea he was 139 and the score 283 for five. He scored 69 in two hours ten minutes between lunch and tea.

Ames was sensibly satisfied to defend when he joined Hammond; once again the attack missed a chance, but it was a tiring attack by this time and probably watched Hammond's and Ames's gentle scoring with the emotion of relief. O'Reilly, I fancied, bowled better at the day's end than at the beginning. But he has much ground to recover before he regains the powers which not long ago made him the finest of his kind in contemporary cricket. Still, he contrived to keep Hammond tolerably quiet this evening at a time when Hammond might have smitten the weary bowlers hip and thigh. Possibly Hammond was wanting a rest, too. All day he had carried a burden, and with a calm which hid from us the weight and magnitude of it. He came to his 200 just before close of play as easily and as majestically as a liner coming into port.

LORD'S, SATURDAY, JUNE 25TH

Irony has played with the Australians this afternoon in the second Test. Fingleton and Brown gave to their innings a solid foundation; each played confidently, almost affably. In an hour England's attack assumed the aspect of resignation. Then Wright bowled his one and only dangerous ball of the day, a spinner which drew Fingleton forward and found the edge of the bat. A case of good cricket. Brown, serene as a post, awaited Bradman; obviously he was going to stay there for hours, ready to keep guard while somebody attacked. Bradman, after a few of those pushes forward which he nowadays strangely exploits in Test matches, began to score at ease. He suddenly pulled a ball from Verity into his stumps. Stupefaction visited all of us; Bradman was a bewildered as well as a disgusted cricketer as he returned to the pavilion.

Now came McCabe, in form at once, prepared to loft his great hook but sure of aim. The English bowling and fielding wavered. Brown went on with his vigil—he was safe enough. McCabe was on the crest of his ability when he cut Farnes to the gully, a blinding stroke. Verity close up, as a good gully should always be, flung himself earthwards and held a catch which none of us could believe in until we saw McCabe walking away. The crowd had unloosed pandemonium at the mishap to Bradman; they roared McCabe out of sight as though the rubber now was England's. Good cricket again.

ENGLAND
First Innings

Hutton, c Brown, b McCormick	4
Barnett, c Brown, b McCormick	18
Edrich, b McCormick	0
W. R. Hammond, b McCormick	240
Paynter, lbw, b O'Reilly	99
Compton, lbw, b O'Reilly	6
Ames, c McCormick, b Fleetwood-Smith	83
Verity, b O'Reilly	5
Wellard, c McCormick, b O'Reilly	4
Wright, b Fleetwood-Smith	6
K. Farnes, not out	5
B 1, lb 12, w 1, nb 10	24
Total	494

AUSTRALIA
First Innings

J. H. Fingleton, c Hammond, b Wright	31
W. A. Brown, not out	140
D. G. Bradman, b Verity	18
S. J. McCabe, c Verity, b Farnes	38
A. L. Hassett, lbw, b Wellard	56
C. L. Badcock, b Wellard	0
B. A. Barnett, not out	6
B 1, lb 5, nb 4	10
Total (for five wickets)	299

To bat: W. J. O'Reilly, E. L. McCormick, A. G. Chipperfield and L. O'B. Fleetwood-Smith.

FALL OF THE WICKETS
ENGLAND—First Innings

1	2	3	4	5	6	7	8	9	10
12	20	31	253	271	457	472	476	483	494

AUSTRALIA—First Innings

1	2	3	4	5
69	101	152	276	276

BOWLING ANALYSIS
ENGLAND—First Innings

	O.	M.	R.	W.		O.	M.	R.	W.
McCormick	27	1	101	4	O'Reilly	37	6	93	4
McCabe	31	4	86	0	Chipperfield	9	0	51	0
F.-Smith	33.5	2	139	2					

McCabe bowled one wide; McCormick nine no-balls; O'Reilly one no-ball.

AUSTRALIA—First Innings (to date)

	O.	M.	R.	W.		O.	M.	R.	W.
Farnes	28	3	99	1	Verity	25	8	59	1
Wellard	17	1	67	2	Edrich	4	2	5	0
Wright	14	2	59	1					

Wright bowled four no-balls.

But in less than half an hour Hassett and Brown created the sense of anticlimax. Neither found much in the bowling to disturb the elegant rhythm of their strokes. Silence descended on the multitude like Sancho Panza's cloak of sleep, but it was a cloak of disappointment really. An hour passed by, and another half-hour. The evening sunshine touched the ground with a soft glow—the bloom which falls on London in the evening was at hand, the bloom which no other city in the world knows, a cadence of atmosphere and light, of colour in sky and stone. Just before six o'clock Hammond asked Wellard to bowl once more. Poor Wellard had so far been only a willing toiler. His first ball, when Hammond resorted to him at this late hour, probably for want of something better to do, was cut for four enthusiastically by Hassett; the third ball hit Hassett's pads, and Hassett was lbw to a straight ball which he missed—just missed, simply that and nothing more. In the same over Badcock played back to a half-volley and was absurdly bowled. I wish to do justice to Wellard, but this was the luckiest over I have ever seen bowled in a Test match. It changed the day. It gave England a chance. Much hard work remains to be done, but the Australians, who are never slow to look facts in the face, realize that they are again in a corner. England's attack may not be capable of consistent deadliness, but there is the Lord's wicket, which on any fourth day is bound to wear at least a little. I do not think that Hammond will ask the Australians to follow on if they do not save it.

The morale of the afternoon for the searcher after the humour of events is this. If Bradman had not chopped into his own stumps Australia by now would probably be in a strong position—300 for one wicket—and history would probably be ready with a ripple of laughter to turn back to a page written at Lord's in 1930, when Australia went in against England's 425 and won by scoring 729 for six. Even yet we might easily look back in time, to four years ago, when Verity on a sticky wicket won the match for England at Lord's.

On a lovely morning of warm wind and sun, Lord's made an imposing sight again. The gates were closed before eleven o'clock, and when the players took the field Hammond and Bradman consulted with the umpires about the crowd, which threatened to overflow the boundary line like the encroaching seas. As soon as the match continued, a pigeon was to be observed strutting well within the playing space; what is more, it threatened to enter the pavilion, and heavens!—it was possibly a woman. Fortunately for tradition and etiquette the pigeon veered respectfully to the left.

The wicket was thoroughly easy, and in vain did McCormick strive to give to the ball an awkward rise. Hammond took up his innings from where he was interrupted last evening, though now he was even more magnificent than at any time yesterday. Using all the proportion I can muster, I declare that Hammond today batted with an ease and style beyond anything he has ever done before; more handsome cricket could not be imagined. He drove almost nonchalantly. The swift velocity of his late cuts seemed an optical illusion, because of the leisurely poise of his body. The wrists were supple as the fencer's steel; the light, effortless, yet thrilling movements of his bat suggested that he had now reached the cadenze of his full-toned and full-sized concerto with orchestra. (I apologize to the purists who resent musical analogies in a cricket report. I have forsworn them for years, but when the game is lifted into music by the art of a glorious cricketer, then I cannot deny the habits of a lifetime.) The innings of the master came to a fitting end. And the cadenza, he put forward a reposeful stroke, missed the ball and was bowled by McCormick. A bruise on the elbow probably incommoded him. It would be high treason to suggest he was dismissed. He withdrew, or let us say, the wheel came full circle. The scene when he came back to the pavilion was surely the grandest tribute ever paid to a cricketer at Lord's. Thirty thousand voices hailed him, and the pavilion stood up and waited for him as he walked home head down and modest.

Ames played excellently in the shadow cast by the sun. Many of his hits were beautifully clean. He did his side much service at a dangerous point in the innings. The ball which got him out was the best bowled so far in the match; Fleetwood-Smith spun it like a top. I hated the sight of it and wished England's total was six hundred. The rearguard this morning failed to consolidate, as the militarists say, the position. The innings ended in howls of merriment. Bradman gave a juggling performance and missed a catch. Farnes endeavoured to hit into Maida Vale, and a terrific skier from a no-ball attracted a whole nest of Australian fieldsmen. Somebody's cap flew off; and

Fingleton deliberately missed the catch and then made fierce gestures of disgust and self-flagellation—to bamboozle the crowd. I did not think a deal of Wellard's innings; he merely 'slogged' and hit high. McCormick caught him with admirable judgment; England had not scored enough runs to allow of so much agricultural nonsense as all this.

Fingleton and Brown made 69 together for Australia's first wicket in less than sixty minutes. For a while Farnes bowled at less than a fast bowler's speed, and he pitched a medium-paced bowler's length frequently. He seemed amiable after McCormick's heroic disregard of the erratic. There is much to be said for an erratic fast bowler. Wright, for a while, kept the ball well up to the bat, and he alone during the first hour of Australia's innings gave the batsmen the slightest trouble. Many times did Fingleton steer Farnes between short-leg and forward-leg; he played this on-side push dexterously. Brown, after one or two speculative traffickings with off-side balls, allowed his innings to grow in the sweet air, confidently as a plant. Bradman sat on the balcony watching the course of things; he wore pads, but I thought he was wearing them formally. The slip catch by Hammond which accounted for Fingleton was a model of balance in spite of the fact that Hammond was suffering from a strained thigh. Fingleton chewed his nether lip as he left the field, where a moment ago he had been so happy.

Bradman turned Farnes audaciously to leg, and in the same over hit him for one of the greatest boundaries of his career, an incredible square-thrust to the on. He groped forward at Wright once or twice; he left the Hindenburg Line of his back foot. I was surprised to see Wright taken off now, for Verity. Australia, at a quarter-past three, was 100 for one; Bradman was seeing the ball almost before the bowler saw it. He bent down to perform an intimate late cut from a rather wide ball which probably came in a little with Verity's arm; it was not a difficult ball, and Bradman is still at a loss to account for his mistimed stroke. But it is good for cricket that accidents should occasionally happen even to Bradman. When he got out the entire crowd stood up to stretch limbs; then everybody sat down, to begin a new match, almost a new life.

Verity used two slips, which was either bluff or significant of a slight dustiness on the wicket. McCabe hooked him loftily for four and flicked him to the on for three, without a sign of effort. He pulled Wellard over short-leg for four and then hit him for six, risking deep mid-on; the stroke was, again, without a sign of effort. Another four, off Verity and off McCabe's pads, defied pursuit. Brown arrived at his fifty, a steady train keeping to time. He played a bad stroke through the slips when he was 54, off Farnes, nearly a chance to Hammond, but proceeded on his way unmoved—a cow on the line, or something. McCabe's innings lived gloriously on the rim; he was ready to take chances. Wright bowled once more, and McCabe pulled and hooked for fours from the first two balls. At ten minutes to four Verity held his catch and saved England a hundred smashing runs.

Verity bowled skilfully, but Wright committed the worst fault of a leg-spin bowler, which is the short length. Farnes was, as usual, subject to strange rises and falls in the temperature of his attack. After he had obtained McCabe's wicket he bestirred himself like a man who had received an injection. He put Brown through a difficult quarter of an hour; Brown indeed, was lucky when he dithered in the nineties; several times he edged or flicked against his own wishes. Hassett was excellent, sound, and surprisingly over the ball for a player of his slight inches. He hooked Farnes and cut him late. But, with his score 32 and Australia's 224 for three, he sent a sharp chance, off Farnes, to Wellard at forward square-leg.

The clouds which had been coming up the heavens passed by, and the afternoon burgeoned. Brown came to his century, his second in consecutive Test matches at Lord's. He was admirably cool, save for the bad patch I have mentioned. His cricket did not strike the eye of the crowd probably, but there was craftsmanship for the connoisseur. And the innings had immense value to his side. I have seldom seen a young man play the veteran's part as easefully as Brown played it today. He and Hassett added 124 in some ninety minutes. Badcock blundered, as I say, against a straight half-volley. The day ended with Barnett entrenched behind Brown's fortifications. Australia, despite unexpected and serious reverses, scored 299 runs in just under four and a half hours.

A grand spectacle during the afternoon was Edrich bowling fast, and trying to bowl faster than anybody else since the world began. He is, as they say, square-armed; he hurls himself at the wicket, prepared to break his neck, back and bootlaces. If he failed to let go the ball he would probably propel himself out of sight. I imagine that when close of play came the groundsman found bootnails in the wicket, and bits of leather and buttons and goodness knows what. I cannot understand how the batsmen see his bowling in the general disturbance he creates. As soon as stumps were drawn a terrific wind blew over the field, scattering newspapers everywhere and suggesting a hurricane and the end of the world. It was, I think, the draught caused by Edrich.

SECOND TEST (THIRD DAY)
ENGLAND

First Innings		Second Innings	
Hutton, c Brown, b McCormick	4	c McCormick, b O'Reilly	5
Barnett, c Brown, b McCormick	18	c McCabe, b McCormick	12
Edrich, b McCormick	0	not out	6
W. R. Hammond, b McCormick	240		
Paynter, lbw, b O'Reilly	99		
Compton, lbw, b O'Reilly	6		
Ames, c McCormick, b F.-Smith	83		
Verity, b O'Reilly	5	not out	5
Wellard, c McCormick, b O'Reilly	4		
Wright, b Fleetwood-Smith	6		
K. Farnes, not out	5		
B 1, lb 12, w 1, nb 10	24	B 7, w 1, nb 3	11
Total	494	Total (for two wickets)	39

AUSTRALIA
First Innings

J. H. Fingleton, c Hammond, b Wright	31
W. A. Brown, not out	206
D. G. Bradman, b Verity	18
S. J. McCabe, c Verity, b Farnes	38
A. L. Hassett, lbw, b Wellard	56
C. L. Badcock, b Wellard	0
B. A. Barnett, c Compton, b Verity	8
A. G. Chipperfield, lbw, b Verity	1
W. J. O'Reilly, b Farnes	42
E. L. McCormick, c Barnett, b Farnes	0
L. O'B. Fleetwood-Smith, c Barnett, b Verity	7
B 1, lb 8, nb 6	15
Total	422

FALL OF THE WICKETS
ENGLAND—First Innings

1	2	3	4	5	6	7	8	9	10
12	20	31	253	271	457	472	476	483	494

Second Innings

1	2
25	28

AUSTRALIA—First Innings

1	2	3	4	5	6	7	8	9	10
69	101	152	276	276	307	308	393	393	422

BOWLING ANALYSIS

ENGLAND—First Innings

	O.	M.	R.	W.		O.	M.	R.	W.
McCormick	27	1	101	4	O'Reilly	37	6	93	4
McCabe	31	4	86	0	Chipperfield	9	0	51	0
F.-Smith	33.5	2	139	2					

McCabe bowled one wide; McCormick nine no-balls; O'Reilly one no-ball.

Second Innings (to date)

	O.	M.	R.	W.		O.	M.	R.	W.
McCormick	7	1	16	1	O'Reilly	6	2	12	1

McCormick bowled one wide and two no-balls; O'Reilly bowled one no-ball.

AUSTRALIA—First Innings

	O.	M.	R.	W.		O.	M.	R.	W.
Farnes	43	6	135	3	Verity	35.4	9	103	4
Wellard	23	2	96	2	Edrich	4	2	5	0
Wright	16	2	68	1					

Wright bowled six no-balls.

LORD'S, MONDAY, JUNE 27TH

The weather has prevented more than three hours' cricket in the Test today, but we have seen some fun. Australia fought to the end of her innings with all the old resolution, and England missed the chance to force home a strong advantage. The seventh Australian wicket fell at 308, and Brown's only helpmates were O'Reilly, McCormick and Fleetwood-Smith, each of them a born bowler, each less a batsman than a conventional position in the order of going in. O'Reilly, as a fact, played a fine innings, in which he not only drove gigantically but, once or twice, performed a cut in style. Verity pitched the length O'Reilly likes; he strangely did not bowl to O'Reilly from over the wicket. I fancy that if he had done so, and swung the ball away from O'Reilly's bat, O'Reilly would have been unable to reach it and also unable to resist trying.

Australia's last three wickets scored 114, so that in the end the balance in England's favour was merely 72. More than that, the last-minute rally, and the rain, imperilled England's position; when Hutton and Barnett batted at half-past five their severe duty was to avoid disaster, as much as it was to get runs, on a turf which

209

enabled a quick ball to rear more than a little. England this evening were obliged, indeed, to think of pushing for victory and of holding off trouble at one and the same time. Barnett and Hutton both lost their wickets endeavouring sorely to save them, and Edrich nearly played on to McCormick and was nearly knocked over by Mc-Cormick, and Verity was missed at second slip off O'Reilly's spin. All in all, half-past six came mercifully in time. But given fine weather tonight the match may be anybody's tomorrow—if Hammond is not Hammond at his strongest again it may be Australia's after all, bless us and protect us.

Brown carried his bat through the Australian innings. It was a bat of exemplary straightness. His craftsmanship was polished, in spite of a few edges through the slips. For all his youthfulness, he was as old in the head as John Nyren's *Guide to the Elegant and Gentlemanly Art of Cricket*. Brown's innings deserved the top-hat of Hambledon. His coolness and the easy way he took charge, after the fall of Bradman and McCabe, were proof of character. The English bowlers did their very best to nourish his admirable stroke-play to leg. Australia could regard with satisfaction a total of 422, compiled in spite of purely nominal contributions from Bradman and McCabe.

Again the crowd packed the ground. The gates were closed before eleven o'clock. Streams of people were propelled through the turnstiles, everybody looking almost as anxious as refugees leaving a city threatened by a devouring army. And from nine o'clock until play began the populace sat and waited, while up in the heavens another Test match was going on between wind and rain. Now the skies darkened, and a faint shower came. Then the wind blew away the wrack of cloud. The trees tossed about their uneasy branches, the weather-cock on the grandstand swayed until Father Time seemed not to know where he was. But, mercifully, the game began promptly, and on a wicket still easy Brown and Barnett continued Australia's innings.

For some dark reason Barnett threw his wicket away trying to drive high and hard into the distance; he let fly at a good-length ball from Verity, and Compton beautifully caught a towering mis-hit on the off side. Chipperfield with his injured hand came next, and was immediately deceived by Verity's flight and pace, and departed leg-before. On the Australian balcony a little toy kangaroo, the mascot, looked wistfully on the field, and Fingleton stroked its back in hopefulness and sympathy. There were other charms and mascots on the balcony; propitiatory of the unfriendly gods. Brown snicked a ball

210

from Farnes behind his back and did not know its direction; O'Reilly clouted Verity for four and took his nose disdainfully away from a rising fast one from Farnes. He lifted Verity to long-off; the ball bounced into the crowd, causing a splash of arms and sticks and umbrellas. Paynter could not catch another mighty thump of O'Reilly's to long-off, a difficult chance needing a trapeze artist. Brown batted with a nicely posed responsibility, and Farnes too often bowled to leg and aided and abetted Brown's favourite stroke, a glance fine and quick. And soon as Wellard came on Brown pulled a long hop almost vindictively.

An over by Verity gave O'Reilly 16 runs, two sixes and a four, colossal heaves with whatever break Verity imparted. Next over, wheeled down by Wellard in the style of Bath Association on Saturday afternoon, Brown drove two fours to the off so easily that he might have been concealing a yawn. The English attack wilted. Wright saw O'Reilly missed on purpose off a no-ball; then he bowled O'Reilly, but it was another no-ball; and the crowd found itself twice taken in and rendered hoarse for nothing. One of O'Reilly's hits, a back-footed cover drive off Farnes, was good enough for the incomparable Woolley. The stand by O'Reilly and Brown added 85 in forty-five minutes; moreover O'Reilly achieved his highest innings in a Test match. It was a stand of importance, calculated to annoy thousands, including Hammond, who saw England's opportunity slipping away. He would not have put Australia in again even if they had collapsed entirely. But he wanted every run—the longest possible lead. Compton missed Fleetwood-Smith in the slips; England were not clinching the issue. I wondered what would have happend to our attack if Bradman had hammered it; even during the O'Reilly foray the bowlers lost control and suffered disruption.

At half-past twelve the rain won in the battle of elements above; the crowd huddled themselves under draughty walls, some queer bodies sat on in the downpour. In all the misery I heard somebody deploring not his own state but the fact that Compton's missed catch had robbed Farnes of a 'hat-trick'. No doubt a hat trick consisting of O'Reilly, McCormick and Fleetwood-Smith would have made a record of an unusual order.

Play was surprisingly possible again at a quarter-past four. Brown then reached his two hundred amidst applause so generous that he might well have though he was for the moment back at Brisbane. The English bowlers could not get Fleetwood-Smith out for forty-five minutes—valuable time filched from England; more annoyance for all patriotic hearts.

Before England's second innings could begin showers drove the players back and forward until they probably felt dizzier than folk lost in the maze at Hampton Court. The crowd howled for cricket, but maybe Hammond was not with them. The wicket, slightly resilient on top, was likely to send McCormick's fast bowling flying upwards and about the batsmen's wrists and vitals. Granted no further rain, the pitch would roll out comfortably enough in the morning; suppose McCormick were to snatch two or three or four good English wickets this afternoon before close of play? That was the question Hammond no doubt pondered when at last the weather cleare and permittedd Barnett and Hutton to face the music.

We quickly were allowed to savour the irony of England's lot now. Barnett and Hutton scored 25 more or less ruefully, until a good-length ball from McCormick rose abruptly, though not unreasonably high, and forced Barnett to send a slip catch. A few moments afterwards a gorgeous leg-spinner, pitched on the wicket and whipping away, confounded Hutton. The young men of England, born to easy living at Nottingham, have so far in this match been taught philosophy. Other studies and instruction in the school of the Stoics may be conducted tomorrow.

SECOND TEST (FOURTH DAY)

ENGLAND

First Innings		Second Innings	
Hutton, c Brown, b McCormick	4	c McCormick, b O'Reilly	5
Barnett, c Brown, b McCormick	18	c McCabe, b McCormick	12
Edrich, b McCormick	0	c McCabe, b McCormick	10
W. R. Hammond, b McCormick	240	c sub, b MacCabe	2
Paynter, lbw, b O'Reilly	99	run out	43
Compton, lbw, b O'Reilly	6	not out	76
Ames, c McCormick, b F.-Smith	83	c McCabe, b O'Reilly	6
Verity, b O'Reilly	5	b McCormick	11
Wellard, c McCormick, b O'Reilly	4	b McCabe	38
Wright, b Fleetwood-Smith	6	not out	10
K. Farnes, not out	5		
B 1, lb 12, w 1, nb 10	24	B 12, lb 12, nb 4	28
Total	494	Total (for eight declared)	242

AUSTRALIA

First Innings		Second Innings	
J. H. Fingleton, c Hammond, b Wright	31	c Hammond, b Wellard	4
W. A. Brown, not out	206	b Verity	10
D. G. Bradman, b Verity	18	not out	102
S. J. McCabe, c Verity, b Farnes	38	c Hutton, b Verity	21
A. L. Hassett, lbw, b Wellard	56	b Wright	42
C. L. Badcock, b Wellard	0	c Wright, b Edrich	0
B. A. Barnett, c Compton, b Verity	8	c Paynter, b Edrich	14
A. G. Chipperfield, lbw, b Verity	1		
W. J. O'Reilly, b Farnes	42		
E. L. McCormick, c Barnett, b Farnes	0		
L. O'B. Fleetwood-Smith, c Barnett, b Verity	7		
B 1, lb 8, nb 6	15	B 5, lb 3, w 2, nb 1	11
Total	422	Total (for six wickets)	204

FALL OF THE WICKETS

ENGLAND—First Innings

1	2	3	4	5	6	7	8	9	10
12	20	31	253	271	457	472	476	483	494

Second Innings

1	2	3	4	5	6	7	8
25	28	43	64	76	128	142	216

AUSTRALIA—First Innings

1	2	3	4	5	6	7	8	9	10
69	101	152	276	276	307	308	393	393	422

Second Innings

1	2	3	4	5	6
8	71	111	175	180	204

BOWLING ANALYSIS

ENGLAND—First Innings

	O.	M.	R.	W.		O.	M.	R.	W.
McCormick	27	1	101	4	O'Reilly	37	6	93	4
McCabe	31	4	86	0	Chipperfield	9	0	51	0
F.-Smith	33.5	2	139	2					

McCabe bowled one wide; McCormick nine no-balls; O'Reilly one no-ball.

Second Innings

	O.	M.	R.	W.		O.	M.	R.	W.
McCormick	24	5	72	3	McCabe	12	1	58	2
O'Reilly	29	10	53	2	F.-Smith	7	1	30	0

McCormick bowled one wide and three no-balls; O'Reilly one no-ball.

AUSTRALIA—First Innings

	O.	M.	R.	W.		O.	M.	R.	W.
Farnes	43	6	135	3	Verity	35.4	9	103	4
Wellard	23	2	96	2	Edrich	4	2	5	0
Wright	16	2	68	1					

Wright bowled six no-balls.

Second Innings

	O.	M.	R.	W.		O.	M.	R.	W.
Farnes	13	3	51	0	Wright	8	0	56	1
Wellard	9	1	30	1	Edrich	5.2	0	27	2
Verity	13	5	29	2					

Farnes bowled one wide; Wellard one wide and one no-ball.

LORD'S, TUESDAY, JUNE 28TH

Before the second Test match came to an exciting draw England was thrust to the wall this morning, and a young boy of Middlesex forced the way out not by fisticuffs but by elegant gestures of persuasion. The score was 76 for five when he went in to bat and 128 for six when Paynter ran himself out. Moreover, the lame Hammond was back in the pavilion and lunch had not come; Australia could win in the time which remained, and, I think, would have won but for Compton. His cricket foretold a luminous future. Wellard also contributed to the rescue work, and Paynter, as usual, was ready with a hand or a fist or two. But it was mortifying to see the need for salvage at all for England. We have had the Australians twice now in the grip which asks for only one more gentle twist to clinch an issue. When are we going to defeat them, and how, after our advantages at Nottingham and Lord's? Frankly, I think we have missed our chance in the rubber. Bradman has yet to play his real Test-match-winning masterpieces, and they are on the way. And we cannot expect to win the toss every time.

England's batting this morning was deplorable. The Australian attack could, apart from McCormick, do nothing. Yet even McCabe for a long time was regarded with awe. Apparently many of our batsmen can deal with fast bowling in two ways only—the blind hook or the myopic grope towards the slips. Once again we must congratulate the Australians on their own remarkable ability to counter-attack from the last ditch. When yesterday I prophesied some trouble for England today I was told I was a pessimist. But I know the Australians—I have known them from my boyhood.

On the fourth morning, which promised the best day's cricket of the match, the crowd was merely numerous, not a multitude. Everybody could walk about the ground in comfort; there was no need now to regard the members of the M.C.C. as bloatedly privileged and see them like so many capitalists straight out of a drawing by Will Dyson, with two cigars in the mouth.

An English disaster occurred at once. McCormick's first ball soared over Edrich's head; then Edrich hooked a short one for four. The last ball, another short, rising length, said in unmistakable Australian: 'Now hook that, my lad, if you can.' And Edrich attempted to hook, head down. McCabe, at forward square-leg, caught him out with ease. Edrich played gallantly on Monday evening, but he should not today have allowed his favourite hit to lead him so openly into the Australian trap. McCormick bowled at a rare pace, very rare nowadays, and several times Verity fortunately could not time velocity on the off side. Paynter heartened us with two capital leg-glances for fours off O'Reilly, who could not, thank heaven, make his spin turn viciously. Another wicket to Australia at this point would, we all knew as well as Bradman, mean a struggling English team.

Verity defended admirably, as he did on Monday's flying pitch. It was much easier now; though not always reliable. But when Verity tried to score he journeyed beyond his territory, and a slice through the slips was terribly fortuitous, or, in Paynter's more English English, 'off t'edge'. Another four by Paynter, a lusty clout from a full toss by O'Reilly, was enough to make the pavilion cat laugh; but the little kangaroo on the Australian balcony watched the stroke with some disdain. At ten minutes past twelve McCormick knocked Verity's off stump out of the ground, and instead of coming from the field he stayed in the middle of the wicket and consulted with Bradman. Optimists thought Bradman was telling, as most of us have wished to be told when we have had our wickets shattered, that it was all a mistake. But no; they were only arranging for a runner for Hammond, whose strained leg was not yet better. Verity's innings deserved praise; he probably saved other and more technical batsmen, though none could well be more academic than Verity, who holds himself at the wicket as though in degree-day gown and mortar-board.

215

A snick by Paynter off McCormick nearly undid him. The crowd gasped, then silently watched Hammond, who obviously batted under a serious physical handicap. He could not play forward strongly. He pushed once at O'Reilly like a man moving on a cork leg. O'Reilly sent a fine over to Paynter at half-past twelve. He beat the bat with a leg-break, and Paynter put his hand to his mouth to conceal a broad grin, which in the circumstances might have seemed irreverent.

Tragedy overwhelmed us now—McCabe bowled for McCormick, and Hammond, pinned down by his injury, scooped helplessly at a potential full-toss, with one hand, and lobbed a catch to short square-leg. He came back to the pavilion with Verity by his side— like blind Samson. England 76 for five—where now were the reserve of runs thrown away by England during the O'Reilly windstorm of Monday? The wonder was that Hammond attempted a forcing stroke at all. Paynter was missed at first slip almost before Hammond could have got his pads off—and from McCabe of all bowlers. The English innings had become suddenly unnerved, as though suffering from vertigo because of a glimpse of a terrible chasm from a height.

Fleetwood-Smith bowled instead of O'Reilly when England was 84 for five, and Compton cut a short ball brilliantly for four. Compton hit two fours in one over from McCabe, excellent and youthfully eager strokes. The game had arrived at the crucial pivot. Bradman gambled with Fleetwood-Smith—he might easily give runs away and put Australia behind the clock. On the other hand, he might run through the side. Bradman, of course, had no great reserve of bowling to support his spearhead McCormick and the steady infantry of O'Reilly. Compton played perfect cricket in this searching period. He used his feet instinctively; his strokes were sound and pretty. He is, I think, likely to go much further than Edrich—he has style and temperament. Bradman declined to trust Fleetwood-Smith. O'Reilly was brought back, for the stand of Paynter and Compton was too quickly (for Bradman) putting England in a position from which to dictate terms.

And now we were sickened. Paynter pulled a poor-length ball from O'Reilly to leg, where Fleetwood-Smith misfielded. Paynter went for a second run and was run out, a frightful blunder. Misfielding should never be trusted. Besides what was the value of a paltry single addition to England's score at such a point in the affairs of the match? When England's sixth wicket fell England was only 200 ahead, and the pitch was good enough for a batsman good as Bradman or McCabe. Ames, with a damaged finger, was caught straight-way after lunch in the slips off McCormick, and England was 142 for seven with four hours to go.

Compton demonstrated how to hook McCormick; he was a model for several of his colleagues. A 'hoick' to leg spoiled the poise of his innings momentarily; but he told eloquently of a great and delightful cricketer in the making. He drove a half-volley from McCormick straight for four and played bumpers down by standing up on his toes. An innings of the highest skill and most likeable flavour. Twice he pulled McCormick for four off consecutive balls; this was the game England needed. Bradman gambled again with Fleetwood-Smith at twenty minutes to three, when England was 244 in front; a few enormous blows by Wellard would place England in a safe way. A delicate persuasion to leg made Compton's score 50, and no young man, playing for England against advancing Australians, could have done better or looked more like a picture of a young man in the part.

Wellard clove and propelled Fleetwood-Smith for three fours in an over, and then Bradman asked McCabe to bowl at Wellard, short and rather to the off, an excellent thing in theory. But Wellard apparently had not read the books on theory, and he hit McCabe for six and four without any show of intellect whatever. McCabe seized the new ball, and Wellard tried to stun it at once into old age. He was bowled in the attempt, but his six boundaries and a six in three-quarters of an hour had served the State and replenished the bank-rupt coffers. He and Compton added 74, the retort brutal to yester-day's outrage by O'Reilly; they actually enabled Hammond to declare the innings closed and leave to Australia the task of scoring 315 for victory in two and three-quarter hours. Compton was un-defeated, and he committed only one dangerous stroke. Taking all things into consideration, the state of the game when he came in, his inexperience and youth, his cricket can be called the finest of the match, after, of course, Hammond's. I have just made this statement to Wilfred Rhodes, and he has shaken hands on it.

Australia began badly whatever policy they had in view. Wellard attacked with a speed and hostility never once seen in his bowling on Saturday. Fingleton touched a vehement out-swinger, and Paynter, keeping wicket in place of Ames, hurled all of himself across and perhaps deflected the ball to Hammond, who caught it amazingly, with as little concern as a conjurer who before breaking an egg into a hot tosses it up into the air for our inspection.

217

Bradman's innings opened uncertainly. He received a rising ball from Farnes with displeasure, and turned another hazardously to leg, then nearly touched an out-swinger from Wellard. The attack of Farnes was fierce and creative of bruises. One ball rocketed over Brown's head, to the open and unashamed amusement of wicket-keeper Paynter. Bradman promptly turned his guns on Wellard and hit him for three fours off successive balls, one of them a stupendous hook—the thunder and lightning of cricket. Next he forced a half-volley from Farnes to the off boundary, and beat the Test-match aggregate of Hobbs. Brown was curiously vague for a while and unhappy; for a brief passage an Australian breakdown threatened yet another staggering turn of the wheel of a great match.

Bradman settled down, and the new ball lost its fury, and Brown, though he continued to hate the bowling of Farnes, gave an imitation of G. T. S. Stevens, the batsman who scarcely lifted his bat from the ground. After tea Bradman showed us a stroke of his very own; I can only describe it as a straight hook. He hit a rising ball off his head crash to the pavilion. A gale arose and blew papers about. Brown was bowled by Verity behind his back, and thought his bails had been removed by the wind. Brown stayed in seventy minutes for his ten runs, and nobody knew for certain when and where he got them. He was out at five o'clock, and optimists said that England would win yet. More likely was it that the gale would blow everybody off the earth.

McCabe hit two fours and sent a high chance to the slips off Farnes, who flung himself against the elements, with his hair in a tangle. Bradman, now at his best, reached fifty in an hour, and another hook off Farnes caused eyes to blink. McCabe pulled Verity for swinging fours off two balls; we were watching now the two greatest stroke players of contemporary cricket, and we could realize how easily Australia would have won but for Compton and Wellard and their eighth-wicket stand.

At half-past five McCabe fell to a slip catch, and, heaven help the poor reporters of cricket matches, the game entered another crisis; and all our articles were in the course of composition, our boats burned, so to say. If Bradman were to fail now, with an hour left, what an hour it would be. We trembled at the thought. Hassett, next man in after McCabe, did not tremble. He drove Wright and cut him, and next over he drove straight, pulled and cut again, every time to the boundary. Hassett is another grand young man. He hit a no-ball from Wright for six; Wright in this match has fallen sadly short of his promise at Nottingham; but he bowled Hassett at five minutes past six with a spiteful leg-break. Poor Badcock got a pair of spectacles, but he need not despair—all the better to see with, he should tell himself. The gorgeous day, which was alive with cricket at its best and most capricious, ended with Bradman's usual Test-match century. He was magnificent. But for him, England would now be, as they say, 'two up'.

FOURTH TEST (FIRST DAY)[1]

ENGLAND
First Innings

Edrich, b O'Reilly	12
Barnett, c Barnett, b McCormick	30
Hardstaff, run out	4
W. R. Hammond, b O'Reilly	76
Paynter, st Barnett, b Fleetwood-Smith	28
Compton, b O'Reilly	14
Price, c McCabe, b O'Reilly	0
Verity, not out	25
Wright, c Fingleton, b Fleetwood-Smith	22
K. Farnes, c Fingleton, b Fleetwood-Smith	2
Bowes, b O'Reilly	3
Lb 4, nb 3	7
Total	223

BOWLING ANALYSIS
ENGLAND—First Innings

	O.	M.	R.	W.		O.	M.	R.	W.
McCormick	20	6	46	1	F.-Smith	25	7	73	3
Waite	18	7	31	0	McCabe	1	1	0	0
O'Reilly	34.1	17	66	5					

O'Reilly bowled two no-balls; McCormick bowled one no-ball.

FALL OF THE WICKETS

1	2	3	4	5	6	7	8	9	10
29	34	88	142	171	171	172	213	215	223

AUSTRALIA
First Innings

J. H. Fingleton, not out	9
W. A. Brown, b Wright	22
B. A. Barnett, not out	1
Total (for one wicket)	32

[1] Rain caused the Third Test Match at Old Trafford, Manchester, to be abandoned without a ball being bowled.

To bat: D. G. Bradman, S. J. McCabe, C. L. Badcock, A. L. Hassett, M. G. Waite, W. J. O'Reilly, E. L. McCormick and L. O'B. Fleetwood-Smith.

BOWLING TO DATE

AUSTRALIA—First Innings

	O.	M.	R.	W.		O.	M.	R.	W.
Farnes	7	1	21	0	Wright	2	2	0	1
Bowes	4	0	11	0					

FALL OF THE WICKETS

$$\frac{1}{28}$$

Umpires: Chester and Smith.

LEEDS, FRIDAY, JULY 22ND

England played an outrageous innings today on an easy pitch. The ball turned frequently, but at so slow a pace for the most part that a comfortable, not to say indolent, stroke was possible and safe—or should have been safe. None but O'Reilly of the Australian attack was more than a useful bowler, and though he no doubt exhibited his finest arts his most valuable ally was an unaccountable diffidence which entered the English outlook. I was reminded of Leeds in 1934, when England were put out for 200 on a lifeless turf. I am afraid that at the crisis of the rubber the English team have weakened in character and allowed the initiative to pass, at least momentarily, to the enemy. The Australians today were obviously perceived as of old—as more than eleven men in buckram green: as, indeed, an army advancing with banners. It was all disappointing and disillusioning after the warlike gestures at Nottingham and Lord's.

The Australian attack surpassed its everyday self for reliability, but, apart from Hammond, no batsman did a thing to put a proper valuation on good length and perseverance. As I say, O'Reilly bowled at the top of his form; the point is that he was given permission to bowl that way. We were back in 1934 once more; only Grimmett and his turnip and candle and winding-sheet were needed to make the English nightmare thoroughly complete and hair-raising.

Again Hammond won the toss, and when Bradman picked up the coin he gave Hammond the sort of smile we give to the dentist when he waves us to the chair. On a grey morning the match began on a slow wicket, which the experts say will show signs of wear and tear before Tuesday afternoon. The dense atmosphere might have suited Bowes enthusiastically when at half-past eleven McCormick opened his attack with an amiable over which had a six o'clock look about it; not one ball rose more than the height of the stumps. But Waite obtained some slight out-swing, and Barnett's first stroke was a two through the slips, a stroke behind his back, so to say. Then Barnett edged Waite for four, also through the slips and also without his full knowledge and consent. The crowd swarmed noisily and the sun came through the haze, and Barnett played an in-swinger from Waite accurately to the middle of O'Reilly's hands at short leg, and O'Reilly dropped the catch without hesitation.

England were then 14 and Barnett 9; the crowd rejoiced unashamedly; it was the easiest and loveliest catch; perhaps O'Reilly imagined the over had come to an end and somebody had thrown him the ball to go on as first change. At noon McCormick went into retirement after half an hour's tranquil work; Waite crossed over, with O'Reilly heaving his arms around at the other end. Barnett promptly sliced Waite direct to Brown at second slip, and again the chance was put to grass; which was enough to make the pavilion cat laugh—if there is a pavilion cat at Leeds, or a pavilion. O'Reilly now spun a leg-break and appealed to high heaven and afterwards to Chester for a catch at the wicket, but entirely in vain. I did not welcome this abrupt appearance so early in the proceedings of O'Reilly's spin; also I was disconcerted to see Arthur Dolphin walking about in the crowd without his hat and umpire's white coat, apparently under the impression that he was still at Manchester waiting for the waters to subside.

Edrich was steady and conscientious; he made eight in fifty minutes, and never once hinted of his hook; he reminded me of a naughty boy under observation concealing in his pocket a violent firework. O'Reilly bowled him at twenty-five minutes past twelve by means of a superb googly; I did not at all like the look of O'Reilly. England's first wicket fell at 29. A quarter of an hour afterwards Hardstaff backed up to a defensive push by Barnett and was run out in a frantic convulsion to regain ground. Thus in spite of two instances of bad fielding England in seventy minutes could score only 34 for two. The pitch, as I say, was generally comfortable, even if it did enable O'Reilly to turn his googly; certainly the Australian attack was steadier than ever before in this summer's Test matches; the pace of the ground discouraged McCormick from efforts to bump, and this was to the gain of length and direction.

Hammond for twenty minutes did nothing but respect the attack, and at one o'clock England were 48 and making terribly heavy weather. Barnett hooked recklessly and no fieldsman could get near the mis-hit, though somebody's cap flew off yards behind him. Barnett was sketchy; an outline of an innings, a wan ghost of the innings he played at Nottingham. O'Reilly bowled at his cleverest, especially the googly, yet it could be detected even by myself in the press box, with, of course, the aid of my spectacles. I noticed that whenever O'Reilly hit the pads and appealed without profit he would immediately send down the googly in the hope that the batsman would be afraid to use the pads again: a clever ruse which took in Edrich, who is still in his green and salad days.

Fleetwood-Smith came on just before lunch, and Hammond struck him for four, but he caused a ball to jump to Barnett's gloves. At half-past one England had scored 62 for two in two hours; the slowest scoring so far in the rubber. Fingleton and Brown were in comparison gay and flippant while saving the match at Trent Bridge. O'Reilly's analysis at lunch was fourteen overs, eleven maidens, four runs, one wicket, and two of the runs had come from a no-ball. No bowler that ever lived, not even Barnes, bowled well enough to deserve this amount of flattery.

During the interval the noise was awful; hoarse voices announced that one wicket was down for Yorkshire; people pushed one another in the small of the back and trod on one another's boots; it was awful and dirty. When the agony went on at a quarter-past two McCormick allowed the slightly faster wicket to tempt him into short stuff, and Hammond drove a no-ball for six and got a four off Fleetwood-Smith. But McCormick at length found the edge of Barnett's bat, and a catch at the wicket ensued: it was an edge which for two and a half hours had been as obvious as the hole in a fence which a hurried hen can seldom find in spite of persistent endeavour. Nearly every over of Barnett's innings was a crisis: the suspense of it became severe. With his side 88 for three Paynter joined his captain in much the same ditch as occurred at Lord's; the expression on his face as he began his responsible job conveyed nothing, neither worry nor the contrary. Hammond greeted him with a four from Fleetwood-Smith's long hop, then the captain drove O'Reilly to the off boundary twice from consecutive balls and reached fifty, both of them strokes of ferocity and dignity and power. Paynter made a contrast by cutting Fleetwood-Smith next over to the boundary, a terrier-yap of a stroke, accompanying the leonine roar.

The English innings was in the balance at three o'clock: 100 for three and a long tail to set in probably if Paynter and Compton should falter. Hammond, thank goodness, looked as safe and permanent as St. Paul's or Sir Pelham Warner. The batsmanship of Hammond had a domed sort of grandeur; it seemed marbled in the stately manner of Alma Tadema. It was as English as a three-volume novel in the library of a country manor house. Now and again his power broke through conventional form, as when he hit Waite for a sudden straight four off his back foot, a terrific smashing volley that scattered the mob. The English innings after three hours of ill-nourished existence promised to grow to life and muscularity: O'Reilly was temporarily reduced to leg theory; apparently Hammond's batsmanship made direct attack merely crude and unconstitutional, as though brickbats were thrown to smash windows in the Royal Albert Hall.

The afternoon mellowed, for the sun had now dispersed the mist and shone a soft light, not spending itself in an excess of power but lending its presence even as Hammond lent his. A delay in the match happened here while refreshments were taken out to the combatants by a man in a steward's coat followed by four waitresses in white aprons and caps and black stockings and starched cuffs. The crowd took the opportunity to stand up, stretch legs and see how Yorkshire were going on. No sooner had we all sat down than O'Reilly clean bowled Hammond—a glorious ball which perhaps nipped in after seducing Hammond into a forward push.

The downfall of the captain shocked everybody; he had appeared to bat by sheer prerogative, by indefeasible right. The position of England was acute when Hammond departed, fourth out at 142, with Price to come in next but one. The boy Compton quickly hit a no-ball from O'Reilly to leg for four and snicked O'Reilly an inch from the wicket-keeper's gloves for four through the slips without a blush. A thumping boundary to the off told us that Paynter held no opinion of McCormick or of the Test match or of anybody or anything. He was simply doing a job of work, and resting when he found himself stuck for bobbins. He and Compton defended ball by ball, and the crowd took refuge in silence, unaccustomed as Leeds crowds are to slow batting and public speaking.

Paynter remained obstinate for an hour and forty minutes, scored 28 by habit, and at the end jumped out to drive Fleetwood-Smith and was stumped, which left England, at 171 for five, swaying on the edge of collapse. Price behind Compton, Verity behind Price, and the others behind one another. Compton was comprehensively bowled while the score was still 171, bowled by the O'Reilly

223

leg-break, which they told me was now no more but obsolete and for-gotten. When we saw after tea the sight of Price and Verity holding England's seventh wicket we knew the spectacle would not afflict us for long; Price was caught in the slips reaching forward ornamentally at nothing or everything, come what may. The innings finished in a comic strip, with no-balls caught and an attempt by Bradman at a run out after he had caught a no-ball off O'Reilly by Wright, while Verity batted like Will Hay in a mortar-board. Then O'Reilly missed a return chance, the crowd making the rowdiest excitement of the day when Verity got two fours in an over by Fleetwood-Smith. We needed only to have Donald Duck coming in now, and we had the next-best thing in Bill Bowes. Wright and Verity batted gamely and scored 41 for the eighth wicket, and during this stand we could understand what staunch measures might have done with the bowl-ing, even O'Reilly's. Bowes walked out in his sweater in humid heat; he reached the wicket at last, made three, and aimed at a six and was bowled. England's innings of 223 lasted five hours, and seemed to last twice as long.

In a declining light Farnes bowled fast, and a glorious break-back was snicked impulsively across Brown's leg stump and the ball flashed wide of Price's left hand for four. The batting then gained in assurance as the threat of a storm passed by, and at a quarter-past six the Australian innings looked as though it were well under way in prosperous waters. Bowes was disappointing, and Wright came on in his place. His first ball made pace off the pitch; Brown tried to pull and was bowled. This was consolation for England at the close of a ruinous day.

On the best authority I learn that hardly a ball turned awkwardly during the whole of England's innings; by superb length and tactics O'Reilly played on weakness of temperament and policy as much as on technical faults.

LEEDS SATURDAY, JULY 23RD

It is not easy to report the happenings at Leeds on Saturday. Towards five o'clock I was proceeding in the direction of the Press Box at Headingley when my attention was attracted to a number of men, amongst whom was the chief culprit William Bowes; I recog-nized him by his spectacles, but the prevailing darkness rendered further identification impossible. I was about to charge these persons with assault and disturbance in a public place when they dis-appeared. This would be at five-twenty.

FOURTH TEST (SECOND DAY)

ENGLAND

First Innings

Edrich, b O'Reilly	12
Barnett, c Barnett, b McCormick	30
Hardstaff, run out	4
W. R. Hammond, b O'Reilly	76
Paynter, st Barnett, b Fleetwood-Smith	28
Compton, b O'Reilly	14
Price, c McCabe, b O'Reilly	0
Verity, not out	25
Wright, c Fingleton, b Fleetwood-Smith	22
K. Farnes, c Fingleton, b Fleetwood-Smith	2
Bowes, b O'Reilly	3
Lb 4, nb 3	7
Total	**223**

BOWLING ANALYSIS

ENGLAND—First Innings

	O.	M.	R.	W.		O.	M.	R.	W.
McCormick	20	6	46	1	F.-Smith	25	7	73	3
Waite	18	7	31	0	McCabe	1	1	0	0
O'Reilly	34.1	17	66	5					

O'Reilly bowled two no-balls; McCormick bowled one no-ball.

FALL OF THE WICKETS

1	2	3	4	5	6	7	8	9	10
29	34	88	142	171	171	172	213	215	223

AUSTRALIA

First Innings

J. H. Fingleton, b Verity	30
W. A. Brown, b Wright	22
B. A. Barnett, c Price, b Farnes	57
D. G. Bradman, b Bowes	103
S. J. McCabe, b Farnes	1
C. L. Badcock, b Bowes	4
A. L. Hassett, c Hammond, b Wright	13
M. G. Waite, c Price, b Farnes	3
W. J. O'Reilly, c Hammond, b Farnes	2
E. L. McCormick, b Bowes	0
L. O'B. Fleetwood-Smith, not out	2
B 2, lb 3	5
Total	**242**

BOWLING ANALYSIS
AUSTRALIA—First Innings

	O.	M.	R.	W.		O.	M.	R.	W.
Farnes	26	3	77	4	Verity	19	6	30	1
Bowes	35.4	6	79	3	Edrich	3	0	13	0
Wright	15	4	38	2					

FALL OF THE WICKETS

1	2	3	4	5	6	7	8	9	10
28	87	128	136	145	195	232	240	240	242

ENGLAND
Second Innings

Edrich, not out	25
Barnett, not out	20
Lb 4	4
	—
Total (for 0)	49

BOWLING TO DATE
ENGLAND—Second Innings

	O.	M.	R.	W.		O.	M.	R.	W.
McCormick	6	2	12	0	O'Reilly	6	4	11	0
Waite	2	0	9	0	F.-Smith	4	0	13	0

It really was a gloomy afternoon, and I am surprised that Bradman did not appeal against the light immediately after lunch. The appeal certainly would have been upheld. As soon as England's second innings began an appeal was made and not rejected. Bradman probably feared a thunderstorm; he no doubt preferred that his side should bat on a good wicket in the dark rather than on a sticky wicket in the sunshine. I have never before seen (or just seen) first-class cricket played for so long in a light as bad as this at Leeds from lunch until late afternoon. Something is wrong somewhere when Bradman is bowled middle stump, and when McCabe plays back repeatedly to fast balls well up to him. I hope I am not doing injustice to England's admirable bowling, or to the way the whole team jumped to an opportunity and changed the prospect of defeat into a prospect of victory. I am as patriotic as most folk; notwithstanding the evidence of my writings, it may be said of me, or even sung, that in spite of all temptations to belong to other nations he remains an Englishman, though he might have been a Roosian, a French or Turk or Prussian, or an Australi-an.

If the sun had not gone from the world on Saturday it would be possible and fair to indict Australia's batting exactly as England's batting was indicted on Friday. But an awkward fact remains—before lunch, while the light was clear, Fingleton and Barnett played all the bowlers comfortably, even Barnett. And I do no injustice to a fine cricketer by saying 'even Barnett'. The point is that he not one of the Australians' first batsmen; he was sent in on Friday evening as a stop-gap. For an hour and ten minutes on Saturday morning Barnett and Fingleton held England's attack in check without much anxiety; shortly after half-past one Australia were 80 for one wicket, and then Fingleton tried to pull a ball from Verity, and was bowled —to his open chagrin, for, like Brown, he assisted at his own undoing. The evidence is accumulating that several of the Australian batsmen are unsound somewhere within the vitals of their technique.

Farnes bowled a stupendous over when McCabe came in—fast and magnificently tempered. It was the last over before lunch, and McCabe groped for it off his back foot. After lunch Farnes sent one of McCabe's stumps flying, and after that the Australians were like lost souls in a November fog—being led about by Bradman and his torch. Once again Bradman played at both ends of the wicket; he made 100 out of 148 scored while he batted. He took the last ball of over after over, took it easily and for the sake of his colleagues. This was his sixth century in six successive Test matches; nobody is likely to break that record, which is the finest of all: it tells of the genius to do well in the greatest kind of cricket.

Possibly one or two of the Australian batsmen erred in hiding their ability as much as they did under Bradman's wing. Hassett did little but stop the ball for an hour. Waite, too, was either self-effacing or entirely without a stroke in his technique. Badcock again failed sadly. There is a lack of the usual Australian toughness in the middle of the team's batting order; time after time in the Test matches this year Bradman has had to carry the side and the situation. The English bowlers, as I say, seized the chance, and in swift and thrilling strokes knocked the Australians from the affable car of anticipation on which they had come riding from Harrogate at the fresh of the morning. Hammond deployed his fast bowlers ruthlessly, and the fielding supported them to a man. You could only see a streak of white when Paynter gave pursuit; he was phosphorescent. And Hammond's catch which got rid of O'Reilly proved that he fields by instinct; a more remarkable slip catch could not possibly occur; the ball flashed low and to the right and away, and Hammond gripped one-handed, curving his body round, lovely and boneless.

Bowes bowled his best as soon as he was moved over to what I shall fancifully call the pavilion end. The heavy miasmatic atmosphere helped swing bowling and made a confident forward stroke perilous. When Bowes knocked the middle stump of Bradman out of the ground the crowd roared itself hoarse; this was their money's worth. It was a grand day for England—even if it was not visible all the time.

When Fingleton and Barnett continued Australia's innings at half-past eleven Bowes was discernible at the position of second slip to Farnes. He bowled at the other end, by which I mean the end opposite to the football stands. For a while both Farnes and Bowes were tame, so that Barnett could use his pretty straight bat with relish, and Fingleton needed to lift his bat not more than an inch; only desperately good bowling causes him to use his strokes, which are excellent if not generally known. Slowly but imperturbably the Australian score reached 48, then Bowes crossed over and Wright bowled for Farnes. Bowes immediately increased a little in pace and swing; but nothing suggested the wrath to come. Wright pitched his spin cleverly, and once or twice lifted up our hopes. On the whole, though, our emotions at present were those of ironical surprise at the spectacle of Barnett's composure and confidence. He pulled Wright with a heave for four, and another pull swept a short ball from Verity for four. Verity took the place of Wright, who came back for Bowes. Clearly Hammond was looking for a bowler to deal with an irritating situation—Barnett threatening a huge stand before the job of attending to serious business presented itself. Barnett hit two fours to leg in an over from Wright, one from a no-ball. He showed first-class skill and much style. At a quarter to one the estimates of Australia's total varied from 400 to four figures. Then Verity put Fingleton into a tangle; he found the edge of the bat and in the same over dropped a ball a shade short, and Fingleton missed aim in an effort at a push to the on. He and Barnett had scored 55 in 70 minutes, and probably some of the other Australian batsmen had chafed all the time to get in on the easy wicket.

Bradman 'foozled' his first ball, which spun from Verity's fingers, and he also pushed forward to Verity and made an uppish stroke for nothing towards mid-off. Verity, who bowled beautifully, gave Bradman a deal of anxiety before the great man broke his duck. A slice for three off Wright was not exactly in Bradman's best manner, and he ran an all-run four at some risk. When Bowes returned Bradman drove him at once to the off for fours off two consecutive balls.

Each stroke was superb and told us that the tuning-up period was over. We could hear almost the rap of the conductor's stick on the desk. Not once after this did Bradman waver in his mastery. Ten minutes before lunch Barnett reached a capital 50, with a square-leg hit for four from Farnes; the next ball was hit for four in the same direction and as lustily. Australia 128 for two—Barnett not out and, what is more, Bradman not out and McCabe not out, and fours to square-leg by Barnes off Farnes. No wonder it went dark.

At twenty-five minutes past one Barnett on the crest of confidence, slashed at Farnes and was triumphantly caught at the wicket by Price, who was excellent all day. McCabe, as I say, just managed to survive the smashing over hurled at him before lunch by Farnes, who is subject to curious changes of mood. He can be docile and ferocious during the passing of a quarter of an hour. Twice he struck McCabe's pads with a thud. Lunch came and with it pandemonium. The Caledonian Market compared to Leeds at lunch is diffident and taciturn. 'One down for Surrey!' 'Soft seats!' 'Ices!' 'Two down for Surrey!' Congestion everywhere, and bricks and old iron and corners that catch you on the knee-cap and tons of grit and stones.

At a quarter-past two Farnes attacked McCabe again, and not once did McCabe look like McCabe. He played inexplicably back to the ball which bowled him. An electrical glance by Bradman off Farnes was saved from the boundary by Paynter at a speed that gave you a headache to watch. Badcock's form in this rubber passes understanding; he was on Saturday a very distant relation of the cricketer who cut and drove England's bowling right and left at Melbourne. His bat was nowhere near the ball from Bowes which bowled him. When Hassett came to the wicket Bradman spoke to him and smiled. Through all of Australia's sudden vicissitudes Bradman remained calm and conversational; he was always laughing between overs, as though enjoying some private joke. From the moment Hassett came in until the end Bradman took charge of the Australian innings without fuss or any effort. Like Hammond on Friday, he seemed something left over from a greater day; the other were, compared to him, so many Porters, Drawers, Sutlers, Beadles, Grooms. He hit Verity for three to square-leg, and reached fifty in eighty-five minutes. If he now and again erred so little in timing the crowd gasped, and the bowler had reason to consider himself clever beyond the common lot. Edrich bowled when Bowes took rest after an hour of sustained and challenging work, and Edrich at once sent a square-arm 'grub' to Bradman. I thought Bradman would appeal against the light now for certain. Hassett, who is a stroke player, made little or no attempt to force the ball away, and he fell to a catch at slip from a nicely flighted leg-break by Wright. Waite spoke to Bradman when he reached the middle; but the game was not stopped, though even Bradman was quiet now, playing as late as he could. At five minutes to four the end of the world appeared imminent, and at last the appeal was submitted and granted. Australia were 205 for six wickets.

Twenty minutes afterwards Bradman drove Farnes to the off for four, and from the new ball hit two fours to the on, great strokes, rapid and entirely foreseen. Waite merely put his bat to the ball at the last second, as though it came to him out of a hole in the wainscot. He stayed in forty-five minutes for three, and was seventh out at 232. Bradman reached one of the finest hundreds of his career after two and a half hours' show of authority; I repeat, only 48 runs other than his were scored in that time. The stroke he made to the ball that bowled him was unbelievably late and out of position; besides, you simply do not knock Bradman's middle stump from the ground when he is 103. At five o'clock Australia were all out, and the match had joined issue again.

The light improved a little, but England rightly appealed against it before McCormick bowled a ball. Bradman laughed heartily when this appeal was lodged and, with hesitation, upheld. The players were scarcely in the pavilion before the day became lighter than at any time since one o'clock. Chester and Smith walked to the wicket not wearing white coats. They inspected the light carefully when they got there, inspected it forcibly, on the spot. Then the game went on, and Edrich was missed at slip by Fleetwood-Smith off McCormick. But he drove McCormick for a straight four; and Barnett put his diffident methods of Friday behind him. No disaster ensued, and at close of play I saw somebody in the crowd wearing sun glasses. The match is anybody's at the moment—with the odds slightly in England's favour.

LEEDS, MONDAY, JULY 25TH

England were, in spite of loyal prophecy, beaten at Headingley today after a shocking collapse. The wicket took the Australian spin more readily than on Friday, but I decline to accept the view that it was a really dangerous wicket. Of course, the ball turned: if two slow bowlers are at work in a Test match, does anybody expect them to bowl straight? When England were all out, many zealots hoped

ENGLAND

First Innings		Second Innings	
Edrich, b O'Reilly	12	st Barnett, b F.-Smith	28
Barnett, c Barnett, b McCormick	30	c Barnett, b McCormick	29
Hardstaff, run out	4	b O'Reilly	11
W. R. Hammond, b O'Reilly	76	c Brown, b O'Reilly	0
Paynter, st Barnett, b F.-Smith	28	not out	21
Compton, b O'Reilly	14	c Barnett, b O'Reilly	15
Price, c McCabe, b O'Reilly	0	lbw, b Fleetwood-Smith	6
Verity, not out	25	b Fleetwood-Smith	0
Wright, c Fingleton, b F.-Smith	22	c Waite, b F.-Smith	0
K. Farnes, c Fingleton, b F.-Smith	2	b O'Reilly	7
Bowes, b O'Reilly	3	lbw, b O'Reilly	0
Lb 4, nb 3	7	Lb 4, w 1, nb 1	6
Total	223	Total	123

BOWLING ANALYSIS

ENGLAND—First Innings

	O.	M.	R.	W.		O.	M.	R.	W.
McCormick	20	6	46	1	F.-Smith	25	7	73	3
Waite	18	7	31	0	McCabe	1	1	0	0
O'Reilly	34.1	17	66	5					

O'Reilly bowled two no-balls; McCormick bowled one no-ball.

FALL OF THE WICKETS

1	2	3	4	5	6	7	8	9	10
29	34	88	142	171	171	172	213	215	223

ENGLAND—Second Innings

	O.	M.	R.	W.		O.	M.	R.	W.
McCormick	11	4	18	1	O'Reilly	21.5	8	56	5
Waite	2	0	9	0	F.-Smith	16	4	34	4

Fleetwood-Smith bowled one wide; McCormick bowled one no-ball.

FALL OF THE WICKETS

1	2	3	4	5	6	7	8	9	10
60	73	73	73	96	116	116	116	123	123

AUSTRALIA

First Innings		Second Innings	
J. H. Fingleton, b Verity	30	lbw, b Verity	9
W. A. Brown, b Wright	22	lbw, b Farnes	9
B. A. Barnett, c Price, b Farnes	57	not out	15
D. G. Bradman, b Bowes	103	c Verity, b Wright	16
S. J. McCabe, b Farnes	1	c Barnett, b Wright	15
C. L. Badcock, b Bowes	4	not out	5
A. L. Hassett, c Hammond, b Wright	13	c Edrich, b Wright	33
M. G. Waite, c Price, b Farnes	3		
W. J. O'Reilly, c Hammond, b Farnes	2		
E. L. McCormick, b Bowes	0		
L. O'B. Fleetwood-Smith, not out	2		
B 2, lb 3	5	B 4, nb 1	5
Total	242	Total (for five wickets)	107

BOWLING ANALYSIS

AUSTRALIA—First Innings

	O.	M.	R.	W.		O.	M.	R.	W.
Farnes	26	3	77	4	Verity	19	6	30	1
Bowes	35.4	6	79	3	Edrich	3	0	13	0
Wright	15	4	38	2					

FALL OF THE WICKETS

1	2	3	4	5	6	7	8	9	10
28	87	128	136	145	195	232	240	240	242

AUSTRALIA—Second Innings

	O.	M.	R.	W.		O.	M.	R.	W.
Farnes	11.3	4	17	1	Verity	5	2	24	1
Bowes	11	0	35	0	Wright	5	0	26	3

Wright bowled one no-ball.

FALL OF THE WICKETS

1	2	3	4	5
17	32	50	61	91

for an Australian breakdown as comprehensive as England's; we were told that on the crumbling turf Verity and Wright would cause the ball to perform all manner of antics. But though Australia batted nearly as tentatively as England, it was not deadly spin which took our five wickets: at any rate, Hammond's faith in fast bowling rather exceeded his faith in the arts of Verity and Wright. The result was a sad disillusionment.

England's grip on the match at the day's beginning was strong: we knew that the pitch would be difficult on Tuesday, undoubtedly difficult: England needed only to score 250 to make victory a matter of logical course. Subsequent events bore out this theory with ruthless emphasis. Three times in the rubber we have had a splendid chance of winning: we have enjoyed the luck of the toss three times. But now we are defeated, one match to the bad, with no hope of getting back the Ashes this year, for even if England win at the Oval Australia will retain them.

For the fifth Test match the Selection Committee should try to choose an England team in which we shall not be disconcerted by the sight of Price coming in to bat at the fall of the sixth wicket. The evidence is that the English team lost confidence this morning as soon as they saw the Australians on the warpath, making all the old Satanic signs. But the quick downfall of Hammond settled the general hash; each side is ludicrously dependent on one great player. I have seldom seen worse batting in a Test match than today's; Australia's scratchings and ditherings to compile 105 runs this afternoon were not much less inglorious than England's. In the two teams there are nine or ten cricketers who may, without slander, be relegated to the company fancifully called 'rabbits'. As the crowd left the shambles of Headingley a man announced to the world that he was going home. 'There's nowt else to do now,' he said, and somehow the remark made a truthful valuation of what we had seen through the dank and dirty air. The one stroke of greatness was a matter of character rather than of technique; the Australians knew that they were doomed unless before lunch they overwhelmed at least five English batsmen. They attacked like Yorkshiremen under Sellars; they again seized the initiative. 'Put Wally Hammond in t'Yorkshire team,' said a voice at the unhappy finish. But another voice answered, dubiously: 'Well, Ah don't mind him, but we want nobody else.'

There seemed more people at the match than ever, and more noise and dust. The cricket was resumed in a frightful din: thousands of voices told a man in a bowler hat to sit down and a dog ran on the field of play. O'Reilly turned his googly at once, but Barnett pulled a no-ball from him for four. The day was warm and cloudy, and, after Saturday's gloom, the light frequently caused the eyes to blink. For a while Barnett and Edrich put us in an affable paradise of hopefulness which became inflated to optimism when Barnett thumped another no-ball from O'Reilly for four. Bradman wore a grim look, and McCormick ran to bowl as though fiends were after him—not after the English.

It was McCormick indeed who began the English collapse, aided and abetted by Barnett, who hinted of indecision when he pushed a not very hair-raising rising ball into the void on the off side where no fieldsman stood. From the first ball of McCormick's next over Barnett blindly hit at another and more pronounced bumper: it was a stroke made head down with the bat cleaving vaguely on high. The consequence was a skier near the wicket to leg, and the Australian Barnett ran and caught it like naturalist chasing a butterfly. This was a clear case of *felo de se*. In the same over Edrich, forced back, sent a ball to his wickets' base, but not hard enough to disturb the bails. Trouble was clearly on the brew, sure as death. Edrich was apparently wearing an amulet; he had now made 28, been missed twice, and had nearly played on. McCormick thumped Edrich's fingers, and a very small boy shouted 'Body line!' Whether or not as a result of this indignant protest McCormick went off and O'Reilly changed his end, and Fleetwood-Smith bowled opposite to him.

Here, we felt, we were at the game's turning-point: to save themselves the Australians needed wickets now at no great cost. Hardstaff affronted us with an innings as wavy as his own hair; he was irresolute until O'Reilly gave him a no-ball, which he drove bravely to the on boundary. The next ball crashed into his stumps swift as a gunshot. And from the next ball Hammond feebly turned a quick googly to short-leg, where Brown caught a left-handed catch amidst leaps of joy from all Australians on the spot.

England were plump in the corner again: only 54 ahead and three wickets gone, including the captain's. Paynter was nearly caught at silly-point by Bradman, who turned a somersault in the attempt to scoop up a desperate push. It was a great over, and the crowd applauded O'Reilly at the end of it. Next over Fleetwood-Smith deceived Edrich, who groped out at a gorgeous googly and found only the encircling air, and was stumped.

Thus at half-past twelve young Compton went in to do his best, with England's total 73 for four; he reached a wicket surrounded by demons at the kill. The next batsman to come in for England would be Price, a thought sobering enough to bankrupt all the bars. Paynter surveyed the proceedings like the village plumber called in to investigate a complicated mess in the bathroom, and at once he struck two fours from consecutive balls off the terrible O'Reilly, a cut and a vast pull. Another no-ball by O'Reilly was sent soaring by Compton for four, and he drove a legitimate ball by O'Reilly for another four. Then two successive balls by Fleetwood-Smith spun viciously and missed Paynter's off stump by a foot after pitching straight. Compton succumbed now rather unluckily; he tried to sweep O'Reilly to leg and was caught at the wicket off either his glove or bat handle or something or other; the ball jumped.

This disaster made England 96 for five, 77 in front, when Price arrived, accompanied by the steward and his bevy of waitresses with drinks. Paynter cut Fleetwood-Smith for a grand square four; he fought like a little man with on top of him sitting on his head a whole scrum which he kicked and bit and occasionally escaped from to do fierce damage. He was heroic in a way that made us laugh as much as it made us proud of him. Price, too, brandished a fist and hoicked O'Reilly for four and generally defended his wicket with the air of a man batting on the extreme end of a diving-board. He was leg before the stumps and the stumper playing a beautifully perpendicular bat. The last four wickets fell for seven and we need not go morbidly into the details. Verity, Wright, Farnes and Bowes got out so quickly that possibly the scorers broke their pencils endeavouring to cope with the rush.

O'Reilly thrived on weak batsmanship, as I say: well as he bowled he was not a combination of Barnes, Spofforth, Trumble and O'Reilly himself. Ten English wickets fell in less than two hours for 74, and the rout left the crowd sick, stupid and blasphemous. Fleetwood-Smith also snatched amongst the spoils; his googly gyrated like something in a Walt Disney film. None the less, his tricks could be seen plainly, and some assault should have been launched against him. It is the fact, though, that O'Reilly and Fleetwood-Smith used whatever naughtiness the pitch contained far more craftily than England's spin bowlers could.

The crowd was afflicted with delirium when Fingleton and Brown began Australia's task after lunch. Whenever a ball missed the bat somebody apparently had a seizure. Farnes bowled with stupendous hostility and soon he defeated Brown, leg-before, with a ball terribly quick from the earth. Bradman walked to the wicket slowly and his face was serious. Bowes lacked conviction, yet it was Farnes who made way for Verity: if England could somehow win now we knew the miracle would be worked by spin. Verity at once spun and popped a ball to Fingleton, and the next ball baffled Fingleton leg-before from the moment if pitched. From Verity's next over 14 were scored, including four overthrows because Bowes misfielded a throw-in.

Thunderclouds loomed up the sky, and McCabe and Bradman wore the expressions not of victors but of men of responsibility. McCabe drove Verity to the on for four with a gesture of impatience. but Bradman remained dour and defensive. Wright bowled at Bowes's end; Bradman edged him for two through the slips, then next ball, to a sound like the roar of beasts, Bradman sliced again and was caught an inch or half an inch from the ground in the slips. Wright ensnared the great man with the ball he likes least of all—a well-flighted leg-break spinning away from the bat. A quarter of an hour after this wonder of wonders McCabe hooked a dreadful long-hop with a huge heave of the bat, hooked it straight into Barnett's hands at mid-on.

Australia 61 for four and the two lions gone: the crowd saw visions and howled and ran about, the dog returned and chased across the field and came to wag his tail at everybody. But the lot of England was too far gone; oh, for the hundred more runs which should have been hit during the second innings! In gathering darkness Hassett set about the bowling and pulled and drove as though saying, 'For Heaven's sake let's get it all over and done with.' His brave and skilful innings was ended when he hit out recklessly and skied to the off: he feared the advent of a thunderstorm and gave his wicket away for the cause: rain was falling when he got out. Badcock was reduced to strokeless resistance. He did his work and Barnett straightway conveyed a full toss from Wright to the square-leg boundary.

Play was stopped for a brief space when Australia, with five wickets in hand, wanted only nine; as far as I could see Hammond led his team off and left the batsmen rather at a loss. The delay was mercifully short; soon after four the match was won. It might be known henceforth as O'Reilly's match, for though without Bradman's hundred England would have won, a hundred by Bradman is neither here nor there, but ten wickets for 122 in a Test match is a performance not common even during the life and career of the best bowler of the age.

THE OVAL, SATURDAY, AUG. 20TH

A week or two ago I suggested in these columns that for the Oval Test match the Yorkshire team should be chosen intact to represent England. People laughed at the idea and said it was one of my little jokes. But I was serious; I would not dream of making little jokes about a Test match. Today England have scored 347 runs and only

236

ENGLAND
First Innings

Hutton, not out	160
Edrich, lbw, b O'Reilly	12
Leyland, not out	156
B 5, lb 9, w 1, nb 4	19
	—-
Total (for one wicket)	347

To bat: W. R. Hammond, Paynter, Compton (D.), Hardstaff, Wood, Verity, K. Farnes and Bowes

BOWLING ANALYSIS TO DATE
ENGLAND—First Innings

	O.	M.	R.	W.		O.	M.	R.	W.
Waite	33	5	62	0	F.-Smith	35	3	121	0
McCabe	17	4	45	0	Barnes	11	2	21	0
O'Reilly	35	10	79	1					

FALL OF THE WICKETS

$$\frac{1}{29}$$

AUSTRALIA: D. G. Bradman, S. J. McCabe, B. A. Barnett, S. Barnes, W. A. Brown, J. H. Fingleton, A. L. Hassett, M. G. Waite, C. L. Badcock, W. J. O'Reilly and L. O'B. Fleetwood-Smith

Umpires: Chester and Walden.

one batsman, a Middlesex man, has got out. Two Yorkshiremen have taken the total from 29 for one wicket to its present altitude. If Sutcliffe had been playing instead of Edrich the chances are that England would not be less comfortably placed than they are as it is. I do not remember a single instance of a plain, unmistakable failure in Test cricket by a chosen Yorkshireman.

Bradman was terribly unlucky to lose the toss again on the easiest wicket conceivable, easier even than Nottingham's. In the absence of McCormick, said to be suffering from neuritis, the Australian attack was the weakest ever seen in representative cricket. O'Reilly laboured alone on the lifeless hearthrug. Fleetwood-Smith turned one or two balls, and off one of them Hutton gave an easy chance of stumping when he was not more than forty. Waite and McCabe, as opening bowlers in a Test match, whetted the appetites of all batsmen present. Bradman was compelled to ask Sidney Barnes to bowl, much to the curiosity of the authentic Sidney Barnes, who looked on

237

and probably wondered what it was all about. Edrich faltered woefully at twenty minutes past twelve; after that, for five hours, Hutton
and Leyland played exactly as they wished to play. There was hardly
ever a hint of the fall of a wicket. During one period which came
under my observation not a ball beat the bat in an hour. Leeds was
revenged—by two Yorkshiremen who took no part in the recent
atrocities there. They will begin again on Monday. If the wicket
holds good an England score of 600 at least should be obtained
comfortably. And on a wicket of the same docility there is every
reason to suppose that Bradman will, in one of his two innings, stay
in until the beginning of the match is lost in the mists of antiquity.
The English batting was watched by an astonishingly small crowd.
Less than 13,000 paid at the gates, and on the whole it was an
apathetic crowd. A voice said, 'They're not trying'—meaning the
Australians,—'they know they've got the Ashes.' The statement
was as untrue as it was hoarse: O'Reilly bowled his hardest, so did
his colleagues. They were beaten by Yorkshiremen and by a
ridiculous wicket, of which we have not yet heard the last.

Edrich and Hutton began quietly, and the crowd also was quiet;
it was almost a congregation. For half an hour Waite and McCabe
bowled with the new ball, both of them amiable as two Cherryble
brothers. McCabe beat Edrich and appealed for leg-before-wicket,
but Walden, with presence of mind, said, or indicated, not out.
Edrich seemed unhappy and far away from Lord's. At twelve o'clock
England were twenty for none. Then O'Reilly came on with Fleetwood-Smith. The stage was ready; the scene-shifters had got the
setting order. Hutton played confidently and forward to O'Reilly.
Edrich played back and interogatively. He missed a quicker one, and
Chester's finger went up terribly when the ball struck the pads. This
was O'Reilly's hundreth wicket in nineteen Test matches. Poor
Edrich departed in silence; he has eaten of the bitter bread of irony
this season. On this occasion he suffered seventy-five minutes with
the rest of us, for twelve penitential runs.

Leyland came in, thick in the arms and broad in the pads. I
expected cheerfulness at once, but the cold weather was not
encouraging. Shortly before Edrich got out Hutton committed a
swift late cut off McCabe; he then pulled himself together. And even
Leyland put levity momentarily aside. Thus in an atmosphere of
gathering depression England contrived to score 89 for one wicket in
two hours. Lunch mercifully intervened. I could not endure this kind
of play so I took a walk and met J. N. Crawford and Braund, who

recalled an occasion at Melbourne when K. L. Hutchings scored 128 against Australia and hit a six and twenty-five fours. It is often more thrilling to talk to an old cricketer than to watch a contemporary one. Towards ten minutes past one Leyland atavistically drove two brilliant fours in front of the wicket off Fleetwood-Smith.

No other incident ruffled the face of the day until after lunch Hutton was given his second innings by Barnett, who missed a most luscious chance of stumping off a ball from Fleetwood-Smith which spun a foot, and Hutton was a long way out of his ground ploughing the off side. Hutton's score was now 40 and England's 91 for one. He then drove O'Reilly through the covers for four, with his body falling beautifully forward; it was a stroke of thanksgiving. Leyland watched it with admiration, and obviously it reminded him of a cricket match, for he struck Fleetwood-Smith promptly for a four to the off, a real drive which went racing along the earth with the illusion of increasing velocity every yard. Next he was bowled by a no ball from O'Reilly, much to his amusement. The match began to wake up and stretch itself. McCabe bowled from the Vauxhall or Houses of Parliament end while O'Reilly changed over; Leyland drove McCabe straight and powerfully, and, of course, no fieldsman protected the boundary behind the bowler. Then Leyland reached 50 in a hundred minutes, and a moment or two later Hutton also reached 50—in the more seemly time of two and a quarter hours. The sun came out, as though to see what all the sudden noise was about, and witnessed another boundary, a perfect forcing hit to the on by Hutton off O'Reilly. Hutton was a model No. 1 batsman, sound yet watchful for the really loose ball and always a Yorkshireman.

Bradman persistently changed the bowling, probably for want of something better to do, and as soon as he asked Waite to try off-breaks Leyland smote a four to the off, and after doing so stood as still as a post and watched the ball's progress towards Westminster. Both batsmen appeared as comfortable now as old inhabitants in their favourite club chairs. O'Reilly made his windmill movements to the wicket, head down, arms wheeling about him, but the drowsy turf changed his arts into merely hopeful industry. He mopped his brow at an over's end and, I thought, took refuge in muttered words. At three o'clock England was 147 for one; the fall of another wicket seemed dependent on some act of absentmindedness on the part of Hutton and Leyland. Seldom did a ball elude the bat; sixty runs were scored in fifty minutes after lunch, as safely and as inevitably as any shelling of peas. Never a ball rose abruptly, seldom a ball spun. Bradman and his men waited for something to turn up, and once, at the end of an over, O'Reilly threw the ball to the other bowler and seized his cap from the umpire with no attempt to disguise his disgusted helplessness. He could make no more impression on Leyland than an argumentative voice on a deaf man; Leyland played him with a rich, comic, wooden sort of assurance, as though saying all the time, 'Hey, Bill, tha'rt a good un, but Ah know all about thi.' So Fleetwood-Smith came to O'Reilly's assistance and, Leyland hit his first ball for four, as though continuing his discourse, 'And tha'rt not what Ah'd call surprising, either.'

Still, Fleetwood-Smith found the edge of Leyland's bat, and Leyland at 68 was glad to snick an isolated spinning-away ball for two—which was the first ghost of a chance the Australian attack had seen since the failure of Edrich nearly two hours ago. Waite's hypothetical off-spinners, from round the wicket, recalled the age of innocence: McCormick's pace was badly missed. But Leyland, at 70, gave another diverting trace of fallibility by prodding a ball from Waite between his back foot and the leg stump, as though saying now, 'Go on, lads, get me out—it can be done; Ah'm pla-ayin' for mi place in t'team, remember.' Another exquisite late cut by Hutton, off Waite this time, told us that England v. Australia is one thing and Lancashire v. Yorkshire another. At 175 for one wicket Bradman resorted to Barnes, who experimented with three or four practice balls to McCabe, or somebody, before launching upon his first over. Probably he wished to make sure which really was his bowling arm, right or left. I myself am not sure yet.

Hutton when he was 86 was nearly caught at first slip off a full-toss from Fleetwood-Smith; I mention this fact as an indication of how unlikely it seemed hereabouts that a wicket would fall in a way relating effect to cause. Two gorgeous fours in an over by Fleetwood-Smith, one to Leyland and one to Hutton, relegated the doldrums of the morning to a primal and empirical past; the English innings came out of the vapours and dispersed them. The Australian attack apparently entered bankruptcy; Barnes as a bowler meant that the brokers were in. At ten minutes to four Hutton achieved another century; he had exhibited a finely organized craftsmanship for more than four hours, and now and again he modulated into the aesthetic; his forward strokes were elegant and effortless and occasionally fruitful in the eyes of the scorers.

Just before tea Leyland came to his destined century after some three and a quarter hours of ripeness; it was as certain as harvest-time that he would score plenteously against this Australian bowling; I have never doubted it. Leyland is always an England batsman; for the purposes of Test matches he should be regarded as in form whenever he is not suffering from a broken leg or a splintered finger. He began soberly today while he investigated the attack; 'Let's be careful for a bit' he seemed to say. 'There's no hurry; we can play this match till Christmas. We'll begin when we're ready.' From O'Reilly's first ball after tea Leyland allowed himself to be bowled—by a no-ball; this was the second time he had allowed O'Reilly to bowl him with a no-ball. He is a man of humour. 'Live and let live; give him a bit of encouragement—it costs nowt.'

A slight shower fell before tea, not of much consequence but scarcely a promise of fine weather over the weekend. At half-past four the game went forward, with great white clouds in a sky of blue, clouds with castles on the edges of cliffs, clouds like islands in a sea. The gas-holder, now painted a severe grey, became transcendental in the soft evening light.

Hutton kept pace with Leyland; he forced Fleetwood-Smith twice in an over with his wrists to the on; he played back strongly and with poise. His footwork was quick and clean; seldom, if ever, did he lose balance or employ the wrong stroke. Even allowing for the poor attack, Hutton's cricket was a guarantee of many long scores for England for days to come, here and in Australia. Leyland, less studious than Hutton, attended to the humanities; his drives were related to the man himself. Sometimes he bent down and enjoyed a late cut, a humorous dab at the ball, a chuckle which contrasted with the broader laughs of his drives.

On and on the Australian bowlers toiled while the score mounted up and up—29 for one, 50 for one, 75 for one, 100 for one, 125 for one, 150 for one, 175 for one, 200 for one, 225 for one, 250 for one, 275 for one, 300 for one and so on until the day's end. Think of the suspense suffered in the countless homes of Australia where whole families were gathered round the radio, listening to a ball-by-ball narrative, while outside the winter winds blew—and there are indeed wintry winds in Australia, especially in Melbourne and Goulburn. Can a more searching trial to the spirit be imagined than that of a patriotic Australian, as he sits looking into a box, while hour after hour his beloved O'Reilly toils in vain, over after over until midnight comes and the fire dies down and the beer and whisky run out? At half-past five, English time, the score became 300 for one, and the

241

crowd let out a roar so loud and abrupt that I thought the gas-holder (or O'Reilly) had gone off. In the last hour the scoring slackened to fifty or fewer; the batsmen rubbed home their lesson. Leyland put his bat to the dog-tired bowling, and it said, as broad and plain as Ilkley Moor, 'So if tha wants Test matches played to a finish, well, here's the way to get off the mark before the Leagues and Littlewood's begin, properly like.'

FIFTH TEST (SECOND DAY)
ENGLAND
First Innings

Hutton, not out	300
Edrich, lbw, b O'Reilly	12
Leyland, run out	187
W. R. Hammond, lbw, b Fleetwood-Smith	59
Paynter, lbw, b O'Reilly	0
Compton, b Waite	1
Hardstaff, not out	40
B 10, lb 18, w 1, nb 6	35
Total (for five wickets)	634

To bat: Wood, Verity, K. Farnes, and Bowes.

BOWLING ANALYSIS TO DATE
ENGLAND—First Innings

	O.	M.	R.	W.		O.	M.	R.	W.
Waite	61	13	121	1	F.-Smith	70	8	235	1
McCabe	29	8	59	0	Barnes	17	2	40	0
O'Reilly	66.2	19	144	2					

FALL OF THE WICKETS

1	2	3	4	5
29	411	546	547	555

AUSTRALIA: D. G. Bradman, S. J. McCabe, B. A. Barnett, S. Barnes, W. A. Brown, J. H. Fingleton, A. L. Hassett, M. G. Waite, C. L. Badcock, W. J. O'Reilly and L. O'B. Fleetwood-Smith.

THE OVAL, MONDAY, AUG. 22ND

The crowd was immense for the final Test match here today, congested to acute discomfort on the stony popular side, and at half-past eleven nearly everybody not in one of the stands received a slight drenching from a shower which held play back until five minutes to twelve.

In O'Reilly's first over Fingleton misfielded, and as the batsman hesitated I thought that the Australians were at once resorting to attempts at run-outs as the most likely way of dealing with their problem—trying to persuade Leyland and Hutton to 'linger out a purposed overthrow'—which is not a quotation from a cricket book but from one of the sonnets of Shakespeare. Hutton got to work immediately with a glorious off-drive from Fleetwood-Smith, and then a roar of applause recognized the fact that the partnership had become the most prolific in all the history of Test matches. Fleetwood-Smith settled into a length of extraordinary steadiness for a bowler who tries as hard as he does to spin, and Hutton played him with an exemplary forward method. O'Reilly, too, needed careful scrutiny; the bowling was less harmless hereabout than it ever was on Saturday. But Leyland drove O'Reilly straight for four, a quick and impertinent hit, late and powerful, a real smack in the face.

At twenty minutes to one Fleetwood-Smith beat Leyland by means of a lovely spinner which flashed inches over the stumps; Leyland was not half as startled as Fleetwood-Smith. Fifty runs only were scored in the first hour, too many of them from absurd short one, with Leyland responsible for the risk; he probably wished to keep himself and the crowd awake, but a better way was a brilliant cover-drive, which he thumped from Waite and sent up the 400. Fleetwood-Smith's bowling in this first hour was beautiful; on a fair pitch he would have taken wickets; his fine art was abused by the groundsmen's drowsy syrups.

Then, at ten minutes past one, the partnership ended in the way, the only way, it had ever seemed likely to end. Hutton pushed a ball to the off from O'Reilly, Hassett misfielded, and Leyland went for a second run comically dangerous and unnecessary. He was out easily, and so we shall never know how long it would have taken the Australian bowlers to break the stand by their own devices. It put on 382 in some six and a quarter hours—which, of course, was the duration of Leyland's innings of 187.

Hammond came in with the score 411 for two and banged Fleetwood-Smith for four straight and pulled him round for four and rifled the over for a dozen. Next over he again pulled Fleetwood-Smith for four, a great scythe of a stroke; he scored twenty in a quarter of an hour before lunch and suggested the cavalry charge after the infantry's sturdy preparation, if one may use obsolete military language, probably incorrectly. But after the interval the plan of campaign was reconsidered, and another dour piece of sapping

243

was undertaken, slow and industrious. Hutton reached 200 after eight hours of incredible accuracy. Then, like a proper Test match batsman, he proceeded to play himself thoroughly in and did nothing perceptible for half an hour, until the green light shone once more in his mind and he hit Waite through the covers for four—as perfect a drive as any connoisseur could wish to see. All in all, though, no risks were taken; so far the only risk taken in the innings was the risk of a short run. Fingleton left the field because of cramp —I wondered that O'Reilly did not leave the field because of Hutton. The Australians stuck to the hopeless toil philosophically and Bradman changed his bowling, and the umpires counted the overs, and the runs mounted, and the clouds rolled on, and the gas-holder went up and down, and the trams went by the ground, and the hours waxed and waned, and somewhere even the weariest river wound safe to sea.

When Hutton was 215 Waite twice beat him, or rather, got a ball past his bat, which in this match meant the same thing. Hammond after lunch compiled 16 in an hour to Hutton's 24. The cavalry had gone back to the stables, while the sky threatened plenty of rain and a pretty wicket for Australia's innings. I wondered what Waite and O'Reilly were thinking about as they bowled and bowled, and also I wondered what Hutton and Hammond were thinking about as they batted and batted. And I could not guess at all why, when they struck a four, they did so off one kind of ball rather than off another of much the same kind. Drinks were served on the field when England were 485 for two, then Hutton made another of his glorious drives to the off. He was, for all his slowness, always pretty to see in the eyes of the close student of batsmanship; technically he is easily the best of our young batsmen; he knows the grammar backwards. His defensive play is elegant because mostly he moves forward. And he never, needless to say, wastes energy.

Hutton at 228 snicked Fleetwood-Smith to leg for four when he was trying to drive. The mishap was a faint proof that we were watching human and fallible batsmen. Five hundred was reached at twenty-five minutes to four, after the innings had lasted for more than nine hours, in which time the Australian bowlers had taken a wicket. Hereabout Fleetwood-Smith beat Hammond twice in an over, which was an achievement. Australia's only two bowlers were noble in their faith and persistence, and a question which may now have occurred to some spectators was whether O'Reilly was bald before the game began on Saturday or had gone bald since then.

Hammond added 27 after lunch in an hour and a half. Hutton out-paced him, passed Hammond's score of 240 made at Lord's, and then stopped another good ball from Fleetwood-Smith with the side of his bat. Fleetwood-Smith enjoyed not the slightest luck and scarcely seemed to expect any.

The crowd did not find the slow batting objectionable. They were revelling in their heart's desire, but I tremble to think what they would have said if the Australians had stone-walled with their grand total 520 for two. The press would have been husky with letters about it tomorrow. Hutton, at 246, cocked a ball from Fleetwood-Smith to the off side. It was a capital ball, too, which actually spun. Few bowlers have bowled as well and for so long as Fleetwood-Smith in this match and for such scant reward. The batsmen continued to take risks with short runs, but nobody would risk a catch in the unguarded acres of the outfield. Hammond's 50 occupied him for two hours, in spite of his busy prelude before lunch. The batting since lunch had become rather unchivalrous. At four o'clock England had increased Saturday's total of 347 for one to 530 for two—183 in three hours and three-quarters. I cannot remember that any Australian team in the same strong, not to say impregnable, position has batted as slowly as this. A pretty late cut by Hutton came as gushing water in a desert.

A quarter of an hour from the tea interval two wickets suddenly fell, to the general bewilderment—it was as though the Gorner glacier had leaped forward. Hammond was leg-before to Fleetwood-Smith, and justly to Fleetwood-Smith. And at 547 Paynter also succumbed lbw to O'Reilly; he made a duck, which was clever of him on this wicket. So far three wickets had fallen lbw and the other was a run out, after ten hours' play for 550. The stumps were a survival from a distant epoch in the game's development; they were like the little toe on the human foot. During the afternoon there was faint evidence that the turf was beginning to take spin a little; at any rate, Fleetwood-Smith caused Hammond to stab late, and, as I say, Hutton once got a ball on to the side of the bat.

During the tea interval rain again descended gently, so that cricket was delayed until five o'clock, when the Australians returned to the field leaping and gambolling like spring lambs. Bradman tossed the ball about and played a sort of 'tick' or 'chase me' game with somebody. You would have thought that they were beating England easily. In Waite's first over after tea Compton played forward and was clean bowled—the most extraordinary occurrence of the match;

I wonder that the bails came off; they might well have been fossil-ized. England were blotting their innings; three wickets had fallen while nine runs were scored—Hammond's, Paynter's and Compton's, and the total was the beggarly one of 555 for five at five o'clock.

Hardstaff forced Waite to the square-leg boundary, one of the best strokes of a generally strokeless day, a stroke quick and supple at the wrists. And slowly Hutton went his way towards passing R. E. Foster's 287 amassed in 1904 in Australia, the highest innings until today by an English batsman, and made because J. T. Tyldesley batted a sticky wicket dry before Foster went in. Hutton reached 288 out of 600 at twenty minutes to six, a remarkable performance.

The cricket grew in style and animation, thanks largely to Hardstaff, whose strokes possessed lustre. An off-drive by him put cricket's clock back nearly half a century—left leg forward and the flashing bat. And this time he played Fleetwood-Smith forward with some confidence, not back, as usually he has done, with the air of a man gulping down a beating heart. At his best Hardstaff is an artist, a spreader of delight, not one of the bricklayers and hod-carriers. He nearly lamed McCabe at silly mid-on with a terrific drive off O'Reilly; McCabe was glad to turn his back on the terrific missile which he saw coming at him. Somebody will (and should) be killed some day fielding in that position of bluff.

One of the sights of the evening was O'Reilly and Fleetwood-Smith chasing a hit to third man, running a race—with both of them I take it, conceding weight. All day the Australians fielded well, and Bradman placed them thoughtfully.

Barnes bowled leg-spin towards six o'clock, and Hardstaff's cricket now suffered the familiar bend at the knees. One ball kept low, and Hardstaff was nearly leg-before. This sign of quick, low spin probably disconcerted Bradman as much as it disconcerted Hardstaff; it may have been a sign of wrath to come, and just as we were proclaiming Hutton's 300 the rain came once more, still gently, but with a sky that probably caused the ghost of a smile to appear on the face of Verity, who as a rule is not given to smiling at small things.

ENGLAND
First Innings

Hutton, c Hassett, b O'Reilly	364
Edrich, lbw, b O'Reilly	12
Leyland, run out	187
W. R. Hammond, lbw, b Fleetwood-Smith	59
Paynter, lbw, b O'Reilly	0
Compton, b Waite	1
Hardstaff, not out	169
Wood, c and b Barnes	53
Verity, not out	8
B 22, lb 19, w 1, nb 8	50

Total (for seven wickets declared) 903

K. Farnes and Bowes did not bat.

BOWLING ANALYSIS
ENGLAND—First Innings

	O.	M.	R.	W.		O.	M.	R.	W.
Waite	72	16	150	1	Barnes	38	3	84	1
McCabe	38	8	85	0	Hassett	13	2	52	0
O'Reilly	85	26	178	3	Bradman	3	2	6	0
F.-Smith	87	11	298	1					

FALL OF THE WICKETS

1	2	3	4	5	6	7
28	411	546	547	555	770	876

AUSTRALIA
First Innings

C. L. Badcock, c Hardstaff, b Bowes	0
W. A. Brown, not out	29
S. J. McCabe, c Edrich, b Farnes	14
A. L. Hassett, c Compton, b Edrich	42
S. Barnes, not out	25
B 4, lb 2, nb 1	7

Total (for three wickets) 117

To bat: D. G. Bradman, B. A. Barnett, J. H. Fingleton, M. G. Waite, W. J. O'Reilly and L. O'B. Fleetwood-Smith.

BOWLING ANALYSIS TO DATE
AUSTRALIA—First Innings

	O.	M.	R.	W.		O.	M.	R.	W.
Farnes	9	2	42	1	Verity	5	1	15	0
Bowes	9	0	21	1	Leyland	2	0	5	0
Edrich	4	0	27	1					

FALL OF THE WICKETS

1	2	3
0	19	70

THE OVAL, TUESDAY, AUG. 23RD

This afternoon just before tea Bradman was bowling and England were 887 for seven, which was the equal of the highest score ever made in a first-class match in England. Suddenly Bradman fell to the ground in utter collapse. He had severely sprained an ankle and was sent from the ground to be X-rayed. For hours Bradman had worked hard and tirelessly, always leading his men, never slackening effort, always cheerful and inspiring. He was carried from the field, and the crowd stood up in silence, as though at a valedictory ceremony. With Fingleton also out of the match, through a strained muscle, Australia's cup was bitter full. As Bradman is unable to bat at all the match has been ruined as a contest, which is wretched luck for England as well as for Australia, because England will be deprived of full credit for victory, after a remarkable, not to say relentless, exhibition of batting.

For seventy-five minutes this morning Hutton kept the great crowd on a rack of suspense, we were all waiting for him to beat Bradman's record of 334, the highest in a Test match between England and Australia. When he was 311 a beautiful ball from Fleetwood-Smith nearly bowled him; Fleetwood-Smith's luck in the English innings was sinful. Slowly the minutes went by, Hardstaff was often uneasy and doubled up against the slow bowling, and though he occasionally made a glorious stroke, we could not enjoy them. Everybody ached for Hutton's sake; we trembled to think that on the verge of achievement he might fail, get run out, or die, or something. At half-past twelve Hardstaff drove a no-ball from O'Reilly straight for four, and then Fleetwood-Smith came on again, with Hutton's total 326. Hutton pulled his first ball to the boundary, and in the same over got a single, which took him opposite O'Reilly, who proceeded to bowl a no-ball, which Hutton missed entirely, while the crowd groaned disappointment. O'Reilly attacked fiercely to keep the record in Australia, but Hutton obtained another single, then against Fleetwood-Smith he made a grand late cut and his score became 336.

The scene which now occurred moved even the hardened critics. Thousands of happy people stood up and cheered. Somebody with a cornet began to play 'For he's a jolly good fellow' and the crowd took up the refrain in that evangelical tone which the British public invariably adopts when it lifts up its heart to rejoice in song. Moreover, the voices and the cornet did not keep together—but in the circumstances I admit that to say so is a piece of pedantic musical criticism. Bradman shook hands with the hero, all the Australians shook hands with him, journeying to the wicket from the remoter parts of the Oval—all except tired Bill O'Reilly, who lay prone on the grass until he saw a man coming out with drinks, when he got up at once and made for him, in a hurry. The cheers broke out again as soon as Hutton went beyond 336 and exceeded Hammond's innings against New Zealand. Hutton took the occasion with a charming modesty. He raised his cap in acknowledgment of the honours done to him, and bent his head. But what a moment for him!—the moment of his life.

As the ground became resonant with the cheering the thought occurred to me that it was being heard far and wide, all over the Empire, not only all over this country. People walking down Collins Street in Melbourne would hear it, and it would roar and echo in Kandy, Calcutta, Allahabad, Penang; they would hear it in the Cocos Islands and join in, and on liners going patiently their ways over the seven seas they would hear it too, and drink Hutton's health. Possibly in some club in Pall Mall a permanent member would wake up and go to the lunch-room and have to be informed who was Hutton.

England proceeded to beat the Australian record of the highest total amassed in a Test match. Little effort was made to increase the rate of scoring. Loose stuff was pushed for careful ones or twos whether McCabe was swinging his arm or any more authentic bowler. At lunch the score was 758 for five, and I observed now a number of Chelsea veterans watching the cricket. I wondered how many of them would live to see the match finished.

After lunch Hardstaff reached his hundred, then at half-past two Hutton got out through sheer exhaustion, caught at cover. His extraordinary innings lasted some thirteen hours and a quarter and he gave an easy chance of stumping when he was 40. He and Hardstaff added 215 for the sixth wicket in three and a half hours; I apologize for these statistics, but there was nothing else to write about. A new game has been invented which employs the implements of cricket.

At 770 for six another Yorkshireman came forth, rugged and ready to hold the fort. But Wood at once hit a boundary or two; the habits of a lifetime are hard to forget. The Australian attack was reinforced by Hassett, who delivered the ball from a little above the height of the bails, or above the peak of Walden's cloth cap. Barnes tried his spin at the other end, and thus the match was at last making a parody of itself—Barnes and Hassett bowling for Australia, in the absence of Grimmett—an absence which Grimmett no doubt would be the first to congratulate himself about. The fantastical position at a quarter to three was this: half of the third day gone and only six wickets down, with 790 on the scoreboard. The joke is that it was the Australians who originally were engaged to do all this; England had stolen their part, and taken the stage first, behind their backs.

Hardstaff having completed his 100, played forward most cautiously at Hassett's slow medium straight maidens, and the crowd began to clap ironically—and no wonder. I can play Hassett's bowling myself. Wood insisted on behaving like a cricketer who enjoys life. He drove Barnes to the off for a cracking four, so that for the first time since the game began the play became play, and not a burden to be sustained. Hardstaff, after he had obtained his 100, dallied forty full minutes for four, with England's aggregate 770 for six. Before the 800 was inflicted on the Australians Bradman came on to bowl, and he too succeeded in sending a maiden to Hardstaff, who does not know, apparently, that he is a stroke player and not a bore. If a man will not play cricket when he has made a hundred in a Test match, and his side is 800 for six, when on earth will he play cricket, and why did he ever think of playing cricket? Bradman pitched a pretty length, and once he turned a ball from leg and caused Hardstaff to stretch and grope; he obviously enjoyed his few overs.

Wood pulled a no-ball from O'Reilly for four with open and unashamed violence and relish, and turned him to leg in the same over for four—his sixth boundary in 34 runs. Sunshine warmed the Oval now, from a summer sky, and a puff of dust went up from the wicket, which though still thoroughly comfortable, was bound in time to suffer the wear and tear of all earthly things. At a quarter-past three England were 820 for six, and Bradman at extra-cover dashed in and stopped a hit by Hardstaff as though England needed six to win with the last men batting. Bradman's fielding and his eager and sensible captaincy throughout a fearful ordeal were beyond praise; he nursed his bowlers, talked to them, put his arm in theirs between overs, and cheered them up; he was not only the team's captain but the father-confessor and philosopher.

Hardstaff persisted in stone-walling, probably under orders. Such is contemporary Test cricket in this our England. Wood compiled 50 in 65 minutes, but in spite of his lack of conscience in the cause England scored only 100 runs in 100 minutes between lunch and four o'clock, against an attack which frequently consisted of Hassett and Barnes. Apologists blamed the played-out Test match for this state of things, but what was wrong was the spirit of the batting. If the spirit is wrong, the game will be wrong under any conditions. Hardstaff increased his score by 48 in an hour and three-quarters after passing his hundred and England more than 750 in hand for six. Wood was caught and bowled at 876, the seventh out, and when he reluctantly departed, with eight fours much to his credit, Hardstaff had acquired 150 in nearly five hours. And, by the way, when Wood got out Yorkshire in the match had scored 604 for three wickets.

At a quarter-past four the day's tragedy occurred. Bradman, as I say, was carried off the field. Shortly afterwards Hammond mercifully declared England's innings closed at 903 for seven, no doubt to the great relief of the men who work the score-boards, for there is no room on them for a total of four figures.

At five o'clock, in a mellow light, the Australians began their forlorn journey and ran into hardship straightway, for in Bowes's first over Badcock lamely pushed a ball into the hands of close mid-on, a stroke of little or no conviction. The score-board now read 0—1—0, a curious sight, like a once prosperous firm gone bankrupt, carpets taken up and nothing left but vacancy. McCabe got a single from Farnes and a fortuitous four through the slips, and Farnes beat him again. The innings seemed under sentence of death and every stroke a case of eating and drinking and merry-making before tomorrow's funeral, or the day after's. McCabe flicked his bat for a brief space until he sent a chance to square-leg, where Edrich held a quick and clever catch.

Hassett began with a brilliant forcing hit to square-leg from Farnes, who bowled his fastest; the English attack was far more hostile than Australia's at any time—it was the hostility of an army clearing up a dispersed and routed foe. The quicker wicket suited both Farnes and Bowes. Another four to the on by Hassett and another to square-leg, both off Farnes, were both magnificent strokes and recognizable as such by everybody. Not half a dozen strokes as good had been seen since Saturday, but, of course, the Australians were in a position to bat with enjoyment—the death sentence puts an end to reponsibility. The Australian batting was a case of 'Pagan, I regret to say'. Brown, though, stood for Puritan Duty. He observed the rules and scored five in half an hour, which really was the game I should have expected my men to play had I been Australia's captain.

Edrich came on for Farnes, and Hassett forced him for another boundary square to the on, a hit as easeful as it was rapid. In forty minutes Australia reached fifty, the swiftest scoring in the match so far. Hassett was guilty of a dangerous slash over the heads of the slips off Edrich, but he hooked magnificently for four in the same over. He was caught next over, at deep long-leg, endeavouring to clear the rails. In half an hour he scored his 42. Danse Macabre.

It was strange to see Australians playing as though the match already was lost beyond the possibility of a single concerted rear-guard action. The change which came over the proceedings after four o'clock was as dramatic as any I can recall—the game seemed becalmed for days to come. The disaster to Bradman was, of course, a cruel blow to a team facing a score of 900; none the less I expected to see the Australians dying in the last ditch, not on their own swords as though dishonour waited for them in a last ditch. The Oval wicket is still full of runs, and there are supposed to be five batsmen still left in the Australian team, all of them batsmen of reputation. The best compliment they could make to England, and the best way they could console their captain in his misfortune, would be an act of serious retaliation, with offence and defence mingled proportionately and governed by discretion.

FIFTH TEST (FOURTH DAY)

ENGLAND

First Innings

Hutton, c Hassett, b O'Reilly	364
Edrich, lbw, b O'Reilly	12
Leyland, run out	187
W. R. Hammond, lbw, b Fleetwood-Smith	59
Paynter, lbw, b O'Reilly	0
Compton, b Waite	1
Hardstaff, not out	169
Wood, c and b Barnes	53
Verity, not out	8
B 22, lb 19, w 1, nb 8	50

Total (for seven wickets declared)   903

K. Farns and Bowes did not bat.

BOWLING ANALYSIS
ENGLAND—First Innings

	O.	M.	R.	W.		O.	M.	R.	W.
Waite	72	16	150	1	Barnes	38	3	84	1
McCabe	38	8	85	0	Hassett	13	2	52	0
O'Reilly	85	26	178	3	Bradman	3	2	6	0
F.-Smith	87	11	298	1					

Waite bowled one wide; O'Reilly seven no-balls; Fleetwood-Smith one no-ball.

FALL OF THE WICKETS

1	2	3	4	5	6	7
28	411	546	547	555	770	876

AUSTRALIA

First Innings		Second Innings	
C. L. Badcock, c Hardstaff, b Bowes	0	b Bowes	9
W. A. Brown, c Hammond, b Leyland	69	c Edrich, b Farnes	15
S. J. McCabe, c Edrich, b Farnes	14	c Wood, b Farnes	2
A. L. Hassett, c Compton, b Edrich	42	lbw, b Bowes	10
S. Barnes, b Bowes	41	lbw, b Verity	33
B. A. Barnett, c Wood, b Bowes	2	b Farnes	46
M. G. Waite, b Bowes	8	c Edrich, b Verity	0
W. J. O'Reilly, c Wood, b Bowes	0	not out	7
L. O'B. Fleetwood-Smith, not out	16	c Leyland, b Farnes	0
D. G. Bradman, absent hurt	0	absent hurt	0
J. H. Fingleton, absent hurt	0	absent hurt	0
B 4, lb 2, nb 3	9	B 1	1
Total	201	Total	123

BOWLING ANALYSIS
AUSTRALIA—First Innings

	O.	M.	R.	W.		O.	M.	R.	W.
Farnes	13	2	54	1	Verity	5	1	15	0
Bowes	19	3	49	5	Leyland	3.1	0	11	1
Edrich	10	2	55	1	Hammond	2	0	8	0

Edrich bowled two no-balls and Hammond one no-ball.

FALL OF THE WICKETS

1	2	3	4	5	6	7	8
0	19	70	145	147	160	160	201

BOWLING ANALYSIS
AUSTRALIA—Second Innings

	O.	M.	R.	W.		O.	M.	R.	W.
Farnes	12.1	1	63	4	Leyland	5	0	19	0
Bowes	10	3	25	2	Verity	7	3	15	2

FALL OF THE WICKETS

1	2	3	4	5	6	7	8
15	18	35	41	115	115	117	123

THE OVAL, WEDNESDAY, AUG. 24TH

The Australians batted today in a manner which, on the whole, reminded us of the hearty breakfast which is formally taken on a morning of execution. Apart from Brown, nobody seemed determined to play himself in on a wicket still full of runs. The batting did much to support the view that this Australian team it terribly dependent on Bradman, and that under the mantle of his genius a deal of mediocrity can be hidden. A side that cannot win a match should try not to be beaten ingloriously. There were spells of fine bowling today by Bowes, but in general the English attack caused us, by its appearance, to thank our stars that Hammond won the toss.

The sudden breakdown of the match has complicated the problem of the duration in future of any of these matches. Up to four o'clock yesterday the chances were that we should be inhabiting the Oval till Saturday at the earliest. Bradman's mishap changed everything. The fact remains that the wicket prepared for this engagement was unfair to skilful bowlers and not in the interests of cricket. The game has left an unpleasant taste in the mouth. To see a fine stroke-player like Hardstaff deliberately patting half-volleys a few yards away from him with his score a hundred and England's score nearly eight hundred—this sight was not one to remember. No cricket match should occur again in which the wicket is contrived so that an innings of 900 is possible against any bowling.

The victory by England confirmed the impression of the rubber as a whole that Australia were the weaker all-round combination. Too much was expected of Australia's young men, and each of them disappointed, for, though Hassett proved himself a magnificent stroke-player, he seemed to lack a concentrated defence. I never expected him to stay long enough to get a century.

The bowling of both sides was moderate; but on the wickets prepared at Trent Bridge and at the Oval perhaps the bowling of Sidney Barnes himself would have had an ineffectual look. Something must be done to protect cricket from the constant danger of records being reared up and broken almost daily. An effort should be made to get back to the conditions when none but the greatest batsmen could hope to score a hundred in a Test-match innings.

For the first half-hour of the warm and lovely morning Brown and Barnes promised us an attempt at a stand, though straightway Brown sliced dangerously through the slips off Farnes, much to the surprise of Bowes, who could not bend in time. Brown then proceeded to play cool and intelligent cricket, straight of bat and erect of poise. His leisurely method caused the bowling to seem merely ordinary. Barnes performed a few good strokes, but with an immature air which scarcely suggested ability to play a long innings, and it was only in accord with expectations that he chopped a swinger from Bowes into his wicket at twelve o'clock.

Barnett in the same over snicked to the off side, and Wood hurled his body, all of it, across and held a clever and noisy catch. Waite became thoroughly bowled by Bowes in an attempt at a forward drive; and O'Reilly was not in form as a batsman. So, when Fleetwood-Smith came in, last man, Australia were 160 for seven. Fleetwood-Smith decided to play one of his most prolific innings, and, as Brown persisted in sensible technique, the last wicket added 41, during which time Hutton on the boundary seemed to kick a ball over the line to enable the bowlers to get at Fleetwood-Smith. Fleetwood-Smith was unbeaten at the end, for Brown tried to sweep a curious ball to leg from Leyland but struck with the top of his bat, from which the mis-hit flew upwards and was caught remarkably by Hammond, who leaped high with the utmost suppleness and grace.

Brown's innings lasted more than three hours, and it should have taught his colleagues a necessary lesson both in technique and moral principle. The attack of Bowes deserved a better opposition; he kept a length and caused his swing to occur late and at a good pace. Still, on such a wicket, an analysis of five for 49 told as plainly of a defeatist batting policy as it did of excellent bowling.

The Australians followed on at ten minutes past one and again Badcock failed, and yet again he failed because he shuffled and played back to a fast length ball. His leg stump was knocked spinning, and poor Badcock returned to the pavilion in dejection. His eight innings in the season's Test matches had brought him 32 runs. On his Australian form I wrote him down as one of the finest young batsmen of the day. An inexplicable failure and a cruel one.

McCabe slashed recklessly at the one or two balls he received and was inevitably caught at the wicket off Farnes. The lunch interval took place when Australia in their second innings were 31 for two; and immediately afterwards Hassett succumbed lbw to Bowes, and then the vigilance of Brown relaxed and he pushed a ball from

Farnes into the clutches of short-leg. So far the Australians had today lost eight wickets, and a Yorkshireman had helped in the taking of seven of them—five to Bowes, one to Leyland, and Farnes one, thanks to a catch at the wicket by Wood. I suggested after the Leeds match that the Yorkshire team should be chosen to play at the Oval for England. In essence it has played, or hasn't it?

Barnett lost no time hitting Farnes for three fours in an over, with crashing pulls which said 'Damn the consequences' or other and less euphemistical words to the same effect. Then Verity came on for Bowes, and the bowler at the other end was Leyland; the Australians were like lost, doomed men in an enchanted wood, where on every hand, here and there and round about, the same awful faces appeared. As soon as Farnes returned to the attack Barnes cut him for four and drove him straight for four. The English attack had a mediocre aspect now, while Bowes rested and Barnett and Barnes preferred to wait for the ball instead of deciding to strike before they saw the nature of it. As I say, any rational show of forward play would have obtained a decent amount of runs today. Farnes was punished severely; an off-drive by Barnett and a pull off consecutive balls went racing for fours. It was for England a lucky chance that disposed of Bradman.

Barnett and Barnes added 74 in an hour, and Barnes got out endeavouring to pull Verity over the roof of Archbishop Tenison's Grammar School; he missed his aim and departed reluctantly leg-before. The next ball removed Waite; and when Farnes bowled Barnett this was only the second wicket of the day not influenced by Yorkshire out of the thirteen that had miserably fallen. Shortly after half-past three the match without a time-limit, in which one batsman stayed in thirteen hours and in which 900 runs were scored in a single innings, was over easily within four days. Providence yesterday decided that something had to be done, and so the one player who could have prolonged the occasion was got out of the way.

The match ended on a note of welcome comic relief; O'Reilly drove Verity high and straight to the deep, where Hardstaff waited for the catch. There was a scramble for the stumps, which were uprooted; but Hardstaff missed the catch, and the stumps had to be put up again. This was the one honest laugh since Saturday morning, which now seems, and mercifully seems, long, long ago.